WORKSHOP MANUAL
for
TRIUMPH HERALD/SPITFIRE RANGE

COMPILED AND WRITTEN
BY

Andy Hugh

PUBLISHED BY
INTEREUROPE
AUTODATA DIVISION
NICHOLSON HOUSE
MAIDENHEAD
BERKSHIRE
ENGLAND

SBN 901610 - 88 - 7

D1345572

Printed in England

History and Type Identification

YOUR MANUFACTURER

The Triumph Motor Company was founded in 1903 under the trade name of Standard Motor Company. In 1945 the firm incorporated the Triumph Motor Co., and in 1968 became part of the British Leyland Motor Corporation's Specialist Car Division.

With the head office and works at Canley, Coventry, Warwickshire, England, the company has assembly plants in many other countries.

YOUR CAR

The Herald 1200 saloon, coupe and convertible versions with a 1,147 c.c. engine were introduced in April 1961 to be followed by the estate car in May 1961. The coupe was discontinued in October 1964, and after October 1967 only the saloon was manufactured. From October 1961 front wheel disc brakes were available on all models, a diaphragm spring clutch was installed from February 1966 and in March 1968, the electrical system polarity was changed to negative earth.

The Herald 12/50 "Skylight Roof" saloon introduced in March 1963 was mechanically similar to the 1200 with the 1,147 c.c. engine developing 51 b.h.p. and was equipped with front wheel disc brakes, BRD roller joint transmission and diaphragm spring clutch.

In October 1967 the 12/50 was discontinued and replaced by the Herald 13/60 in saloon, convertible and estate versions with a Vitessse chassis, restyled bonnet and full width grille. A collapsible steering column and two spoke steering wheel accompanied a new style fascia and better sited controls. Engine capacity was 1296 c.c. and the electrical system had negative earth polarity.

The Spitfire "4" with the 1147 c.c. engine, twin carburettors and front wheel disc brakes was introduced in October 1962 and overdrive and a hard top version were made optional extras in September 1963.

In March 1965 the Mk. II version brought a water-heated manifold, new camshaft and diaphragm clutch together with redesigned seats, new grille and badges.

The Mk. III arrived in March 1967 with a twin carburettor version of the 1296 c.c. engine and improved clutch and brakes. The front and rear bumpers were raised, the front lamps clusters were re-designed and a reversing lamp became standard. Negative earth polarity was applied to the electrical system and a "no loss" cooling system was introduced. A new sports type steering wheel and improved padding appeared in August 1969, together with new badges, matt black windscreen surround and a wheel rim increased in size to 4 1/2J. In October 1970 the Mk. IV was introduced with a close-ratio all synchromesh gearbox and improved suspension. A new matt black grille modified the front end and the bonnet rib joints were removed while the rear end was restyled on "Stag" lines. Re-designed seats, repositioned instruments and heater controls and standard fitment of an anti-theft lock on the steering column were other modifications together with opening rear quarter lights. An alternator was incorporated into the charging system to replace the generator.

GENERAL DIMENSIONS AND WEIGHTS

Length:

Herald	12 ft. 9 in. (3.886 m.)
Spitfire 4 & Mk. II	12 ft. 1 in. (3.683 m.)
Mk. III	12 ft. 2 1/2 in. (3.721 m.)
Mk. IV	12 ft. 5 in. (3.764 m.)

Width:

Herald	5 ft. 0 in. (1.524 m.)
Spitfire 4, Mk. II & Mk. III	4 ft. 9 in. (1.448 m.)
Mk. IV	4 ft. 10 1/2 in. (1.486 m.)

Height:

Herald	4 ft. 4 in. (1.320 m.)
Spitfire	3 ft. 11 1/2 in. (1.207 m)

Track:

Front -	Herald	4 ft. 0 in. (1.219 m.)
	Spitfire	4 ft. 1 in. (1.245 m.)
Rear		4 ft. 0 in. (1.219 m.)

Wheelbase:

Herald	7 ft. 7 1/2 in. (2.320 m.)
Spitfire	6 ft. 11 in. (2.109 m.)

Herald 1200, 12/50

Saloon	15 3/4 cwt. (800 kg.)
Coupé	15 1/4 cwt. (770 kg.)
Convertible	14 7/8 cwt. (725 kg.)
Estate	16 1/8 cwt. (820 kg.)

Herald 13/60

Saloon	16 cwt. (815 kg.)
Convertible	15 1/2 cwt. (785 kg.)
Estate	17 cwt. (865 kg.)

Spitfire 4 & Mk. II	13 1/4 cwt. (675 kg.)
Mk. III	14 cwt. (712 kg.)
Mk. IV	14 1/2 cwt. (734 kg.)

Index

Introduction

Our intention in writing this Manual is to provide the reader with all the data and information required to maintain and repair the vehicle. However, it must be realised that special equipment and skills are required in some cases to carry out the work detailed in the text, and we do not recommend that such work be attempted unless the reader possesses the necessary skill and equipment. It would be better to have an **AUTHORISED DEALER** to carry out the work using the special tools and equipment available to his trained staff. He will also be in possession of the genuine spare parts which may be needed for replacement.

The information in the Manual has been checked against that provided by the vehicle manufacturer, and any peculiarities have been mentioned if they depart from usual workshop practice.

A fault finding and trouble shooting chart has been inserted at the end of the Manual to enable the reader to pin point faults and so save time. As it is impossible to include every malfunction, only the more usual ones have been included.

A composite conversion table has also been included at the end of the Manual and we would recommend that wherever possible, for greater accuracy, the metric system units are used.

Brevity and simplicity have been our aim in compiling this Manual, relying on the numberous illustrations and clear text to inform and instruct the reader. At the request of the many users of our Manuals, we have slanted the book towards repair and overhaul rather than maintenance which is covered in our **"Wheel" series** of handbooks.

Although every care has been taken to ensure that the information and data are correct
WE CANNOT ACCEPT ANY LIABILITY FOR INACCURACIES OR OMISSIONS,
OR FOR DAMAGE OR MALFUNCTIONS ARISING FROM THE USE OF THIS BOOK,
NO MATTER HOW CAUSED.

intereurope

1. Fibre washer
2. Plain washer
3. Nyloc nut
4. Filler cap
5. Copper/asbestos washer
6. Sparking plug
7. Nut
8. Adaptor
9. Gasket
10. Rear engine plate
11. Bolt
12. Rear oil seal
13. Bolt
14. Gasket
15. Oil pump drive shaft bush
16. Oil pressure switch
17. Crankshaft thrust washer
18. Rear bearing shell
19. Rear bearing cap
20. Relief valve
21. Spring
22. Copper washer
23. Cap nut
24. Oil pump body
25. Oil pump end plate
26. Centre bearing shell
27. Centre main bearing cap
28. Sump plug
29. Sump
30. Sump gasket
31. Front bearing shell
32. Front main bearing cap
33. Sealing wedges
34. Sump bolt
35. Slotted screw
36. Front sealing block
37. Front engine mounting
38. Gasket
39. Front engine plate
40. Oil seal
41. Gasket
42. Front timing cover
43. Slotted setscrew
44. Bolt
45. Plain washer
46. Split pin
47. Chain tensioner
48. Pivot pin
49. Bolt
50. Generator pedestal
51. Dipstick
52. Bracket
53. Nyloc nut
54. Bolt
55. Nyloc nut
56. Breather pipe
57. Cylinder block
58. Cylinder head gasket
59. Cylinder head
60. Generator adjusting link
61. Rocker cover gasket
62. Rocker cover

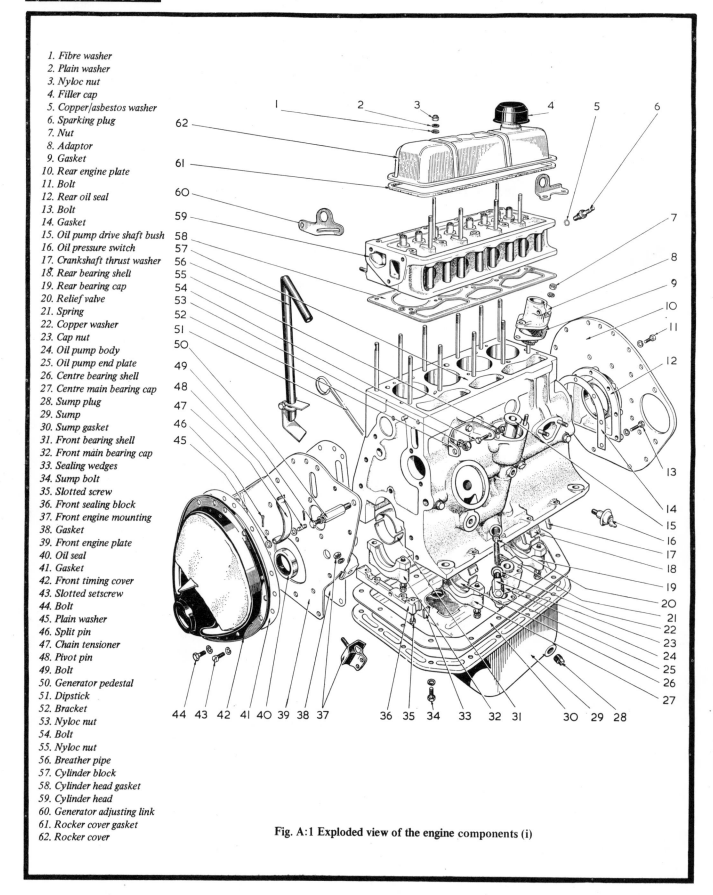

Fig. A:1 Exploded view of the engine components (i)

Engine

GENERAL

The four cylinder in-line water cooled engine installed in each of the Herald and Spitfire variants is similar in design and construction, a larger cylinder bore giving the Herald 13/60 and the later Spitfires the increased 1296 c.c. capacity against the original 1,147 c.c. All variants have high and low compression versions denoted by the suffix HE or LE in the unit number, except for the Herald 12/50 and Spitfire Mk. IV which are high compression only. Fig. A:1 shows the fixed and moving parts of the engine. Tighten nuts and bolts to the specified torque values given in TECHNICAL DATA.

VALVE CLEARANCES - Measurement and Adjustment

1. Disconnect breather pipe where fitted, and remove rocker cover. Renew gasket if damaged or distorted.

2. Rotate crankshaft and with screwdriver and spanner (Fig. A:2) adjust and lock the adjusting screw to give a gap of 0.010 in. (0.25 mm.) at each valve when the following sequence is followed:

   Adjust Nos. 1 and 3 valves with Nos. 8 and 6 valves open
   Adjust Nos. 5 and 2 valves with Nos. 4 and 7 valves open
   Adjust Nos. 8 and 6 valves with Nos. 1 and 3 valves open
   Adjust Nos. 4 and 7 valves with Nos. 5 and 2 valves open

3. Refit rocker cover with servicable gasket and connect breather pipe if applicable.

CYLINDER HEAD - Removal and Installation

Removal

1. Isolate battery.

2. Drain cooling system (see COOLING SYSTEM section for details).

3. Disconnect radiator hoses at thermostat housing and water pump inlet.

4. Remove radiator header tank (Spitfire only).

5. Disconnect heater hoses at engine.

6. Remove air filter(s).

7. Slacken generator/alternator bolts and remove fan belt.

8. Remove water pump bolts and move pump away from engine.

9. Disconnect fuel pipe and throttle and choke controls at carburettor(s).

10. Disconnect breather pipe from rocker cover and servo-vacuum pipe from rocker.

11. Remove HT leads and sparking plugs.

12. Disconnect exhaust down pipe and remove inlet and exhaust manifolds.

13. Remove rocker cover.

14. Evenly slacken and remove rocker pedestal nuts and lift off rocker assembly.

    Withdraw push rods and cam followers and keep in correct order.

15. Remove cylinder nuts, initially in small increments, in the reverse sequence to that shown in Fig. A:3. Lift off cylinder head complete with gasket.

Installation

1. Ensure faces of head and block are clean.

2. Smear servicable cylinder head gasket with grease before assembling head. Fit washers and tighten nuts in small increments in sequence shown in Fig. A:3.

3. Install push rods and cam followers in correct order. Fit rocker shaft assembly to engage with the push rod caps. Fit washers and tighten nuts evenly. Check and if necessary adjust valve clearances. Install rocker cover with servicable gasket.

4. Secure water pump, fit fan belt and adjust and secure generator with total lateral movement of 3/4 in. to 1 in. midway in longest run of belt.

5. Assemble manifolds, connect pipes and controls to carburettor(s).

6. Connect hoses and install air filter(s).

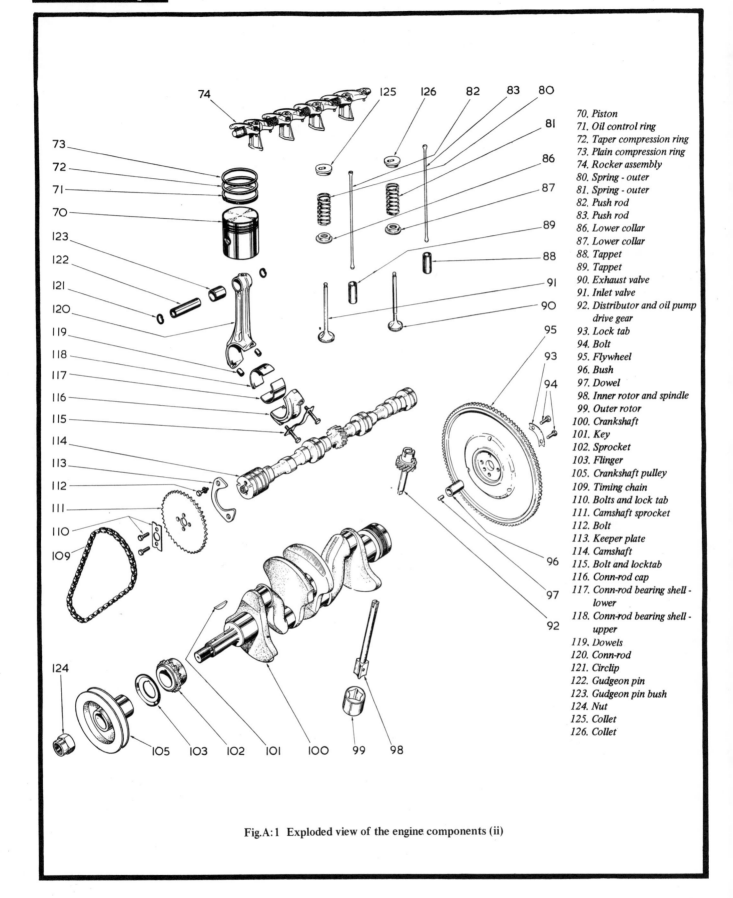

70. Piston
71. Oil control ring
72. Taper compression ring
73. Plain compression ring
74. Rocker assembly
80. Spring - outer
81. Spring - outer
82. Push rod
83. Push rod
86. Lower collar
87. Lower collar
88. Tappet
89. Tappet
90. Exhaust valve
91. Inlet valve
92. Distributor and oil pump drive gear
93. Lock tab
94. Bolt
95. Flywheel
96. Bush
97. Dowel
98. Inner rotor and spindle
99. Outer rotor
100. Crankshaft
101. Key
102. Sprocket
103. Flinger
105. Crankshaft pulley
109. Timing chain
110. Bolts and lock tab
111. Camshaft sprocket
112. Bolt
113. Keeper plate
114. Camshaft
115. Bolt and locktab
116. Conn-rod cap
117. Conn-rod bearing shell - lower
118. Conn-rod bearing shell - upper
119. Dowels
120. Conn-rod
121. Circlip
122. Gudgeon pin
123. Gudgeon pin bush
124. Nut
125. Collet
126. Collet

Fig.A:1 Exploded view of the engine components (ii)

7. Fill cooling system and connect battery.

8. Start engine, bring to normal temperature and check for leaks. If necessary re-adjust valve clearances.

CYLINDER HEAD - Decarbonising

1. Plug all push rod water-way and oil-way apertures in the cylinder head and also in the block. Bring pistons to top of cylinders in turn.

2. With suitable tool scrape all carbon deposits from cylinder head and block faces, valve heads, combustion chambers and piston crowns. Avoid scratch damage to all surfaces particularly the piston crowns. Remove all particles of carbon and dirt from cylinder head and block.

For valve grinding refer to "CYLINDER HEAD - Inspection and Overhaul" below.

CYLINDER HEAD - Inspection and Overhaul

1. Remove thermostat elbow and thermostat.

2. On Herald engines, release each valve spring by placing a wooden block under the valve, compressing the spring and sliding the valve cap aside (Fig. A:4). On Spitfire engines use a valve spring compressor (Fig. A:5) to remove split collets (Fig. A:6).

3. Clean all parts.

4. Check valves for wear or distortion, reface or renew as necessary. A valve must be renewed if, after refacing, the thickness of the valve head is less than 1/32 in. (0.8 mm.) (Fig. A:7).

5. Check valve springs for cracks and distortion. Check fitted length and load, see TECHNICAL DATA. If any springs are defective a new set is recommended. (Fig. A:8).

6. Check valve caps, spring seats and collets for damage and distortion. Renew as necessary.

7. Inspect the cylinder head for cracks and scratches or burrs on the machined face. Renew if cracked, remove scratches or burrs with oilstone. Out of true machined faces may be skimmed within specified limits.

8. Inspect valve seats for wear, scores or pitting. Reface or recut as necessary. When recutting seat ensure that the cutter pilot is a good fit in the valve guide. Maximum dimensions for "A" "B" and "C" are given. It is particularly important not to exceed "B" when using a 15° cutter (Fig. A:9).

A = 0.060 in. (1.52 mm.)

	B Inlet	Exhaust
Spitfire	1.378 in. (35.0 mm.)	1.252 in. (31.8 mm.)
Herald	1.440 in. (36.5 mm.)	1.252 in. (31.8 mm.)

C = 0.10 in. (0.25 mm.)

When valve seats cannot be restored by refacing, new inserts may be fitted to pocket dimensions given in TECHNICAL DATA. If both inserts are to be replaced, fit inlet insert before boring for the exhaust insert. Remove all swarf after boring, drive insert squarely into pocket and secure by careful peening (Fig. A:10).

9. Check valve guides for wear with a new valve raised 1/8 in. (3.2 mm.) approx. from its seat and moved diametrically in the guide (Fig. A:11). If movement of the valve head across the seat exceeds 0.020 in. (0.5 mm.) the guide should be renewed. Use a good fitting drift to remove the old guide and tool No. S60A for fitting the new guide, which should project by 0.75 in. (19.05 mm.). (Dimension "X", Fig. A:12). Limiting distance pieces to ensure correct protrusion are available.

10. After valve and seat refacing, grind the valves in their respective positions (Fig. A:13). Remove all traces of grinding paste and swarf before beginning assembly.

11. Lubricate valve stems and guides, enter valve in guide and place spring seat, spring and valve cap over guide. Compress spring and fit split collets (Spitfire) or slide valve cap to centre position (Herald). Use a compressor for the Spitfire assembly. Repeat for all valves.

12. Remove cotter pin at end of rocker shaft and slide off rockers, springs, pedestals and washers from front end noting location and position of components. (Figs. A:14 & A:15). On Herald 13/60 and late Spitfire models, remove rear pedestal locating screw and withdraw rear pedestal and rocker. Clean all parts. Renew rocker shafts if worn or scored and rockers if pivot holes or tips are worn. Tips are chill hardened to a depth of 0.060 in. (1.525 mm.) and grinding to restore profile is not recommended. Renew adjusters if ball ends are worn or screw driver slots or threads damaged. Renew nuts with worn corners or damaged threads. Rebuild rocker gear as shown in Figs. A:14 or A:15 as appropriate, ensuring all oilways are clear, components are in correct order and rockers move freely on shaft. Ensure rear pedestal screw is correctly located in shaft. (Fig. A:15).

OIL SUMP - Removal, Inspection and Installation

Removal

1. Isolate battery.

2. Remove sump drain plug and drain oil. Withdraw dipstick.

3. Raise front of vehicle on to stands.

4. Remove bolts and washers and remove sump and gasket. (It may be necessary to remove lower bell housing bolts).

Inspection

1. Clean sump, strainer if fitted, and engine joint face. Remove all traces of gasket and rectify any distortion.

2. Renew damaged or block strainer (secured by self-tapping screws). Renew oil filter if oil is being changed.

3. Renew gasket.

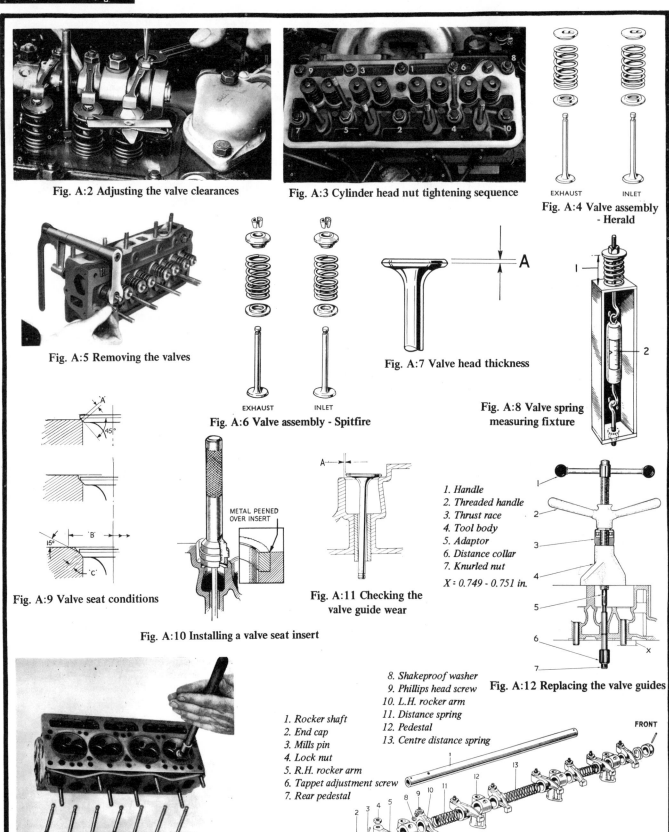

Fig. A:2 Adjusting the valve clearances

Fig. A:3 Cylinder head nut tightening sequence

Fig. A:4 Valve assembly - Herald

EXHAUST   INLET

Fig. A:5 Removing the valves

Fig. A:7 Valve head thickness

A

Fig. A:8 Valve spring measuring fixture

EXHAUST   INLET

Fig. A:6 Valve assembly - Spitfire

45°

15°

'B'

'C'

Fig. A:9 Valve seat conditions

METAL PEENED OVER INSERT

Fig. A:10 Installing a valve seat insert

A

Fig. A:11 Checking the valve guide wear

1. Handle
2. Threaded handle
3. Thrust race
4. Tool body
5. Adaptor
6. Distance collar
7. Knurled nut

$X = 0.749 - 0.751 in.$

Fig. A:12 Replacing the valve guides

8. Shakeproof washer
9. Phillips head screw
10. L.H. rocker arm
11. Distance spring
12. Pedestal
13. Centre distance spring

1. Rocker shaft
2. End cap
3. Mills pin
4. Lock nut
5. R.H. rocker arm
6. Tappet adjustment screw
7. Rear pedestal

FRONT

Fig. A:14 Details of the rocker gear - Herald 1200, 12/50, Spitfire 4 and Mk II.

Fig. A:13 Grinding-in the valves

Installation

1. Install in reverse order ensuring the two short bolts are fitted at the front sealing block and tightening bolts to specified torque only.

2. Fit drain plug and fill with oil.

3. Connect battery, run engine and check for leaks.

OIL PUMP - Removal and Installation

1. Remove sump as described above.

2. Remove three attachment bolts and remove pump.

3. Clean and inspect as described in LUBRICATION SYSTEM section.

4. Secure pump to crank case.

5. Install sump.

TIMING COVER OIL SEAL - Replacement

1. Isolate battery.

2. Remove radiator as described in COOLING SYSTEM section.

3. Slacken generator/alternator bolts and remove fan belt.

4. Remove securing nut and withdraw crankshaft pulley.

5. Remove attachment bolts and washers and remove cover and gasket.

6. Carefully lever oil seal out avoiding damage to timing cover.

7. Press new seal evenly in housing with seal lip towards sprocket.

8. Lubricate seal lip and pulley running surface.

9. Position servicable gasket on front plate and check oil flinger is in position.

10. Position timing cover with tensioner compressed with bent wire (see Fig. A:16) on locating dowels and evenly tighten attachment bolts.

11. Fit and secure crankshaft pulley, install and tension fan belt.

12. Install and fill radiator.

13. Connect battery.

TIMING CHAIN - Removal and Installation

1. Remove timing cover as previously described and straighten locking tabs on camshaft sprocket bolts.

2. Bring No. 1 piston to T.D.C. on compression stroke.

Timing marks should now be aligned. (Fig. A:17).

3. Check timing chain wear, (Fig. A:18). Dimension "A" must not exceed 0.4 in. (10 mm.).

4. Remove camshaft sprocket bolts, ease sprocket off camshaft and detach chain from crankshaft sprocket.

5. Install chain and sprocket with timing marks aligned.

   NOTE: If new sprocket is being fitted proceed as described in "ENGINE - Overhaul: Valve Timing".

6. Install timing cover as previously described.

CAMSHAFT - Removal and Installation

Removal

1. Remove cylinder head, timing cover and camshaft sprocket and timing chain as previously described.

2. Lift out cam followers.

3. Remove distributor as described in IGNITION SYSTEM section. Remove drive gear. Remove fuel pump.

4. Remove camshaft keeper plate.

5. Extract camshaft, avoiding damage to cams and bushes.

Installation

1. Lubricate journals and bearings and insert camshaft with care to avoid damage.

2. Fit keeper plate and check camshaft end-float is within 0.004 - 0.008 in. (0.10 - 0.20 mm.). If necessary correct with new keeper plate.

3. Install fuel pump and distributor.

4. Fit cam followers.

5. Assemble camshaft sprocket, timing chain and cover, and cylinder head.

6. Adjust valve timing and ignition timing.

MAIN BEARING SHELLS - Replacement

1. Proceed in accordance with "SUMP - Removal" and "OIL PUMP - Removal".

2. Remove front sealing block and side packing pieces.

3. Remove main bearing caps.

4. Slide upper bearing shells into crank case with tab ends leading.

5. Slide new upper shells into crank case with tab ends trailing. Ensure tabs are seated correctly.

6. Renew shells in bearing caps, replace caps and tighten

Fig. A:15 Rocker gear - Herald 13/60,
Spitfire Mk III and IV

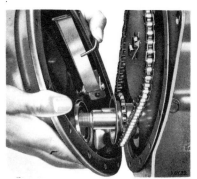

Fig. A:16 Installing the timing cover

Fig. A:17 Valve timing alignment marks

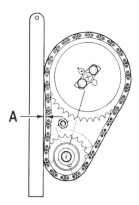

Fig. A:18 Checking the timing chain wear

Fig. A:19 Right-hand view of the engine

Fig. A:20 Left-hand view of the engine

Fig. A:21 Gearbox installation

attachment bolts to specified torque.

CAUTION: Leave crankshaft unsupported for no longer than necessary, as compression of the oil seal lips may cause subsequent leakage.

NOTE: Crankshaft thrust bearings may be renewed by removing rear bearing cap only.

7. Thoroughly clean front sealing block and crankcase before fitting sealing block as described in "ENGINE - Assembly".

8. Proceed in accordance with "SUMP - Installation", and "OIL PUMP - Installation".

CONNECTING ROD BEARINGS - Replacement

1. Proceed in accordance with "SUMP - Removal".

2. Rotate crankshaft until required connecting rod is at B.D.C.

3. Remove bearing cap bolts and cap and remove shells.

4. Renew shells as necessary and ensure that tab ends are correctly seated.

5. Fit caps and tighten bolts to specified torque.

6. Proceed in accordance with "SUMP - Installation".

CONNECTING RODS AND PISTONS - Removal and Installation

1. Proceed in accordance with "SUMP - Removal"

2. Proceed in accordance with "CYLINDER HEAD - Removal".

3. Remove connecting rods bearing caps and shells. Do not intermix.

4. Push pistons and connecting rods through top of bores.

5. Check in accordance with "ENGINE - Inspection".

6. Replace pistons and connecting rods in their respective cylinders. (See "ENGINE - Assembly").

7. Proceed in accordance with "CONNECTING ROD BEARINGS - Replacement".

8. Install cylinder head.

ENGINE UNIT - Removal and Installation

Removal

1. Isolate battery and drain cooling system, oil sump and gearbox.

2. Remove bonnet by disconnecting front lighting and horn cable connectors on top grille centre, removing overriders and stay bolt, and then hinge bolts. Support bonnet while hinge bolts are removed.

3. Remove radiator as described in COOLING SYSTEM section.

4. Remove air cleaner (1) and disconnect carburettor controls (2) and (3), heater hoses (5) and (6), exhaust down pipe connection (4) and bracket to clutch housing (Fig. A:19).

NOTE: Spitfire air cleaners are double element.

5. Disconnect starter motor cable and engine earth strap.

6. Disconnect HT and LT coil cables (7) and (8), oil pressure switch connection (9) generator cables (10) and (11) and disconnect and plug fuel line (12) at fuel pump. (Fig. A:20).

7. On Spitfire only, disconnect tachometer cable.

8. Remove front seats and carpets and gearbox cover. On Spitfire, remove facia support.

9. Disconnect speedometer drive from right hand side of gearbox extension, remove clutch slave cylinder (7) attachment bolts and move cylinder clear, and remove bolts (13) at front universal flange. (Fig. A:21).

10. Disconnect overdrive solenoid cables, if applicable.

11. Remove gearchange extension and blank opening.

12. Attach hoist cable to lifting eyes, support engine and remove front and rear mounting bolts.

13. Lift engine unit until sump is above chassis cross member and then up, and forward to clear bulkhead.

Installation

1. Lower engine unit into position, and secure front and rear mounting bolts.

2. Attach gearchange extension and front universal flange to gearbox.

3. Install speedometer cable and clutch slave cylinder.

4. Connect overdrive solenoid cables, if applicable.

5. Fit gearbox cover and floor carpets. Fit facia support on Spitfire. Install seats.

6. Connect starter cable and engine earth strap.

7. Secure exhaust down pipe and clutch housing bracket.

8. Connect heater hoses, carburettor controls and install air cleaner.

9. Connect fuel pump supply pipe.

10. Connect electrical cables to coil, generator/alternator and oil pressure switch.

11. Install radiator and bonnet.

12. Fill cooling system, engine and gearbox, and connect battery.

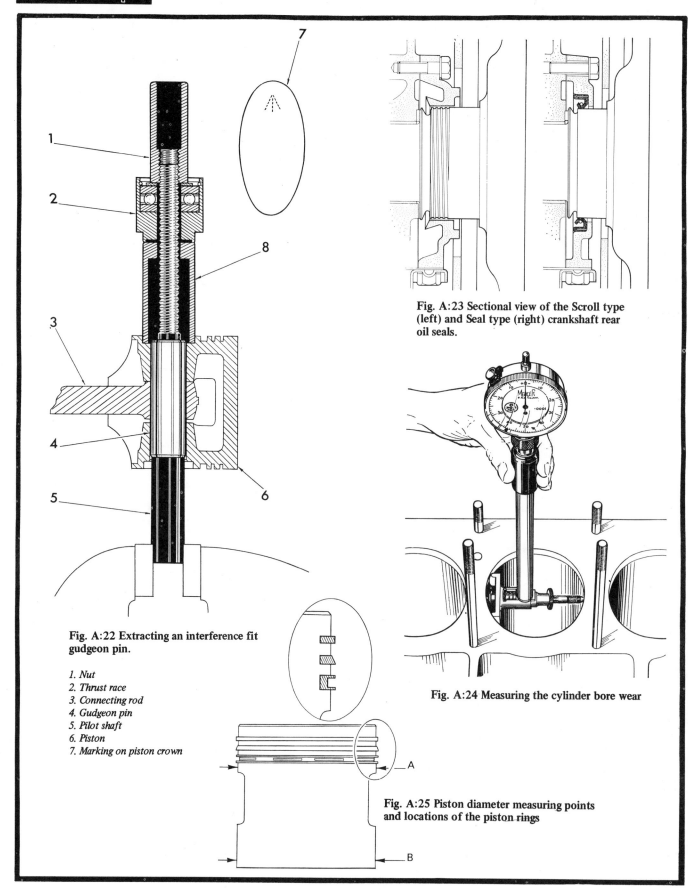

Fig. A:23 Sectional view of the Scroll type (left) and Seal type (right) crankshaft rear oil seals.

Fig. A:22 Extracting an interference fit gudgeon pin.

1. Nut
2. Thrust race
3. Connecting rod
4. Gudgeon pin
5. Pilot shaft
6. Piston
7. Marking on piston crown

Fig. A:24 Measuring the cylinder bore wear

Fig. A:25 Piston diameter measuring points and locations of the piston rings

13. Run engine and tune carburettor(s).

ENGINE - Preparation for Reconditioning

The following items must be removed before reconditioning or despatch for reconditioning:-

1. Fan belt.

2. Radiator header tank - early Spitfire.

3. Water pump, thermostat housing and thermostat.

4. Alternator/generator and starter motor.

5. Fuel pump and fuel pipe.

6. Manifolds.

7. Distributor, pedestal and vacuum pipe.

8. Sparking plugs.

9. Oil pressure switch.

10. Oil filter, relief valve, dipstick and breather pipe.

11. Gearbox and clutch.

ENGINE - Dismantling

Remove cylinder head, push rod and cam followers, also oil sump and oil pump as described in "in position" procedures.

Flywheel and Backplate

1. Remove four bolts securing flywheel and withdraw flywheel.

   NOTE: Early models have lockplates to secure instead of self-locking bolts which are interchangeable.

2. Remove backplate bolts and washers and remove backplate.

Timing Gear and Camshaft

1. Remove securing nut and withdraw crankshaft pulley.

2. Remove bolts and washers and remove timing cover complete with tensioner and oil seal. Remove gasket and oil thrower.

3. Straighten lock tabs on camshaft sprocket bolts and remove bolts. Ease camshaft sprocket off camshaft and detach chain from crankshaft sprocket. Remove crankshaft sprocket and shims.

4. Remove camshaft keeper plate bolts and remove plate.

5. Remove attachment bolts and remove front plate and gasket.

6. Carefully withdraw camshaft to avoid damaging cams and journal bearings.

Connecting Rods and Pistons

NOTE: On original and current engines, con-rods and pistons are connected by floating gudgeon pins secured by circlips. Intermediate engines have interference fit gudgeon pins which are self-securing in the con-rod.

1. Straighten lock tabs on each connecting rod bearing cap, remove bolts, separate caps and remove both half shell bearings.

NOTE: Connecting rod/piston assemblies must be kept together and identified with their respective cylinders.

2. Remove piston and con-rod through the top of the cylinder.

3. Remove floating gudgeon pins by extracting circlips and pushing pin from piston and con-rod. A tight pin is removed more easily when the piston is immersed in hot water.

   Remove interference gudgeon pins with Churchill tool S334 assembled to piston as shown in Fig. A:22, noting that sleeve (8) will locate on one side only. Tighten nut (1) until gudgeon pin is drawn into sleeve. Avoid repeated removal and insertion as each operation reduces the interference fit. Use normal lubricating oil only on tool to ensure assembly torque readings are correct.

Crankshaft

NOTE: A scroll on the rear end of the crankshaft with a matched housing formed the oil seal on early engines. The housings were aluminium up to commission Nos. Herald 1200 GA 115730; Herald 12/50 GD 8314; Spitfire FC 2794, and were subsequently of cast iron with a smaller clearance. A lip type seal is currently fitted, and both sealing methods are shown on Fig. A:23.

1. Remove rear oil seal housing and gasket. Where applicable drive seal from housing using a drift inserted in each of two holes alternately.

2. Remove front sealing block and packing pieces.

3. Remove bearing cap bolts - with lock tabs on earlier engines - and remove bearing caps and lower half shell bearings. Lower crankshaft and remove upper half shell bearings and thrust washers.

ENGINE - Inspection and Overhaul

Thoroughly clean all parts removing all traces of gasket and jointing material from mating faces.

Cylinder Block

1. Inspect cylinder bores for scores and wear (Fig. A:24). If necessary rebore cylinders for oversize pistons or alternatively for liners. See TECHNICAL DATA for dimensions.

   NOTE: When new pistons or rings are fitted, light honing or careful use of medium grade carborundum will assist

Fig. A:26 Checking the run-out at the flywheel face.

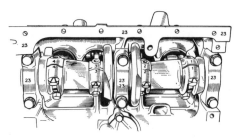

Fig. A:27 Main and big end bearing markings

Fig. A:29 Installing the wedge pieces in the front sealing block.

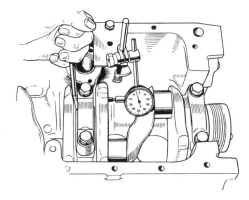

Fig. A:28 Checking the crankshaft end-float with a dial gauge.

Fig. A:31 Centralising the housing for the Scroll type oil seal

Fig. A:30 Aligning the front sealing block

Fig. A:32 Centralising tool for the lip type oil seal

bedding in of rings.

2. Inspect camshaft bearings for wear and damage.

3. Insert distributor drive shaft into its bush and rock to check bush wear. Remove a worn bush with a stepped drift positioned in the crankcase and carefully drive replacement bush into pedestal flange.

4. Clean oilways and water passages where necessary.

5. Smooth any burrs from joint faces.

6. Check studs and core plugs for damage. Rectify or renew as necessary.

Crankshaft

1. Inspect journals and crank pins for wear and scoring. If necessary, grind to next undersize. See TECHNICAL DATA for permitted undersizes which are stamped on the web and on the back of undersize bearing shells.

2. Renew shell bearings if worn or scored or if crankshaft is reground.

Camshaft

1. Check journal diameters for wear (see TECHNICAL DATA for specifications).

2. Inspect for cracks and burrs. Remove burrs with carborundum stone.

3. Check distributor drive for damage.

Connecting Rods and Pistons

The diameters of normal size pistons are graded "F", "G" and "H" with appropriate identification letter on piston crown and cylinder bore face. Grading is not applied to oversize pistons which are available in +0.010 in., +0.020 in. and +0.030 in. sizes. Piston diameter measurement points and also the location of the piston rings are shown in Fig. A:25.

The top compression ring is chromium plated, the middle ring, also compression, was plain but is now taper-faced as illustrated and the bottom oil scraper ring is in three pieces on the Herald 13/60 and Spitfire Mks. III and IV models.

Weight difference between the heaviest and lightest of a connecting rod set should not exceed 4 drams. Piston set weight difference is also 4 drams. except on the Herald 13/60 and Spitfire Mks. III and IV where the maximum weight difference is 2 drams. When building con-rod piston sets, assemble heaviest to lightest to reduce overall weight difference.

1. Renew shell bearings if showing signs of wear or scoring.

2. Check connecting rods for bowing and twist with suitable checking equipment. Rectify or renew if deformation exceeds 0.0015 in. (0.038 mm.) in gudgeon pin length.

3. Inspect pistons for burning and damage. Renew if necessary.

4. On the floating gudgeon pin assemblies, check that a thumb push will pass a dry pin through the connecting rod bush. A pin passing through under its own weight is too loose and a replacement bush is necessary. Use a press and adaptor to press out the old bush avoiding direct contact with con-rod. Ensure that oil holes are in alignment before pressing in new bush. Fine bore or broach the new bush to size - see TECHNICAL DATA for specifications.

5. Where interference fit gudgeon pin assemblies have been separated, examine piston and con-rod bores for evidence of picking up and renew parts where this is present. Check interference fit on assembly.

6. Insert each piston ring into cylinder in which it is to operate, and square up with the head of a piston. Measure the ring gap with feelers and check that the gap is to the dimensions given in TECHNICAL DATA.

Flywheel Assembly

1. Inspect flywheel clutch face for scores which may be removed by skimming in a lathe to a maximum thickness reduction of 0.030 in. (0.762 mm.). Run-out at 3.0 in. (76.2 mm.) radius must not exceed 0.002 in. (0.051 mm.) when checked in lathe or as shown in Fig. A:26. Balance should remain within 1 dram. (1.8 g.).

2. Inspect the starter ring for damaged teeth and security. Renew if necessary by supporting flywheel on hard wood blocks with clutch side up and with no obstruction to ring gear. Evenly drive off ring in small movements. Reverse flywheel on blocks and thoroughly clean rim and new starter ring. Evenly heat the ring and, with chamfered edge of teeth towards clutch face, place ring on flywheel.

Timing Cover and Gears Assembly

1. Inspect timing cover for cracks or distortion. Rectify distortion and, with a straight edge, ensure the flanges are flat.

2. Renew tensioner if damaged or distorted by opening the blade sufficiently to spring it over the pin.

3. Renew oil seal by positioning lip towards cover and applying even pressure.

4. Inspect chain sprockets for worn or damaged teeth, Renew as necessary.

5. Renew timing chain if excessively slack when checked before dismantling, or if damaged or distorted.

ENGINE - Assembly

Crankshaft and Bearings

Bearing cap and cylinder block are bored as an assembly and are not interchangeable. Identification markings on caps and block are shown on Fig. A:27.

1. Fit main bearing shells to cylinder block housings and to bearing caps with tabs correctly located.

Fig. A:33 Measuring the piston ring gap

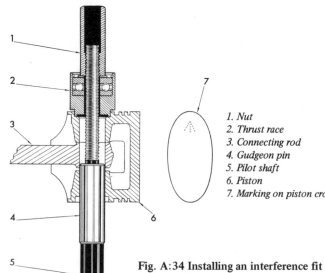

Fig. A:34 Installing an interference fit gudgeon pin

1. Nut
2. Thrust race
3. Connecting rod
4. Gudgeon pin
5. Pilot shaft
6. Piston
7. Marking on piston crown

Fig. A:35 Checking the alignment of the timing sprockets.

Fig. A:37 Determining the point of balance at No. 4 cylinder

Fig. A:38 Determining the required gasket thickness for the distributor adaptor

1. Adaptor
2. Feeler blade
3. Driving gear
4. Washer (1/2 in. I/D)
5. Bush
6. Oil pump shaft
7. Pin

Fig. A:36 Crankshaft sprocket adjustment shims

Fig. A:39 Assembling the distributor pedestal and packing gaskets

2. With clean engine oil, lubricate journals and bearings and position crankshaft in crankcase.

3. Fit a thrust bearing at each side of the rear main bearing with thrust faces against crankshaft.

4. Assemble bearing caps - with locking tabs where self-locking bolts are not used - and evenly tighten bolts.

5. Lever crankshaft in each direction to check if end float is 0.004 - 0.008 in. (0.10 - 0.20 mm.).

   Reduce excessive float with oversize thrust bearings. Check end float with feelers or with dial gauge (Fig. A:28).

6. Bend locking tabs where fitted.

Front Sealing Block

1. Smear jointing compound on sealing block ends and assemble to cylinder block. Do not fully tighten screws.

2. Smear wedge pieces with jointing compound and drive into sealing block slots (Fig. A:29).

3. With a straight edge align sealing block with front face and tighten screws (Fig. A:30).

4. Trim wedge pieces flush with crankcase.

Crankshaft Rear Oil Seal - Lip Type

1. Coat new gasket on both sides with jointing compound and position on housing joint face.

2. For scroll type seal assemble housing with three bolts only nipped up and adjust with hide hammer until a 0.003 in. (0.076 mm.) feeler gauge will pass all round, then fully tighten bolts (Fig. A:31). For cast iron housings on commission Nos. Herald 1200 GA115730, 12/50 GD8314, Spitfire FC2794 and subsequent models with scroll type seals, the clearance is 0.002 in. (0.051 mm.).

3. With lip facing forward press oil seal into housing. Lubricate seal lip, crankshaft and Churchill centralising tool S335, push tool over crankshaft and slide up to joint face. Evenly tighten attachment bolts and remove tool (Fig. A:32).

Front and Rear Engine Plates

1. Position new paper gasket and front plate on the front face of cylinder block and secure with one 3/4 in. long centre bolt and two 7/8 in. long bottom corner bolts.

   NOTE: The top centre stud breaks through into the water jacket and if removed the threads must be coated with jointing compound before replacement to avoid leaks.

2. Fit rear plate to engine and tighten attachment bolts evenly and in turn.

Flywheel

1. Ensure the mating faces of flywheel and crankshaft spigot are clean and free from burrs.

2. Smear spigot bush with zinc oxide grease and insert in crankshaft.

3. Offer up flywheel to engage crankshaft dowel.

4. Fit and tighten self-locking bolts.

   Early models are fitted with lock plates which can be discarded if self-locking bolts are introduced.

5. With dial indicator mounted on backplate check that run-out at 3 in. (76.2 mm.) does not exceed 0.002 in. (0.051 mm.) and concentricity is within 0.004 in. (0.10 mm.). Check run-out with crankshaft pressed against one or the other thrust washer to eliminate end float error.

   NOTE: When fitting a new flywheel the T.D.C. position should be marked and is best done when the pistons are fitted but before the cylinder head is assembled. Set piston Nos. 1 and 4 to T.D.C. and scribe a line across the periphery of the flywheel in line with the marking on the backplate. Accentuate the scribe line with a small chisel, and mark "1" and "4" at the line.

Connecting Rods and Pistons

1. Place each piston ring inside the bore in which it will operate, square up with piston and check ring gap with feelers (Fig. A:33).

   Ring gap should be:-

   Herald 1200, 12/50 and Spitfire 4 & Mk. II
     0.008 - 0.013 in. (0.20 - 0.33 mm.)
   Herald 13/60, Spitfire Mks. III and IV
     0.012 - 0.022 in. (0.30 - 0.85 mm.)

2. Using a ring handling tool or thin plaster strips to avoid breakage, assemble rings to piston beginning with scraper (bottom) ring (Fig. A:25).

   Fit taper faced second compression rings with surface marked "TOP" towards piston crown. Three piece scraper rings fitted to Herald 13/60 and Spitfire Mk. II and IV engines are assembled with middle corrugated section first and then top and bottom flat rings to fit above and below the corrugated section. Stagger ring gaps on each piston.

3. Assemble connecting rod to piston with bearing cap in position towards camshaft direction when arrow on piston crown is at engine forward position.

   For assembly with floating gudgeon pin, lubricate pin and connecting rod bush, correctly align bush with piston boss, slide pin into position and secure with circlips. Preheating of piston in hot water or oil will facilitate gudgeon pin insertion.

   For assembly with interference fit gudgeon pin, lubricate parts, correctly position in Churchill tool No. S334 and turn nut (1) with torque wrench until pin contacts limit stop (Fig. A:34). Correct torque is 5lb./ft. to 30 lb./ft. and results outside these limits indicate incorrect interference fit, and new connecting rod is required. With tool removed check for uneven pivoting of piston on pin which indicates metal pick-up and transfer from con-rod to piston boss requiring new complete assembly.

4. With Nos. 1 and 4 crankpins at B.D.C. lubricate cylinder bore and piston with engine oil, fit piston ring sleeve or compressor and enter con-rod and piston into No. 1 bore with arrow to front of engine. Press piston into bore until clear of ring tool. Lubricate crankpin and bearing shells, fit shells to con-rod and bearing cap with tabs correctly located and assemble to crankpin. Fit and bend locktabs if self-locking bolts not fitted. Install and secure remaining piston assemblies.

Oil Pump and Sump

1. Lubricate pump rotors, assemble cover and secure to crank-case.

2. Use new gasket and evenly tighten sump attachment bolts.

Camshaft

Insert camshaft, secure with keeper plate and check and correct end float if necessary.

Cylinder Head Assembly

Carry out relevant operations of "CYLINDER HEAD - Assembly". Do not fit rocker cover.

Sprocket Installation

1. Mount sprockets on camshaft and crankshaft with the short hub boss outwards on the crankshaft pulley, and without key.

2. With straight edge check alignment of sprockets (Fig. A:35).

3. Shim crankshaft sprocket as necessary (Fig. A:36).

4. Press crankshaft sprocket into position over key.

5. Assemble original (marked) camshaft sprocket with timing chain as shown in Fig. A:17.

6. Fit oil thrower, timing cover and crankshaft pulley.

Valve Timing

When an unmarked timing chain sprocket is installed the following procedure should be followed:

1. Turn crankshaft until No. 1 piston is at T.D.C. and cam-shaft until No. 1 push rod is at highest point. Set No. 8 valve clearance at 0.040 in. (1.00 mm.).

2. Turn camshaft until No. 2 push rod is at highest point. Set No. 7 valve clearance at 0.040 in. (1.00 mm.).

3. Turn camshaft until inlet valve of No. 4 cylinder is about to open and exhaust valve is about to close, check with feelers that clearance at valve Nos. 7 and 8 are equal (Fig. A:37).

4. With camshaft and crankshaft positions unchanged, assemble timing chain on sprockets, fit crankshaft sprocket with keyway aligned and adjust camshaft sprocket inside chain until two attachment holes are aligned with camshaft holes. Four holes in the camshaft sprocket are offset from a tooth centre so that a 90° rotation gives half tooth adjust-ment, sprocket reversal gives a quarter tooth difference, and reversal and 90° rotation give three-quarter tooth variation.

5. Secure camshaft sprocket, re-check that clearances at valve Nos. 7 and 8 are equal and secure bolts with lockplate.

6. Adjust all valve clearances to 0.010 in. (0.25 mm.), assemble oil thrower, timing cover and crankshaft pulley and fit rocker box.

Distributor Drive Gear and Pedestal

It is essential that an end-float of 0.003 - 0.007 in. (0.076 - 0.178 mm.) exists between drive gear and bottom of pedestal after assembly. This is obtained by fitting packing washers under the pedestal. To determine packing thickness required, proceed as illustrated in Fig. A:38.

1. Set No. 1 piston at T.D.C. on compression.

2. Place 0.5 in. (12.7 mm.) inside diameter washer (4) of measured thickness over drive gear shaft and insert assembly into bush to mesh with camshaft gear and engage with oil pump shaft (6).

3. Place pedestal in position and measure pedestal to cylinder block gap. Subtract this from washer thickness to obtain end-float without packing washers, and determine packing washer thickness required to produce specified end-float.

Example

Thickness of gauging washer 0.062 in. (1.57 mm.).
Gap width   0.060 in. (1.52 mm.).
End-float without packing washers
                              0.002 in. (0.05 mm.).

This end-float is less than stipulated tolerance and thus packing washer thickness required to give nominal 0.005 in. (0.12 mm.) float is 0.003 in. (0.051 mm.).

4. Remove drive gear to extract gauging washer, replace gear to mesh with camshaft gear and engage oil pump shaft and fit pedestal with correct thickness of packing washers (Fig. A:39).

ENGINE - Preparation for Installation

Refit items removed in preparation for reconditioning following relevant section procedures.

Technical Data

GENERAL

Type . . . . 4 cylinder "in line" O.H.V.
Bore:-
    Herald 1200, 12/50, Spitfire 4 & Mk. II . . . . 2.728 in.   (69.30 mm.)
    Herald 13/60, Spitfire Mk. III & IV . . . . 2.900 in.   (73.6 mm.)
Stroke . . . . 2.992 in.   (76.00 mm.)
Cubic capacity:-
    Herald 1200, 12/50, Spitfire 4 & Mk. II . . . . 70 cu. in.   (1147 c.c.)
    Herald 13/60, Spitfire Mk. III & IV . . . . 79.2 cu.in. (1296 c.c.)
Compression Ratio:-
    Herald 1200 . . . . 6.8 : 1, 8.0 : 1, or 8.5 : 1
    Herald 1250 . . . . 8.5 : 1
    Herald 1360 . . . . 7.5 : 1, or 8.5 : 1
    Spitfire 4 and Mk. II . . . . 7.0 : 1, or 9.0 : 1
    Spitfire Mk. III . . . . 7.5 : 1, 8.5 : 1, or 9.0 : 1
    Spitfire Mk. IV . . . . 9.0 : 1

DIMENSIONS AND TOLERANCES

Crankshaft:
Main bearing journal dia. . . . . 2.0005 - 2.001 in.   (50.81 - 50.83 mm.)
Undersize bearings available . . . . 0.010, 0.020, 0.030 and 0.040 in.
                              (0.254, 0.508, 0.762 and 1.016 mm.)
Crankpin dia. . . . . 1.6250 - 1.6255 in. (41.27 - 41.28 mm.)
Undersize bearings available . . . . 0.010, 0.020 and 0.030 in. (0.254, 0.508 and 0.762 mm.)
Rear journal width . . . . 1.2976 - 1.2995 in. (32.95 - 33.01 mm.)
Thrust washer thickness . . . . 0.091 - 0.093 in.   (2.31 - 2.36 mm.)
Oversize thrust washer . . . . 0.096 - 0.098 in.   (2.44 - 2.49 mm.)
Connecting Rod:
End float on crankpin:-
    Herald 1200, 12/50 and Spitfire 4 & Mk. II . . . . 0.0105 - 0.0126 in. (0.266 - 0.320 mm.)
    Herald 13/60 and Spitfire Mk. III & IV . . . . 0.0025 - 0.0086 in. (0.063 - 0.218 mm.)
Small end bush internal dia. . . . . 0.8126 - 0.8128 in. (20.65 - 20.66 mm.)
Gudgeon pin dia. . . . . 0.8123 - 0.8125 in. (20.63 - 20.64 mm.)
Cylinder Bores:
Standard cylinder bore gradings:-
Herald 1200, 1250 and Spitfire 4 & Mk. II
    Grade F . . . . 2.7280 - 2.7283 in. (69.29 - 69.30 mm.)
    Grade G . . . . 2.7284 - 2.7287 in. (69.30 - 69.31 mm.)
    Grade H . . . . 2.7288 - 2.7291 in. (69.31 - 69.32 mm.)
Herald 13/60 and Spitfire 4 Mk. III and IV
    Grade F . . . . 2.899 - 2.900 in.   (73.64 - 73.66 mm.)
    Grade G . . . . 2.9001 - 2.9005 in. (73.66 - 73.67 mm.)
Piston Rings:
Piston ring width:-
    Compression ring:-
    Herald 1200, 12/50 and Spitfire 4 & Mk. II . . . . 0.077 - 0.078 in.   (1.97 - 1.99 mm.)
    Herald 13/60 and Spitfire Mk. III & IV . . . . 0.0620 - 0.0625 in. (1.575 - 1.587 mm.)
    Oil control ring:-
    Herald 1200, 12/50 and Spitfire 4 & Mk. II . . . . 0.1540 - 0.1560 in. (3.90 - 3.96 mm.)
    Herald 13/60 and Spitfire Mk. III and IV . . . . 0.1540 - 0.1560 in. (3.90 - 3.96 mm.)
Piston ring groove width
    Compression ring
    Herald 1200, 12/50 and Spitfire 4 & Mk. II . . . . 0.0802 - 0.0812 in. (2.03 - 2.06 mm.)
    Herald 13/60, Spitfire Mk. III and IV . . . . 0.064 - 0.065 in.   (1.625 - 1.65 mm.)
    Oil control rings . . . . 0.157 - 0.158 in.   (3.99 - 4.01 mm.)

NOTE: From engine numbers GA 137545, GD 21229 and FC 24449 a solid skirt piston was introduced with compression ring groove of 0.0797 - 0.0807 in.

Piston ring fitted gap:
    Herald 1200, 12/50 and Spitfire 4 & Mk. II . . . . 0.008 - 0.013 in.   (0.20 - 0.33 mm.)
    Herald 13/60, Spitfire Mk. III and IV . . . . 0.012 - 0.022 in.   (0.30 - 0.85 mm.)

Camshaft journal dia:

    Herald 1200, 12/50 and Spitfire 4 & Mk. II . . . . 1.8402 - 1.8407 in.   (46.74 - 46.75 mm.)

    Herald 13/60, Spitfire Mk. III and IV . . . . 1.9649 - 1.9654 in.   (49.91 - 49.92 mm.)

Rocker shaft diameter . . . . 0.5607 - 0.5612 in.   (14.24 - 14.26 mm.)

Rocker shaft clearance . . . . 0.0008 - 0.0023 in.   (0.02 - 0.06 mm.)

Valve Gear:

Valve springs:

Fitted Length:-

    Herald 1200, and 13/60 . . . . 1.36 in.   (34.54 mm.)

    Herald 12/50 and Spitfire . . . . 1.38 in.   (35.03 mm.)

Fitted load:-

    Herald 1200, and 13/60 . . . . 27 - 30 lbs. (12.25 - 13.61 kgs.)

    Herald 12/50 and Spitfire . . . . 32 - 42 lbs. (14.51 - 19.05 kgs.)

Cutting dimensions for valve seat inserts:-

    Exhaust Pt. No. 132242

             Diameter . . . . 1.249 - 1.250 in. (31.72 - 31.75 mm.)

             Depth . . . . 0.248 - 0.250 in. (6.15 - 6.35 mm.)

    Inlet Pt. No. 132241 (Herald 1200, 12/50)

             Diameter . . . . 1.437 - 1.438 in. (36.50 - 36.52 mm.)

             Depth . . . . 0.248 - 0.250 in. (6.15 - 6.35 mm.)

    Inlet Pt. No. 130814 (Herald 13/60 and Spitfire)

             Diameter . . . . 1.375 - 1.376 in. (34.92 - 34.95 mm.)

             Depth . . . . 0.248 - 0.250 in. (6.15 - 6.35 mm.)

TIGHTENING TORQUES

Connecting rod bolts . . . . 38 - 42 lbs./ft.   (5.25 - 5.81 kg./m.)

Cylinder head bolts . . . . 42 - 46 lbs./ft.   (5.81 - 6.36 kg./m.)

Engine mounting to frame . . . . 18 - 20 lbs./ft.   (2.49 - 2.77 kg./m.)

Fly wheel attachment . . . . 42 - 46 lbs./ft.   (5.81 - 6.36 kg./m.)

Fan to pulley . . . . 6 - 8 lbs./ft.   (0.82 - 1.11 kg./m.)

Front engine bracket and front plate . . . . 18 - 20 lbs./ft.   (2.49 - 2.77 kg./m.)

Camshaft keeper plate . . . . 18 - 20 lbs./ft.   (2.49 - 2.77 kg./m.)

Generator bracket to block . . . . 16 - 18 lbs./ft.   (2.21 - 2.49 kg./m.)

Generator to engine plate . . . . 16 - 18 lbs./ft.   (2.21 - 2.49 kg./m.)

Rear engine plate . . . . 12 - 14 lbs./ft.   (1.66 - 1.94 kg./m.)

Main bearing caps . . . . 50 - 55 lbs./ft.   (6.91 - 7.60 kg./m.)

Oil pump attachment . . . . 6 - 8 lbs./ft.   (0.83 - 1.11 kg./m.)

Rear oil seal . . . . 18 - 20 lbs./ft.   (2.49 - 2.77 kg./m.)

Rocker cover nuts . . . . 1 1/2 lbs./ft.   (0.11 kg./m.)

Rocker pedestal . . . . 24 - 26 lbs./ft.   (3.32 - 3.60 kg./m.)

Starter motor attachments . . . . 26 - 28 lbs./ft.   (3.60 - 3.87 kg./m.)

Sump . . . . 16 - 18 lbs./ft.   (2.21 - 2.49 kg./m.)

Sump to front and rear seal . . . . 10 - 12 lbs./ft.   (1.38 - 1.66 kg./m.)

Timing cover setscrew . . . . 14 - 16 lbs./ft.   (1.94 - 2.21 kg./m.)

Timing cover setscrew slotted . . . . 8 - 10 lbs./ft.   (1.11 - 1.38 kg./m.)

Lubrication System

GENERAL

Oil from the engine sump is pressurised by a rotor type oil pump and delivered to a filter via a passage in the block. A relief valve between the pump and filter regulates the pressure and returns excess oil to the sump. Filtered oil is distributed through the main oil gallery to the crankshaft and camshaft journals, and through drillings to the big end bearings which splash lubricate the cylinders. The rear camshaft journal meters oil to the rocker gear and valve gear. (Fig. B:1).

The timing gear is lubricated by mist from the crankcase and seepage from the front camshaft journal. The crankshaft is sealed by lip type seals at the front and rear. On early models rear sealing was affected by a reverse scroll on the crankshaft in a close fitting housing (see Fig. A:23). A full-flow sealed unit filter, screwed to the cylinder block, incorporates a relief valve which opens when filter blockage occurs and permits unfiltered oil to enter the supply line. (Fig. B:2).

Crankcase ventilation on the Herald 1200, 12/50 and Spitfire 4 and Mk. II is through an open pipe to the atmosphere, while closed circuit systems are incorporated on other models. On the Herald 13/60 a pipe from the rocker cover to the air cleaner or alternatively to an emission valve on the inlet manifold is provided. A similar rocker cover to emission valve arrangement exists on the Spitfire Mk. III, and on the Mk. IV the pipe is connected to the depression side of the carburettor. The closed circuit breather pipe relieves excessive crankcase pressure and admits air as demanded by air intake velocity balanced against crankcase pressure. The emission control valve responds to induction manifold depression to restrict crankcase gas flow when the depression is greatest, and a non-return valve in the oil filler cap balances crankcase and ambient pressures. Fig. B:3 shows the Herald 13/60 crankcase ventilation system and Fig. B:4 the crankcase breather valve system used on the Spitfire Mk. II.

ROUTINE MAINTENANCE

Every 250 miles (400 km.) or before beginning a long journey

Check the oil level. Allow oil to settle with vehicle on level ground, remove and clean dipstick, insert fully and withdraw again. Read level on dipstick and replenish if necessary.

Every 6000 miles, (10,000 km.) or six months whichever is earlier

Drain engine at sump drain plug, replace plug and replenish through rocker cover oil filler cap. Change oil more frequently if dusty roads are used or short journeys made.

Every 12,000 miles (20,000 km.)

Unscrew the oil filter from the block and fit new unit ensuring the mating faces are clean and smeared with oil (Fig. B:5). At the same time clean the breather pipe with petrol and allow to dry before re-fitting. Where a breather valve is installed, release clip (1), remove cover, diaphragm (2), valve pin and spring, wash parts in methylated spirits and inspect for serviceability before re-assembly. (Fig. B:6).

Clean oil filler cap and ensure vent hole is clean.

OIL PUMP - Inspection

1. Remove pump as detailed in engine dismantling.

2. With pump components cleaned and dry, assemble without cover intake pipe assembly and check that clearances are as given in TECHNICAL DATA. (Figs. B:7, B:8 and B:9). Renew worn parts.

3. Assemble and install pump.

RELIEF VALVE - Inspection

1. Remove cap nut, copper washer, spring and valve.

2. Clean parts, examine washer and valve for wear or damage and check spring rate (see TECHNICAL DATA for specifications). Renew parts as necessary.

3. Assemble relief valve.

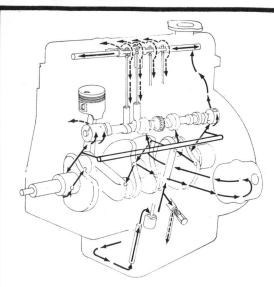

Fig. B:1 Engine lubrication system.

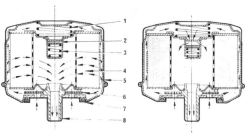

1. Spring
2. By-pass valve
3. By-pass valve spring
4. Filter element
5. Filter casing
6. Non-return valve
7. Sealing ring
8. Union

Fig. B:2 Sectional view of the oil filter assembly. Normal flow - left: By-pass flow - right.

Fig. B:4 Crankcase ventilation system with breather valve.

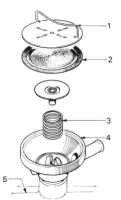

Fig. B:6 Details of the crankcase breather valve

1. Clip
2. Diaphragm
3. Spring
4. Valve body
5. Inlet manifold

Fig. B:3 Closed type crankcase ventilation system

Fig. B:5 Removing the oil filter.

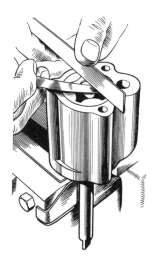

Fig. B:7 Checking the clearance of the oil pump rotors.

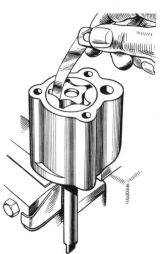

Fig. B:8 Checking the clearance between the inner and outer rotors.

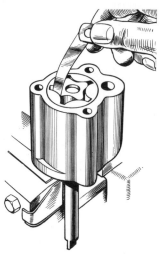

Fig. B:9 Checking the clearance between the outer rotor and the pump housing.

Technical Data

Sump Capacity   -   Dry . . . . 8 Imp. pts.   (9.6 U.S. pts.; 4.6 litres)
               -   Refill . . . . 7 Imp. pts.   (8.4 U.S. pts.; 4.0 litres)

Recommended Oils

  British Isles

    B.P. . . . . Super Visco   -   Static 20 W-50

    Castrol . . . . G.T.X.

    Duckhams . . . . Q 20 - 50

    Esso . . . . Extra Motor Oil 20 W/50

    Mobil . . . . Mobiloil Super SAE 10W/40 or Special 20W/50

    Petrofina . . . . Fina Multigrade Motor Oil SAE 20W/50

    Regent . . . . Havoline Motor Oil 20W/50

    Shell   . . . . Super Motor Oil 100

  Overseas

    Over 30°C (80°F) A.P.I. MM or MS. . . . . SAE 30

    0 - 30°C (30° - 80°F) A.P.I. MM or MS . . . . SAE 20

    Below 0°C (30°F) A.P.I. MM or MS . . . . SAE 10

Single or Multigrades to specification may be used.

Oil Filter:

Type . . . . Full-flow "throw-away" unit

Oil Pump:

Type . . . . Hobourn - Eaton, double eccentric rotor

Pressure at 2,000 r.p.m. (engine hot) . . . . 40 - 60 p.s.i. (4.2 kg/sq.cm.)

Permissable clearances:

  Outer rotor to body   -   Herald 1200, 1250, Spitfire 4 & Mk. II   0.008 in.   (0.203 mm.) max.

                        -   Herald 13/60, Spitfire Mk. III & IV . .   0.0075 in. (0.190 mm.) max.

  Outer to inner rotor   . . . . 0.010 in.   (0.254 mm.) max.

  Rotor end to end face . . . . 0.0005 - 0.0025 in.   (0.0127 - 0.0635 mm.)

Relief valve spring:

  Free length . . . . 1.54 in.   (39.11 mm.)

  Fitted length . . . . 1.25 in.   (31.75 mm.)

  Loaded at fitted length . . . . 14.5 lbs.   (6.58 kg.)

TIGHTENING TORQUES

  Oil filter to cylinder block . . . . 15 - 18 lbs./ft.   (2.07 - 2.49 kg./m.)

  Oil pump to cylinder block . . . . 6 - 8   lbs./ft.   (0.83 - 1.11 kg./m.)

  Oil pump to cylinder block (13/60 only) . . . . 8 - 10 lbs./ft.   (1.11 - 1.38 kg./m.)

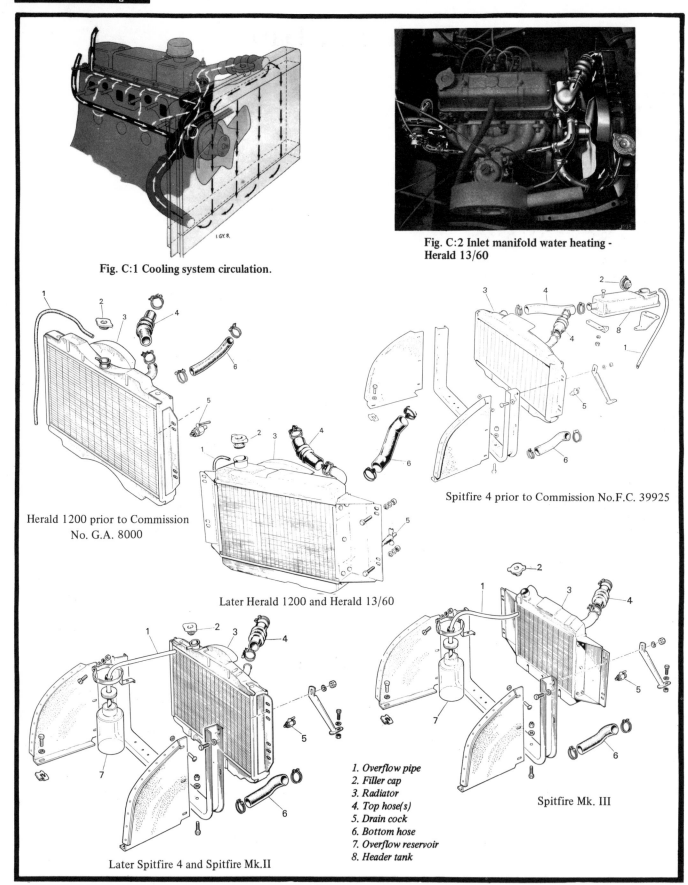

Fig. C:1 Cooling system circulation.

Fig. C:2 Inlet manifold water heating -
Herald 13/60

Herald 1200 prior to Commission
No. G.A. 8000

Later Herald 1200 and Herald 13/60

Later Spitfire 4 and Spitfire Mk.II

Spitfire 4 prior to Commission No.F.C. 39925

Spitfire Mk. III

1. Overflow pipe
2. Filler cap
3. Radiator
4. Top hose(s)
5. Drain cock
6. Bottom hose
7. Overflow reservoir
8. Header tank

Fig. C:4 Details of the various radiator assemblies.

Cooling System

GENERAL (Fig. C:1)

The circulation of coolant through the radiator and the cylinder block is assisted by a centrifugal water pump located at the front of the cylinder head and belt driven from the crankshaft pulley. A filler cap, which incorporates pressure relief and recuperating valves, seals the system, relieves excess pressure during heat expansion and relieves inwardly during cooling contraction. On Spitfire 4 models from commission number FC 39926, the pressure relieves into a translucent coolant reservoir, making a closed circuit, self-recuperating system. Prior to this, a separate header tank was mounted alongside the cylinder head. A thermostat isolates, and then controls, flow to the radiator during the warming up period, and a fan on the water pump pulley assists air flow through radiator. Drain cocks are fitted at the bottom of the radiator and at the right-hand side of the cylinder block. The interior heater is fed from the rear of the cylinder head.

On Herald 13/60 and the Spitfire models, hot water from the cooling system is used to heat the inlet manifolds. (Figs. C:2 and C:3).

Fig. C:4 shows the various radiator installations which were wider and thinner on early Herald and Spitfire models.

ROUTINE MAINTENANCE

CAUTION. If the engine is hot, rotate filler cap one half-turn only to allow pressure to dissipate before fully removing cap.

Weekly

Check water level by removing filler cap or examining translucent reservoir, as applicable. If required, replenish with soft water until level is one inch below filler neck or reservoir is at least half full. Should reservoir become empty, fill radiator before replenishing reservoir.

Annually

1. Remove plug at water pump, screw in 1/8 in. taper Briggs grease nipple and apply grease gun until grease exudes from a release hole in pump. Replace plug (Fig. C:5).

2. Flush out the system at least once a year when adding anti-freeze. Remove drain cocks completely and use plenty of clean running water. Add anti-freeze to required concentration (see TECHNICAL DATA), run engine and check for leaks at all joints. See draining and filling.

3. Remove thermostat from water pump (Fig. C:8).

Inspect for wear, damage or corrosion. If accuracy is suspect, check as described later in "THERMOSTAT - Testing". Replace thermostat.

4. Examine filler cap for damage, wear and corrosion and check fastening device for correct functioning. Filler cap can be checked with a pressure tester as detailed in "FILLER CAP - Testing".

COOLING SYSTEM - Draining

1. Set heater control to "HOT" and remove radiator or header tank filler cap.

2. Open drain cocks at bottom of radiator and on cylinder block. Remove cylinder block drain plug on engines where cock is not fitted.

    NOTE: Draining does not completely empty the heating system and is therefore not a safeguard against frost damage.

COOLING SYSTEM - Filling

1. Set heater control to "HOT" and ensure drain cocks are closed.

2. Remove filler cap and fill system with clean soft water. Replace cap.

3. Run engine until warmed up to circulate water. Stop engine.

4. Check level and replenish as necessary.

5. If installed, half fill overflow reservoir.

COOLING SYSTEM - Pressure testing (Fig. C:6)

1. Ensure water system level is correct and run engine until coolant is warm.

2. Remove filler cap and attach a suitable pressure tester to filler neck.

3. Pump tester until pressure marked on filler cap is indicated on dial.

    This pressure should be maintained for 10 seconds.

    Rectify leakage if necessary.

Fig. C:3 Inlet manifold water heating - Spitfire.

Fig. C:5 Water pump lubrication hole plug

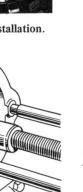

Fig. C:8 Thermostat installation.

Fig. C:6 Testing the cooling system with a pressure tester.

Fig. C:7 Testing the radiator filler cap.

1. Nut
2. Plain washer
3. Drive pulley
4. Circlip - outer bearing to housing
5. Circlip - inner bearing to shaft
6. Housing
7. Sealing gland
8. Impeller
9. Thermostat

10. Gasket - Body to cyl. head
11. Pump body
12. Gasket - housing to body
13. Spindle
14. Spinner
15. Spring washer
16. Inner bearing
17. Spacer tube
18. Outer bearing

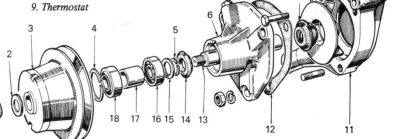

Fig. C:9 Exploded view of the water pump components.

Fig. C:10 Pressing the pump spindle out of the impeller.

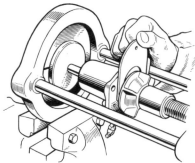

Fig. C:11 Using a 0.030 in gauge to set the correct impeller clearance.

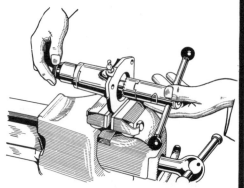

Fig. C:12 Recutting the pump sealing gland face.

4. Remove tester and replace filler cap.

NOTE: This test is more stringent if carried out with engine running.

With this procedure, pressure fluctuation with no evidence of external leakage points to a defective cylinder head gasket.

FILLER CAP - Pressure testing

1. Clean filler cap with water and, while still wet, attach pressure tester.

2. Pump tester until relief valve operates. Indicator should read within +/- 1.0 p.s.i. (0.06 kg./cm^2) of pressure stamped on cap, and maintain pressure for 10 seconds. Reject cap if requirements are not met.

3. Remove tester and refit cap if serviceable.

RADIATOR - Removal and Installation (Fig. C:4)

Removal

1. Drain system and remove bonnet.

2. Disconnect top and bottom radiator hoses and pull off overflow pipe.

3. Remove four bolts, nuts and washers. Tilt radiator rearwards and carefully lift out without fouling fan blades.

Installation

1. Place radiator in position without fouling fan blades, and secure with nuts, bolts and washers.

2. Connect top and bottom radiator hoses and overflow pipe.

3. Install bonnet, fill system, run engine and check for leaks.

THERMOSTAT - Removal and Installation (Fig. C:8)

Removal

1. Drain system sufficiently to empty cylinder head water jacket.

2. Disconnect hose to outlet elbow and remove both attachment bolts.

3. Remove outlet elbow with gasket and remove thermostat.

Installation

1. Place thermostat in position.

2. Assemble elbow with serviceable gasket.

3. Replenish system.

THERMOSTAT - Testing

1. Immerse the thermostat in water together with a thermometer and apply heat to the vessel. Move thermostat to circulate water around bellows.

2. On the thermometer, read off the temperature at which the valve begins to open. This should be within 5°F of temperature marked on the thermostat flange and should be fully open with a further temperature rise of 25°F.

WATER PUMP - Removal and Installation

1. Isolate battery and drain coolant system.

2. Slacken generator/alternator bolts, pivot unit towards engine and remove fan belt.

3. Disconnect hoses from pump and top elbow.

4. Disconnect temperature transmitter cable.

5. Release vacuum pipe and fuel pipe clip where applicable.

6. Remove bolts and lift pump complete with fan from engine. Remove gasket.

7. Reverse removal procedure to install pump. Renew gasket.

8. Run engine and check for leaks.

WATER PUMP - Overhaul (Fig. C:9)

Dismantling

1. Remove fan and pulley. Retain key.

2. Detach bearing housing (6) and gasket from body.

3. Using Churchill tool S4221A with adaptor FTS 127 withdraw impeller (8) from spindle (Fig. C:10).

4. Remove seal (7) from impeller.

5. Remove circlip (4) and drift out spindle complete with bearing assembly.

6. Remove spinner (14) circlip (5) and washer (15).

7. Press bearings and spacer (17) from spindle.

Inspection

1. Clean all parts and examine for wear, damage and corrosion.

2. Examine bearings for cracks, rough rotation, and excessive play. Renew if in doubt.

3. Renew seals if damaged or deformed.

4. Renew spindle if scored or worn.

5. Inspect gland face of bearing housing for scores, particularly if pump has been leaking, and, if necessary, re-cut the face with Churchill tool S126 as described below.

6. Renew gaskets.

Assembly

1. Fit circlip (5) and washer (15) to spindle and press on ball races with distance piece (17) between them. The sealed faces on the ball races must be away from distance piece. Fit seal (14) next to circlip.

2. Pack the space between bearings with high melting point grease and press spindle and races into housing (6). Use a tube on the outer race of the bearing to insert assembly and secure with circlip (4).

3. With sealing gland (7) in the rear recess, press impeller on to spindle until a clearance of 0.030 in. (0.76 mm.) is obtained between impeller and rear face of housing. (Fig. C:11).

4. Solder impeller to end of spindle to prevent water leakage.

5. Smear grease on new gasket (12) and secure bearing housing assembly to pump body.

6. Key and attach pulley to spindle, and assemble fan.

7. Install serviceable thermostat (see "THERMOSTAT - Testing"), fit new gasket and secure elbow. Install temperature transmitter.

WATER PUMP - Restoring Sealing Gland Face (Fig. C:12)

1. Insert pilot of Churchill tool S126 into gland side of housing, until it protrudes at pulley side.

2. Slide bush - with small diameter leading - on pilot and follow with tool bearing and then knurled nut.

3. Turn knurled nut to bring cutter against gland face and steadily turn tommy bar simultaneously applying light even pressure on cutter with knurled nut. Continually remove tool to clear swarf and check gland face surface. Remove only sufficient material to produce a score-free and polished surface.

IMPORTANT: Gland face depth from mounting face of housing must not exceed 0.256 in. (6.7 mm.).

Technical Data

Cooling System Capacity (inc. heater):-
Herald . . . . 8.5 Imp. pts. (10.2 U.S. pts.; 4.8 litres)
Spitfire 4 & Mk. II . . . . 9.5 Imp. pts. (11.4 U.S. pts.; 5.4 litres)
Spitfire Mks. III & IV . . . . 8 Imp. pts. (9.6 U.S. pts.; 4.5 litres)
System Working Pressure:-
Herald, prior to engine numbers GA 204782E and GE 22521E . . . 7 p.s.i.
All others . . . . 13 p.s.i.
Anti-freeze Solution Specification . . . . B.S.I. 3151 or 3152
Anti-freeze Protection:-

	25%	30%	35%
Concentration	25%	30%	35%
Complete protection (Vehicle may be driven away immediately from cold)	10°F (-12°C)	3°F (-16°C)	-4°F (-20°C)
Safe limit (Coolant in mushy state. Short warm up before driving away)	0°F (-17°C)	-8°F (-22°C)	-18°F (-28°C)
Lower protection limit (Front damage prevented. Engine should NOT be started until thawed out).	-14°F (-26°C)	-22°F (-30°C)	-28°F (-33°C)

Pump drive belt Tension . . . . 1 in. (26 mm.) total deflection

TIGHTENING TORQUES

Water elbow attachment	16 - 18 lb.ft.	(2.2 - 2.5 kg.m.)
Water pump pulley attachment	14 - 16 lb.ft.	(2.0 - 2.2 kg.m.)
Water pump attachment	18 - 20 lb.ft.	(2.5 - 2.8 kg.m.)
Fan attachment	6 - 8 lb.ft.	(0.8 - 1.1 kg.m.)
Header tank attachment	6 - 8 lb.ft.	(0.8 - 1.1 kg.m.)

Ignition System

GENERAL

The coil type ignition system includes a Lucas coil on all models, a Lucas distributor on the Herald series and a Delco distributor on the Spitfire range. The coil on the Spitfire IV is used with a ballast resistor to improve starting in adverse conditions.

ROUTINE MAINTENANCE

Interior and exterior of distributor cap, high tension leads and sparking plug ceramics should be kept clean to prevent tracking.

Every 6,000 miles (10,000 km.)

1. Remove distributor cap and rotor arm. On Herald (Fig. D:1), apply a few drops of thin oil to screw (1) and pivot (2) and lightly grease rotor cam (3). On Spitfire (Fig. D:2), lightly oil points (1), (2) & (3), lightly grease cam (4) and inject 5 c.c. of engine oil at hole (5).

2. Remove contact breaker points and clean up faces evenly with fine carborundum stone. Renew contact if excessively worn or pitted.

3. Refit contacts and adjust gap between points.

4. Remove and clean sparking plugs, inspect for worn electrodes and cracked or loose ceramic insulators and renew if necessary. Set plug gaps to 0.025 in. (0.64 mm.).

Every 12,000 miles (20,000 km.)

Fit replacement sparking plugs with correct gap setting.

CONTACT BREAKER POINTS - Adjustment

Herald (Fig. D:3)

1. Remove distributor cap and rotor arm and rotate crankshaft until moving contact is on cam peak.

2. Slacken fixed contact screw (arrowed).

3. With screwdriver in slot and with feeler gauge between contacts, adjust fixed contacts until 0.014 - 0.016 in. (0.356 - 0.406 mm.) gap is obtained.

4. Tighten fixed contact screw and re-check gap.

5. Replace rotor arm and distributor cap.

Spitfire (Fig. D:2)

1. Proceed as for Herald

2. Slacken fixed contact screw (7).

3. Turn eccentric screw (6) until 0.014 - 0.016 in. (0.356 - 0.406 mm.) gap is obtained.

4. Proceed as for Herald.

CONTACT BREAKER POINTS - Replacement

Herald (Fig. D:4)

1. Remove distributor cap and rotor arm.

2. Remove nut (3) insulator (2) and L.T. and capacitor lead terminals.

3. Remove moving contact (1) and fibre washers (29) and (30).

4. Remove lock screw (28) with washer and remove fixed contact (27).

5. Clean preservative from new contact faces.

6. Position fixed contact and fit lock screw and washer.

7. Fit insulation washers and position moving contact.

8. Connect L.T. and capacitor leads, insulator (2) and secure with nut.

9. Adjust contact breaker points.

10. Assemble rotor arm and distributor cap.

Spitfire (Figs. D:5 & D:6)

1. Remove distributor cap and rotor arm and separate L.T. lead at connector.

2. Remove lock screw (9) and raise contact breaker assembly sufficiently to turn nut (1, Fig. D:6).

3. Remove nut, washer, (2) and L.T. and capacitor lead terminals.

Fig. D:1 Distributor lubrication points - Herald.

Fig. D:2 Distributor lubrication and adjustment points - Spitfire.

Fig. D:3 Contact breaker points adjustment - Herald.

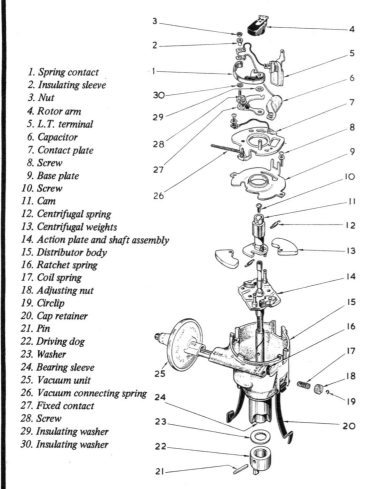

1. Spring contact
2. Insulating sleeve
3. Nut
4. Rotor arm
5. L.T. terminal
6. Capacitor
7. Contact plate
8. Screw
9. Base plate
10. Screw
11. Cam
12. Centrifugal spring
13. Centrifugal weights
14. Action plate and shaft assembly
15. Distributor body
16. Ratchet spring
17. Coil spring
18. Adjusting nut
19. Circlip
20. Cap retainer
21. Pin
22. Driving dog
23. Washer
24. Bearing sleeve
25. Vacuum unit
26. Vacuum connecting spring
27. Fixed contact
28. Screw
29. Insulating washer
30. Insulating washer

Fig. D:4 Exploded view of the distributor components - Herald.

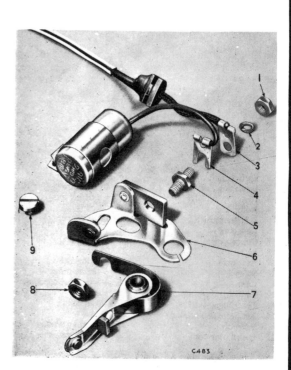

Fig. D:5 Details of the contact breaker assembly - Spitfire

1. Nut
2. Lock washer
3. L.T. cable
4. Capacitor
5. Terminal stud
6. Fixed contact
7. Moving contact
8. Nut
9. Screw (Fixed contact)

4. Remove contacts (6) and (7) and separate by removing nut (8) from stud (5).

5. Clean preservative from new contact faces.

6. Assemble contacts with stud (5) and nut and position in distributor.

7. Attach electrical leads to outside of stud and secure with nut and washers.

8. Fit lock screw (9) and connect L.T. lead.

9. Adjust contacts gap.

10. Assemble rotor arm and distributor cap.

IGNITION TIMING - Adjustment

1. Remove distributor cap and loosen pedestal clamp bolt.

2. Set vernier adjuster to fully retarded.

3. With ignition switched on, rotate distributor until contact breaker points begin to open. Check by observing spark or when test lamp connected to distributor L.T. terminal and good earth illuminates.

4. Re-tighten clamp bolt and turn micro adjusting screw until correct ignition setting is obtained. (Refer to TECHNICAL DATA for specified settings).

   NOTE: On Herald models, one division on the vernier scale equals four crankshaft degrees and on Spitfire models one adjusting screw click equals one crankshaft degree.

   On Spitfire Mk. III Emission Control, fine setting is obtained with engine running at 800 - 850 r.p.m. using stroboscope.

DISTRIBUTOR - Removal and Installation

1. Disconnect L.T. lead to distributor.

2. Disconnect H.T. cables from sparking plugs and coil.

3. On Spitfire models, disconnect tachometer drive cable from distributor.

4. Disconnect vacuum pipe from distributor.

5. Remove bolt securing distributor clamp to pedestal and remove distributor.

   NOTE: Do not slacken clamping bolts unless dismantling.

6. Install in reverse order. If clamping bolt has been released or pedestal drive gear disturbed, set number 1 piston at T.D.C. on compression stroke, and ensure respective rotor arm positions are as in Figs. D:7, D:8 and D:9 before proceeding to ignition timing.

DISTRIBUTOR - Overhaul

Herald (Fig. D:4)

1. Remove distributor cap and rotor arm.

2. Remove contact breaker points, capacitor (6) and L.T. terminal (5).

3. Disconnect vacuum control spring (26) from contact plate (7) remove two screws (8) and take out contact plate and baseplate (9).

4. Remove circlip (19), adjuster (18) and spring (17) taking care not to retain ratchet spring (16). Withdraw vacuum control unit (25).

5. Release springs (12) from base of cam (11) and from action plate (14). Remove screw (10) and draw cam from shaft.

6. Before driving out pin (21) to release driving dog (22) washer (23) and shaft from distributor body, check shaft end-float which should not exceed 1/32 in. (0.8 mm.).

7. With new shaft or checking bar of 0.49 in. (12.45 mm.) diameter check sleeve (24) for wear. Renew sleeve if worn. Reduce excessive end-float by renewing nylon spacer under action plate (14) and washer (23). Clean all parts, inspect for wear or damage and renew as necessary.

8. Fit nylon spacer under action plate and assemble weights, springs and cam to action plate. Secure cam with screw (10).

9. Fit washer (23) and driving dog (22), insert pin (21) and peen over ends.

10. Assemble contact plate (7) to base plate (9) by springing clip over base plate slot edge, inserting contact plate peg into a slot on base plate and turning it slightly clockwise. Secure assembly to body with screws (10).

11. Insert vacuum control unit (25) into body and assemble ratchet spring (16) spring (27) adjuster (18) and circlip (19). Hook spring (26) on to lug.

12. Assemble capacitor, L.T. leads and contact breaker points to contact plate and adjust points.

13. Refit rotor arm and cap.

Spitfire

1. Remove distributor cap and rotor arm.

2. Remove contact breaker points, capacitor and L.T. lead.

3. Remove vacuum control unit and contact breaker plate assembly.

4. With a 7/32 in. dia. steel bar turned down at one end to 0.15 in. dia. by 1/8 in., drive out tachometer gear, thrust washer and end cap.

5. Remove clamp and oil seal bush.

c

Fig. D:6 Replacing the contact breaker assembly - Spitfire.

Fig. D:7 Distributor position with No. 1 piston at T.D.C. on the firing stroke - Herald 1200 & 12/50

Fig. D:8 Distributor position with No. 1 piston at T.D.C. on the firing stroke - Herald 13/60.

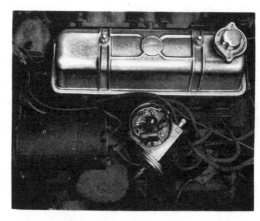

Fig. D:9 Distributor position with No. 1 piston at T.D.C. on the firing stroke - Spitfire.

6. Remove securing rivet and withdraw driving dog and spacer.

   NOTE: Driving dog teeth are offset to left when facing rotor arm locating slot.

7. Remove shaft assembly with spacer from distributor. Release spring at bottom of distributor bowl and remove oil retaining felt.

8. Clean all parts, inspect for wear or damage, and renew as necessary. Soak felt in clean engine oil, shake off surplus and secure felt in position with spring clip.

9. Fit shaft spacer washer on shaft and thread shaft into distributor. Fit driving dog washer, correctly position dog and secure with rivet.

10. With thrust washer on tachometer drive gear shaft, cover assembly with petroleum jelly and push into position. Fit new end cover and secure with four equally spaced centre punch indentations at edge of bore.

11. Fit oil seal bush and clamp to bottom of shaft.

12. Assemble contact breaker base plate and vacuum control assembly.

13. Fit contact breaker points, capacitor and L.T. lead. Adjust points.

14. Refit rotor arm and distributor cap.

Technical Data

Ignition Coil:
Type - Herald 1200, 12/50, Spitfire 4, Mk. II and III . . . . . . Lucas HA12

      - Herald 13/60 . . . . Lucas LA12

      - Spitfire Mk. IV . . . . Lucas 16C6 (6-volt with ballast resistor coil)

Distributor
Type - Herald (Prior to Engine Nos. GA67436 & GA86619) . . . Lucas DM2

      - Herald (From Engine Nos. GA67436 & GA86619) . . . . Lucas 25D4

      - Spitfire . . . . Delco D200

Contact breaker gap:-

      - Spitfire 4 and Mk. II . . . . 0.020 in.   (0.5 mm.)

      - All others . . . . 0.015 in.   (0.4 mm.)

Moving contact spring tension:

      - Herald . . . . 18 - 24 oz.

      - Spitfire 4, Mk. II & Mk. IV . . . . 17 - 21 oz.

      - Spitfire III . . . . 22 - 26 oz.

Rotation - (viewed on rotor) . . . . anti-clockwise

Firing angles . . . . $90^\circ \pm 1^\circ$

Dwell angle - Herald . . . . $60^\circ \pm 3^\circ$

           - Spitfire 4, Mk. II & Mk. IV . . . . $36^\circ \pm 1^\circ$

           - Spitfire III . . . . $41^\circ \pm 1^\circ$

Open angle - Herald . . . . $30^\circ \pm 3^\circ$

          - Spitfire 4, Mk. II & Mk. IV . . . . $54^\circ \pm 1^\circ$

          - Spitfire III . . . . $49^\circ \pm 1^\circ$

Firing order . . . . 1 - 3 - 4 - 2

Ignition timing (static) - Herald 1200, 12/50 . . . . 15° B.T.D.C.

                 - Herald 13/60 . . . . 9° B.T.D.C.

                 - Spitfire 4 & Mk. II . . . . 13° B.T.D.C.

                 - Spitfire III & IV . . . . 6° B.T.D.C.

                 - Spitfire III (emission control) . . . . . 2° A.T.D.C.

Sparking Plugs
Type - Herald 1200, 12/50 . . . . Champion L87Y

      - Herald 13/60, Spitfire Mk. III & IV . . . . Champion N-9Y

      - Spitfire 4 and Mk. II . . . . Lodge CNY

Electrode gap . . . . 0.025 in. (0.64 mm.)

Fig. E:1 Topping up the carburettor damper - Stromberg.

Fig. E:2 Topping up the carburettor damper - S.U.

Fig. E:3 Details of the fuel pump
1. Bolt
2. Washer
3. Cap
4. Gasket
5. Gauze filter
6. Sediment bowl

Fig. E:4 Details of the air cleaner assembly - Herald 1200 & 12/50

1. Clamp bolt
2. Rubber ring
3. Washer
4. Nut
5. Clamp
6. Closing plate
7. Gasket
8. Filter element
9. Case
10. Sealing washer
11. Retaining screw

Fig. E:5 Details of the air cleaner assembly - Herald 13/60

1. Gasket (to carburettor)
2. Closing plate
3. Gasket
4. Filter element
5. Gasket
6. Case
7. Retaining bolt

Fig. E:6 Details of the air cleaner assembly - Spitfire 4.

Fig. E:7 Details of the air cleaner assembly - Spitfire Mk. III.

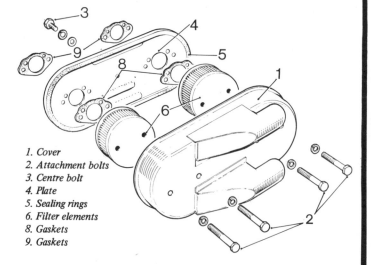

1. Cover
2. Attachment bolts
3. Centre bolt
4. Plate
5. Sealing rings
6. Filter elements
8. Gaskets
9. Gaskets

Fig. E:8 Details of the air cleaner assembly - Spitfire Mk IV

Fuel System

GENERAL

The fuel system main components are the fuel tank, fuel pump, air cleaner with a single carburettor on the Herald and twin carburettors on the Spitfire. The fuel tank is located behind the rear seat squab and incorporates a filler neck with cap and overflow pipe, a fuel gauge transmitter and a fuel feed/drain connection. The Herald 1200 & 12/50 fuel tank contains a reserve fuel compartment controlled by a tap on the top of the tank. The mechanical diaphragm type pump is mounted on the left-hand side of the engine with a rocker arm which is operated by the camshaft.

A single Solex down draught carburettor is fitted to the Herald 1200 & 12/50. A sidedraught Stromberg unit is used on the Herald 13/60, and the Spitfire has twin S.U. sidedraught carburettors. One or two air cleaner elements, as applicable, are housed in a container attached to the carburettor intakes, two hoses direct air from the front of the vehicle to the container on the Spitfire Mk. IV, and the Herald 13/60 container has a breather pipe connection when an emission valve is not fitted. Separate containers are provided on the Spitfire 4 and Mk. II which, together with the Herald 13/60, has a gauze element alternative to the normal paper item. Heated inlet manifolds are provided on the Herald 13/60 and Spitfire Mk. II and subsequent models.

On the Spitfire Mk. III, emission controlled versions of the S.U. H.S.2 carburettors are fitted for the U.S.A. market. These are special units designed to conform to the stringent anti-pollution standards and must not be replaced by other units. The Mk. III 1970 model for the U.S.A. market was equipped with a single Stromberg carburettor also built to conform to these special anti-pollution standards but forming part of a complete emission and fuel evaporation control system.

ROUTINE MAINTENANCE

Every 6,000 miles (10,000 km.)

1. Top up carburettor damper on Herald 13/60 and Spitfire models with seasonal grade of engine oil until threaded plug of damper is 0.25 in. (6 mm.) above dashpot before resistance is felt. (Fig. E:1 or E:2).

2. Lubricate throttle and choke control linkages.

3. Remove and clean air cleaner elements.

Clean paper elements with low pressure air line or soft brush and clean wire gauze elements in petrol, allow to dry, and dip in engine oil allowing surplus to drain. See later for removal and installation procedure of air cleaner.

Every 12,000 miles (20,000 km.)

1. Renew paper type air cleaner element.

2. Clean fuel pump as follows (Fig. E:3):-

   (a) Disconnect and plug inlet pipe to cut off fuel supply from tank.

   (b) Remove bolt (1) and washer and remove cap (3) and gasket (4).

   (c) Remove gauze filter (5) and clean in petrol using fingers to remove dirt.

   (d) Loosen sediment in bowl with small screwdriver and blow out with air pump.

   (e) Renew gasket if damaged or deteriorated.

   (f) Assemble with filter gauze face downwards and connect inlet pipe.

3. Adjust idling control if necessary.

4. Check exhaust system for deterioration, leakage and security. Rectify or renew parts as necessary.

AIR CLEANER - Removal and Installation

Herald 1200, 12/50 (Fig. E:4)

1. Release clamp (5) and remove assembly from carburettor.

2. Remove bolt (11) and washer, separate cover, (9) and plate (6) and remove gaskets (7) and element.

3. Assemble and install in reverse order ensuring that gaskets (7) and rubber sleeve (2) are serviceable and correctly positioned.

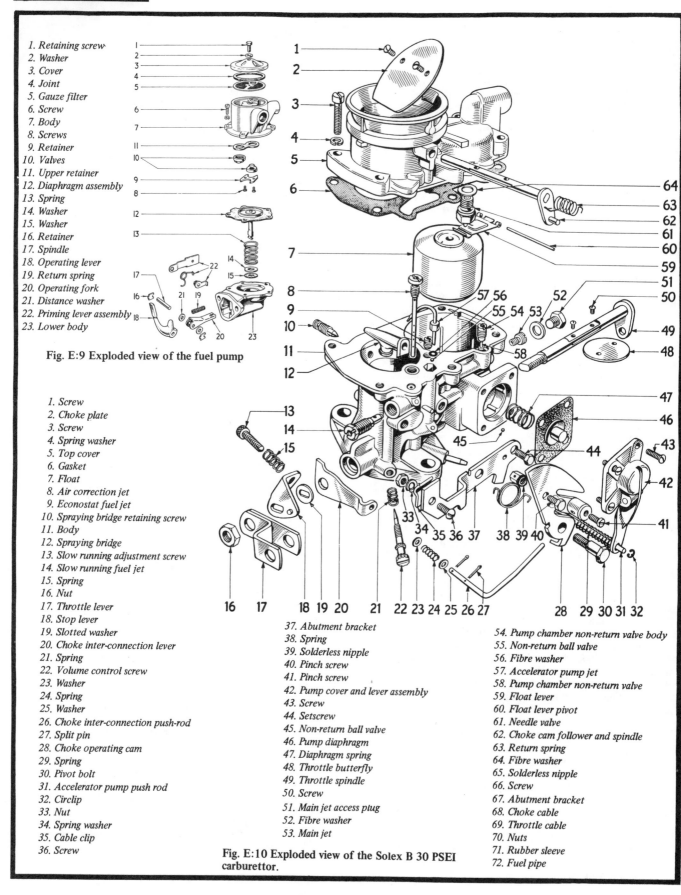

1. Retaining screw
2. Washer
3. Cover
4. Joint
5. Gauze filter
6. Screw
7. Body
8. Screws
9. Retainer
10. Valves
11. Upper retainer
12. Diaphragm assembly
13. Spring
14. Washer
15. Washer
16. Retainer
17. Spindle
18. Operating lever
19. Return spring
20. Operating fork
21. Distance washer
22. Priming lever assembly
23. Lower body

Fig. E:9 Exploded view of the fuel pump

1. Screw
2. Choke plate
3. Screw
4. Spring washer
5. Top cover
6. Gasket
7. Float
8. Air correction jet
9. Econostat fuel jet
10. Spraying bridge retaining screw
11. Body
12. Spraying bridge
13. Slow running adjustment screw
14. Slow running fuel jet
15. Spring
16. Nut
17. Throttle lever
18. Stop lever
19. Slotted washer
20. Choke inter-connection lever
21. Spring
22. Volume control screw
23. Washer
24. Spring
25. Washer
26. Choke inter-connection push-rod
27. Split pin
28. Choke operating cam
29. Spring
30. Pivot bolt
31. Accelerator pump push rod
32. Circlip
33. Nut
34. Spring washer
35. Cable clip
36. Screw

37. Abutment bracket
38. Spring
39. Solderless nipple
40. Pinch screw
41. Pinch screw
42. Pump cover and lever assembly
43. Screw
44. Setscrew
45. Non-return ball valve
46. Pump diaphragm
47. Diaphragm spring
48. Throttle butterfly
49. Throttle spindle
50. Screw
51. Main jet access plug
52. Fibre washer
53. Main jet

54. Pump chamber non-return valve body
55. Non-return ball valve
56. Fibre washer
57. Accelerator pump jet
58. Pump chamber non-return valve
59. Float lever
60. Float lever pivot
61. Needle valve
62. Choke cam follower and spindle
63. Return spring
64. Fibre washer
65. Solderless nipple
66. Screw
67. Abutment bracket
68. Choke cable
69. Throttle cable
70. Nuts
71. Rubber sleeve
72. Fuel pipe

Fig. E:10 Exploded view of the Solex B 30 PSEI carburettor.

Fig. E:11 Solex carburettor installation (see Fig. E:10 for key).

Fig. E:12 Details of the float chamber and jets - Solex.

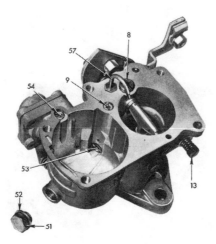

Fig. E:13 Locations of the jets - Solex.

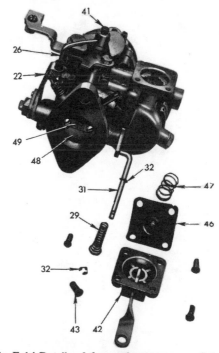

Fig. E:14 Details of the accelerator pump - Solex.

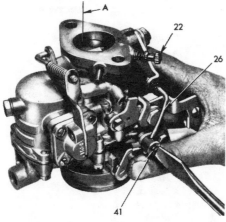

Fig. E:15 Setting the choke and throttle interconnection - Solex.

Fig. E:16 Stromberg carburettor installation.

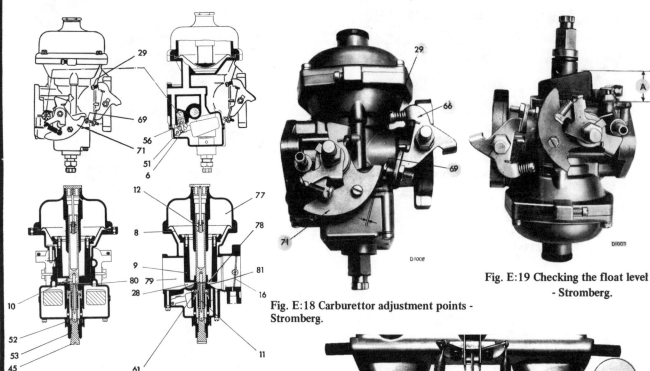

Fig. E:18 Carburettor adjustment points - Stromberg.

Fig. E:19 Checking the float level - Stromberg.

Fig. E:17 Functional diagram of the Stromberg Carburettor

6. Needle	52. "O" ring
8. Diaphragm	53. Bushing screw
9. Air valve	56. Needle valve
10. Needle locking screw	61. Bush
11. Metering needle	69. Stop screw
12. Air valve damper	71. Choke cam lever
16. Throttle butterfly	77. Chamber
28. Starter bar	78. Air valve drilling
29. Throttle stop screw	79. Bore
45. Jet adjusting screw	80. Jet orifice
51. Float assembly	81. Bridge

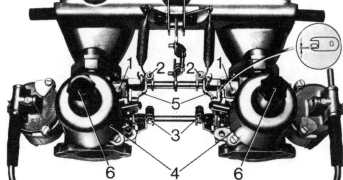

Fig. E:22 Top view of the S.U. carburettor installation

1. Throttle adjusting screw	4. Suction chamber
2. Clamp screw	5. Forked lever
3. Clamp screw	6. Damper knob

1. Clip
2. Pipe protection
3. Mixture cable
4. Spring
5. Lever
6. Balance pipe
7. Throttle rod
8. Fuel feed pipe
9. Fuel connecting pipe
10. Spring
11. Throttle control lever
12. Pinch screw
13. Inner cable
14. Attachment bolts
15. Sleeve

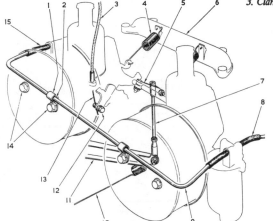

Fig. E:21 Details of the fuel pipe and control connections - S.U.

Herald 13/60 (Fig. E:5)

1. Disconnect breather pipe from container plate if applicable.
2. Remove attachment bolts (7) and washer and remove assembly from carburettor. Retain gasket (1).
3. Separate cover (6) and plate (2) and remove gaskets (3 and 5) and element.
4. Assemble and install in reverse order ensuring that gaskets (3 and 5) and gasket (1) are serviceable and correctly positioned.

Spitfire 4 (Fig. E:6)

1. Disconnect clips securing elements to carburettors balance pipe.
2. Remove two attachment bolts and remove each element in turn from its carburettor. Retain gaskets.
3. Assemble in reverse order ensuring gaskets are serviceable and correctly positioned.

Spitfire Mk. III (Fig. E:7)

1. Remove attachment bolts and remove assembly from carburettors. Retain gaskets.
2. Remove centre bolt and separate cover and plate and re-move elements.
3. Assemble and install in reverse order ensuring gaskets are serviceable and correctly positioned.

Spitfire Mk. IV (Fig. E:8)

1. Remove air intake tubes from cover.
2. Remove carburettors balance pipe.
3. Remove attachment bolts (2) and remove assembly from carburettors. Retain gaskets (9).
4. Remove centre bolt (3) and washers, separate cover (1) and plate (4) and remove elements and inside gaskets (8).
5. Assemble and install in reverse order ensuring sealing ring (5) and gaskets (8 and 9) and serviceable and correctly positioned.

FUEL PUMP - Removal and Installation

1. Disconnect fuel feed and outlet pipes and blank off inlet pipe to avoid loss of fuel. Remove attachment nuts and washers and remove pump and gasket.
2. Clean joint faces, smear new gasket with jointing compound and place gasket and pump on mounting studs. Secure with nuts and washers. Connect fuel pipes and check for correct operation and for leaks.

FUEL PUMP - Dismantling and Re-assembly (Fig. E:9)

1. Dismantle in sequence given in Fig. E:9. Rotate diaphragm (12) 90° anti-clockwise to remove.
2. Clean all parts and inspect for damage and deterioration. Renew parts as necessary.
3. Re-assemble by reversing the sequence. Ensure valves (10) point in the direction shown in Fig. E:9).

CARBURETTOR (HERALD 1200 & 12/50)

Removal (Fig. E:11)

1. Remove air cleaner.
2. Disconnect fuel pipe (72) and pull off vacuum pipe rubber sleeve (71).
3. Disconnect choke cable (68) at bracket (37) and cam screw (40) and throttle cable (69) from lever.
4. Remove attachment nuts (70) and detach carburettor and gasket.

Installation

1. Ensure mating faces are clean, position carburettor on manifold studs using new gasket and secure with two nuts.
2. Connect throttle and choke cables adjusting operating length of choke cable to ensure the butterfly cam plate is against adjustment bracket, stop when choke knob if fully in.
3. Connect fuel and vacuum pipes.
4. Install air cleaner.

Idling Adjustment (Fig. E:11)

1. With engine running, turn slow running screw (13) until idling speed is about 500 r.p.m.
2. Open volume control screw (22) until hunting is evident, then gradually screw in until hunting ceases and engine idles smoothly.
3. Reduce engine speed to 500 r.p.m., if necessary, with slow running screw and correct any consequent slight hunting with volume control screw.

    NOTE: The volume control screw must never be fully screwed in.

Routine Cleaning (Figs. E:11, E:12, E:13 and E:14)

1. Remove air cleaner and disconnect fuel pipe.

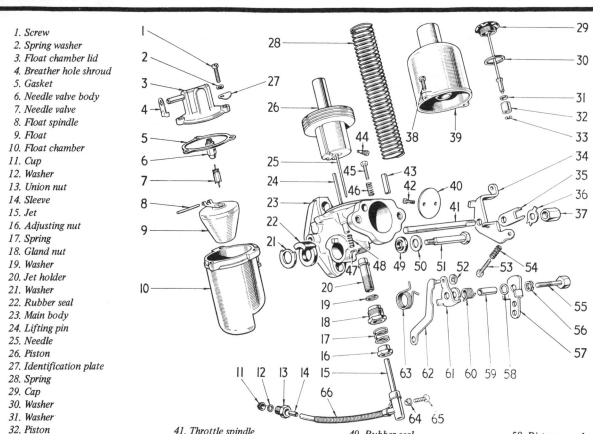

1. Screw
2. Spring washer
3. Float chamber lid
4. Breather hole shroud
5. Gasket
6. Needle valve body
7. Needle valve
8. Float spindle
9. Float
10. Float chamber
11. Cup
12. Washer
13. Union nut
14. Sleeve
15. Jet
16. Adjusting nut
17. Spring
18. Gland nut
19. Washer
20. Jet holder
21. Washer
22. Rubber seal
23. Main body
24. Lifting pin
25. Needle
26. Piston
27. Identification plate
28. Spring
29. Cap
30. Washer
31. Washer
32. Piston
33. Circlip
34. Throttle adjusting bracket
35. Throttle fork
36. Lock tab
37. Nut
38. Screw
39. Vacuum chamber
40. Throttle disc

41. Throttle spindle
42. Screw
43. Mixture enrichment cable abutment
44. Needle retaining screw
45. Throttle adjusting screw
46. Spring
47. Circlip
48. Spring

49. Rubber seal
50. Plain washer
51. Bolt
52. Circlip
53. Throttle adjusting screw
54. Spring
55. Bolt
56. Spring washer
57. Cam lever

58. Distance washer
59. Tube
60. Return spring
61. Pick-up lever
62. Jet lever
63. Return spring
64. Shouldered washer
65. Screw
66. Flexible pipe

Fig. E:20 Exploded view of the S.U. HS-2 carburettor

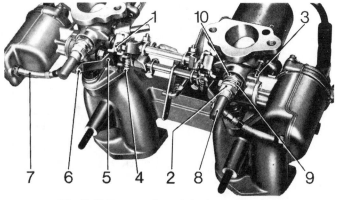

Fig. E:23 Bottom view of the S.U. carburettor installation

1. Choke cable pinch screw
2. Jet adjuster
3. Piston lifting pin
4. Throttle adjusting screw
5. Jet lever
6. Jet lever screw
7. Jet fuel pipe
8. Jet
9. Spring
10. Gland nut

Fig. E:24 Setting the throttle lever-to-pin clearance - S.U.

2. Remove top cover attachment screws and washers and remove top cover assembly and gasket.

3. Remove pin (60), lever (59) and float (Fig. E:12).

4. Screw out slow running jet (14) (Fig. E:11).

5. Remove plug (51) with washer and use a long screwdriver to extract main jet (53). Unscrew air connection jet (8), and remove valve body (54) with valve (54). Remove accelerator pump jet (57) retaining ball valve (55) beneath it. (Fig. E:13).

6. Remove screws (43), pivot accelerator pump cover (42) on pump lever and remove diaphragm (46) and spring (47) retaining ball valve inside pump chamber. (Fig. E:14).

7. Clean float chamber, jets and fuel passages with petrol and air line.

8. Re-assemble in reverse order renewing top cover gasket, if necessary.

Dismantling (Fig. E:10)

1. Remove carburettor and remove top cover and jets as in Routine Cleaning.

2. Remove jet (61) with washer (64) from top cover and, after removing screws (1) and strangler (2), withdraw spindle (62) and spring (63).

3. Remove nut (16) to remove levers (17), (18), (20), and washer (19).

4. Remove screws (50) detach butterfly (48) and withdraw spindle (49).

5. Detach circlips (32) from each end and extract push rod (31) and spring (29).

6. Release screw (41) to free rod (26) and remove split pins (27) to free lever (20) washers (23) and (25) and spring (24).

7. Detach bracket (37), cam plate (28) and spring by removing screws (44) and (30).

8. Withdraw volume control screw (22) with spring (21) and Econostat jet (9).

9. Remove screw (10) to detach spraying bridge (12).

10. Clean all parts with petrol, inspect for wear or damage and renew items as necessary.

Re-assembly

1. Secure spraying bridge (12) with screw (10) and assemble bracket (37) spring (38) and cam plate (28) to body and secure with screw (44) and pivot bolt (30).

2. Fit volume control screw (22) with spring (21) and screw in Econostat jet (9).

3. Position throttle spindle (49) in body and attach butterfly (48).

4. Fit washer (25) spring (24) lever (20) and washer (23) on to rod (26), secure with split pins and thread rod into cam plate boss and secure with pinch screw.

5. Thread items (20), (19), (18) and (17) to throttle spindle (49) and secure with nut (16).

6. Hook rod (31) to butterfly spindle, fit circlip, spring (29) pump lever (42) and secure with second circlip.

7. Assemble ball valve (45), spring (47), diaphragm (46) and pump cover and lever assembly (42) to body. Fit plug (51) with serviceable washer.

8. Fit valve body (54) with valve (58) and insert ball (55) washer and pump jet (57).

9. Screw in jets (8) and (9) and position float, lever (59) and pin (60).

10. Assemble spindle (62) with spring (63) to top cover and attach strangler (2). Fit needle valve (61) with serviceable washer.

11. With new gasket (6) assemble top cover to body with strangler held in open position.

12. Adjust throttle/strangler connecting rod (26) by lodging a piece of 0.027 in. (0.7 mm.) dia. wire "A" between butterfly and bore, holding strangler (2) closed and tighten screw (41) (See Fig. E:15).

13. Install carburettor.

CARBURETTOR (HERALD 13/60)

Removal and Installation (Fig. E:16)

1. Remove air cleaner.

2. Disconnect and plug fuel feed pipe and disconnect vacuum pipe.

3. Disconnect throttle and choke controls.

4. Remove two attachment bolts and remove carburettor.

5. Install in reverse order. Ensure gasket is serviceable and adjust carburettor as necessary.

Idling Adjustment (Fig. E:17)

NOTE: Satisfactory idling depends on general engine condition as well as tappet adjustment, spark plug condition and ignition timing. These points should, therefore, be checked if satisfactory idling is unobtainable.

1. Ensure screw (69) is set to give gap of one sixteenth of an inch (1.58 mm.) at choke lever cam (71) and set throttle stop screw (29) one complete turn back from contact with body flange (Fig. E:18).

2. Bring engine to normal working temperature, remove air cleaner, hold air valve (9) down on to bridge (81) through throttle bore, and with a coin turn jet adjustment screw (45) until jet contacts bottom of air valve. From this

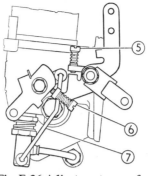

Fig. E:26 Adjustment screw for the jet and throttle inter-connection - S.U.

Fig. E:27 Jet assembly and piston lifting pin - S.U.

Fig. E:25 Setting the jet and throttle linkage clearance - S.U.

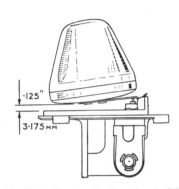

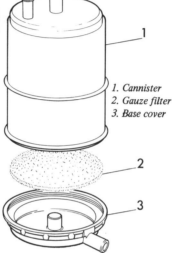

1. Cannister
2. Gauze filter
3. Base cover

Fig. E:30 Fuel line filter.

Fig. E:28 Setting the float level - S.U.

Fig. E:29 Details of the activated carbon filter.

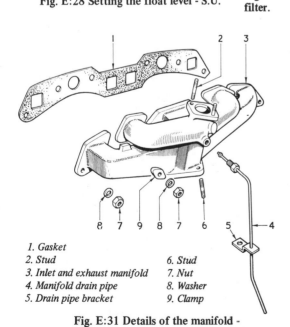

1. Gasket
2. Stud
3. Inlet and exhaust manifold
4. Manifold drain pipe
5. Drain pipe bracket
6. Stud
7. Nut
8. Washer
9. Clamp

Fig. E:31 Details of the manifold - Herald 1200

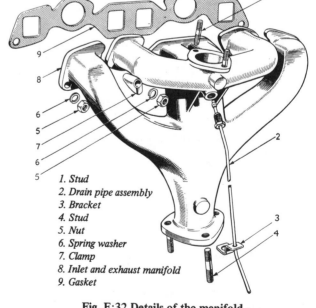

1. Stud
2. Drain pipe assembly
3. Bracket
4. Stud
5. Nut
6. Spring washer
7. Clamp
8. Inlet and exhaust manifold
9. Gasket

Fig. E:32 Details of the manifold - Herald 12/50

position turn down adjustment screw three turns to establish a jet position from which to work.

3. Run engine until thoroughly warm and adjust stop screw (29) to give idling speed of 600/650 r.p.m.

4. Turning jet adjustment screw clockwise to weaken mixture and anti-clockwise to enrich, adjust until engine beat is smooth and regular. Check by lifting air valve a small amount (1/32 in. approx.) with piston lifting pin. Properly adjusted engine speed will remain constant or fall slightly. If engine speed rises appreciably mixture is too rich, and if engine stops it is too weak.

Checking Float Chamber Level (Fig. E:19)

1. Remove carburettor and detach float chamber with gasket.

2. Invert carburettor and check that highest point of float with needle against its seating is 18.00 mm. above the main body face, see "A". If required reset level by carefully bending needle abutment tag. A thin fibre washer under needle valve seat will lower fuel level.

3. Assemble float chamber with new gasket and install carburettor.

Jet Centralising Procedure (Fig. E:17)

Efficient operation of the carburettor requires a freely moving air valve and a correctly centered needle in the jet valve. Check by lifting and releasing the air valve. A valve failing to fall freely indicates a sticking valve or off-centre jet. Rectify the former by removing valve and cleaning bore and valve in paraffin, and the latter by centralising the jet as follows:-

1. Lift air valve and fully tighten brushing screw (53).

2. Screw up orifice adjuster until top of orifice (80) is just above bridge (81).

3. Slacken jet bushing screw (53) to release orifice bush (61).

4. Allow air valve to fall and needle to enter and centralise orifice.

5. Slowly tighten bushing screw (53) frequently checking that needle is free in orifice by raising air valve (9) .25 in. and allowing it to fall freely. Valve should stop firmly on bridge.

6. Proceed as in Idling Adjustment.

CARBURETTORS (SPITFIRE)

Removal and Installation (Fig. E:21)

1. Remove air cleaner.

2. Remove fuel pipe (9) and disconnect pipe (8).

3. Disconnect choke cable (3), throttle control rod (7) and return springs (4).

4. Remove attachment nuts and detach carburettors from

inlet manifold complete with linkage. Remove and discard gaskets.

5. Install in reverse order using new gaskets and adjusting carburettors as necessary.

Routine Cleaning (Fig. E:20)

1. Scribe a locating mark at joint of vacuum chamber (39) with main body and remove screws (38).

2. Remove damper, chamber and piston (26) complete with needle and spring.

3. Clean inside of chamber, piston and needle with petrol.

4. Assemble dry apart from few drops of thin oil on piston rod. Replenish damper reservoir.

5. Repeat for other carburettor.

6. Disconnect fuel feed pipes from carburettors.

7. Remove float chamber tops (3) and float assemblies.

8. Clean sediment from float chambers.

9. Install float chamber tops with float assemblies and connect fuel pipes.

Tuning Procedure

NOTE: Satisfactory tuning depends on general engine condition as well as tappet adjustment, spark plug condition and ignition timing. These points should therefore be checked before attempting to tune the carburettors.

1. Bring engine to normal running temperature and remove air cleaners. Adjust each carburettor in turn.

2. Release clamp bolts (2) and (3) and set throttle adjusting screws (1) just clear of stop with throttle closed (Fig. E:22).

3. Turn in adjusting screw 1 1/2 turns to open throttle.

4. Scribe vacuum chamber joint and remove chamber and piston assembly.

5. Disconnect choke cable from jet lever (1) and turn in jet adjuster (2) until jet is level with bridge. Set both carburettor jets in same relative position to bridge (Fig. E:23).

6. Replace chamber and piston assembly.

7. Press up and release piston lifting pin and check piston falls freely and clicks against bridge. If not proceed as in Jet Centralising Procedure.

8. Unscrew jet adjusting nut two full turns.

9. Start engine and set both throttle adjustment screws to give approx. 800 r.p.m.

10. With length of small bore tubing listen to hiss at intakes and adjust throttles until an equal hiss is heard at both intakes.

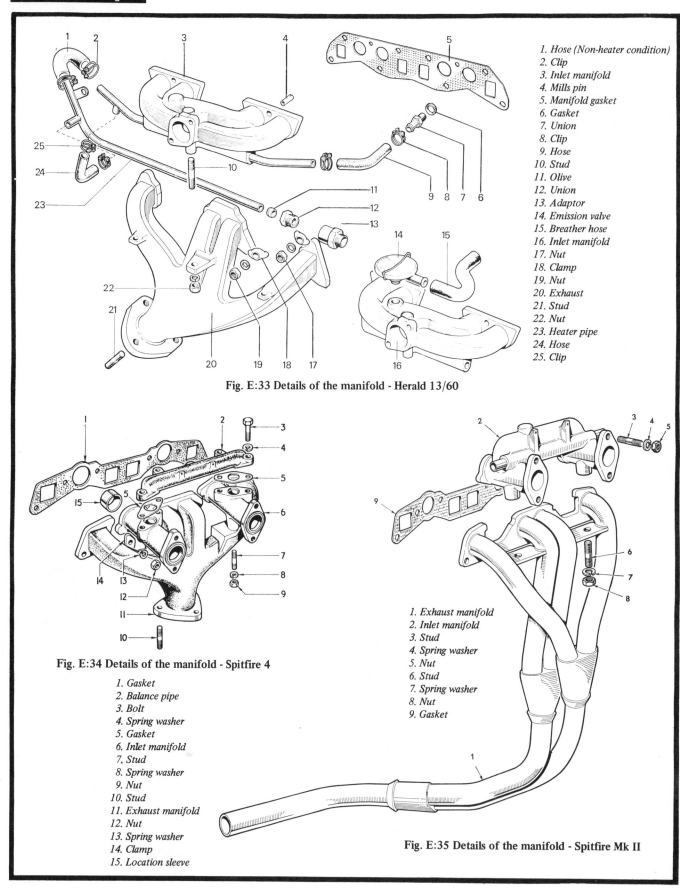

1. Hose (Non-heater condition)
2. Clip
3. Inlet manifold
4. Mills pin
5. Manifold gasket
6. Gasket
7. Union
8. Clip
9. Hose
10. Stud
11. Olive
12. Union
13. Adaptor
14. Emission valve
15. Breather hose
16. Inlet manifold
17. Nut
18. Clamp
19. Nut
20. Exhaust
21. Stud
22. Nut
23. Heater pipe
24. Hose
25. Clip

Fig. E:33 Details of the manifold - Herald 13/60

Fig. E:34 Details of the manifold - Spitfire 4

1. Gasket
2. Balance pipe
3. Bolt
4. Spring washer
5. Gasket
6. Inlet manifold
7. Stud
8. Spring washer
9. Nut
10. Stud
11. Exhaust manifold
12. Nut
13. Spring washer
14. Clamp
15. Location sleeve

1. Exhaust manifold
2. Inlet manifold
3. Stud
4. Spring washer
5. Nut
6. Stud
7. Spring washer
8. Nut
9. Gasket

Fig. E:35 Details of the manifold - Spitfire Mk II

11. Position each clamping lever (5) with its pin 0.015 in. (0.38 mm.) above bottom of throttle lever fork and tighten clamp bolts (2). (Fig. E:24).

12. Set both jet levers at lowest position and tighten clamp bolts (3) (Fig. E:22).

13. Reconnect choke cable with 1/16 in. (1.6 mm.) free movement of control knob before jet levers commence movement.

14. Gently press piston lifting pin on front carburettor 1/32 in. (0.8 mm.) to check mixture strength. Properly adjusted, engine speed will rise slightly or remain constant. If engine speed increases appreciably mixture is too rich, and if it falls mixture is too weak.

15. Repeat piston lifting check on rear carburettor and if adjustment is necessary recheck front carburettor.

    NOTE: Exhaust indications of mixture strength are as follows:-

    (a) Smooth and regular note - correct.

    (b) Uneven note with splashy misfire and colourless gas - too weak.

    (c) Regular misfire with blackish gas - too rich.

16. Pull choke knob until carburettor jets (8) are on point of movement by lever (5) and adjust screws (4) to give engine speed of 1,000 r.p.m. when hot. (Fig. E:23).

17. Install air cleaners and re-check mixture strength as in operation 14.

Jet and Throttle Linkage Setting (Figs. E:25 and E:26)

1. Run engine until at normal working temperature.

2. With choke control in and throttle closed set screw (6) with 0.015 in. (0.4 mm.) clearance between end of screw and cam lever.

    NOTE: This clearance must be checked whenever throttle adjusting screw (5) is altered.

Jet Centralising Procedure (Fig. E:27)

1. Disconnect jet lever at jet and jet fuel pipe at float chamber.

2. Hold jet (15) in topmost position and slacken gland nut (16).

3. Remove damper and with pencil gently press down piston and needle. Tighten gland nut.

4. Raise and release piston lifting pin (24) with jet in upper and lower positions and check that a similar click is heard from falling piston in each position. Repeat centering procedure until free fall in both positions is obtained.

5. Connect fuel pipe and jet lever and replenish damper.

Checking Float Chamber Lever (Fig. E:28)

1. Disconnect fuel feed pipe to carburettor.

2. Remove float chamber top cover and invert.

3. With gauge or 10 SWG material check gap between float and cover with float lever on needle valve is .125 in. (3.175 mm.). Bend lever to correct gap if necessary.

4. Replace cover and connect fuel pipe.

EMISSION CONTROL SYSTEM

The twin S.U. Emission carburettors installed on the Spitfire Mk. III for the American market are built to stringent anti-pollution requirements. Special procedure and equipment are necessary for assembly, installation and tuning which must be carried out by authorised personel. Servicing by the owner/driver is therefore limited to maintenance of damper oil level, control cables and attachments.

Similarly with the Stromberg single carburettor on the Spitfire Mk. III 1970 Model for the American market which is, additionally, part of a comprehensive emission control system entailing complementary modifications to engine and ignition system and installed in conjunction with fuel evaporation control system.

On models with emission control it is particularly important that associated routine maintenance on the distributor, spark plugs, valve rocker clearances, air cleaner and fuel filter should also be meticulously carried out.

The evaporative control system (Fig. E:29) consists of a sealed fuel tank with an overflow tank to allow for thermal expansion of the fuel and tank venting through an activated carbon filter which is purged by a connection to a rocker cover/carburettor breather pipe. The high level pipe run around the luggage compartment prevents fuel escaping to the carbon filter at any vehicle angle.

Carbon Filter (Fig. E:29)

Every 12,000 miles (20,000 km.) the filter gauge is replaced as follows:-

1. Disconnect pipes from top of filter canister.

2. Release mounting bracket and remove canister.

3. Unscrew base (3) and remove and discard gauze (2).

4. Clean base, fit new gauze and replace base.

5. Refit canister and connect pipes.

    Every 48,000 miles (80,000 km.) renew canister complete.

Fuel filter (Fig. E:30)

Every 12,000 miles (20,000 km.) the complete filter should be renewed as follows:-

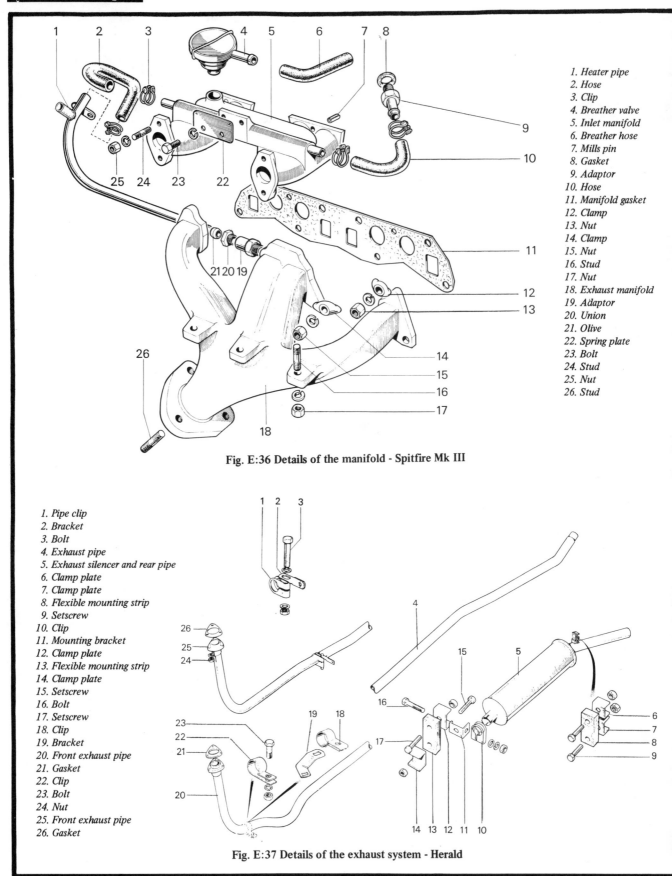

1. Heater pipe
2. Hose
3. Clip
4. Breather valve
5. Inlet manifold
6. Breather hose
7. Mills pin
8. Gasket
9. Adaptor
10. Hose
11. Manifold gasket
12. Clamp
13. Nut
14. Clamp
15. Nut
16. Stud
17. Nut
18. Exhaust manifold
19. Adaptor
20. Union
21. Olive
22. Spring plate
23. Bolt
24. Stud
25. Nut
26. Stud

Fig. E:36 Details of the manifold - Spitfire Mk III

1. Pipe clip
2. Bracket
3. Bolt
4. Exhaust pipe
5. Exhaust silencer and rear pipe
6. Clamp plate
7. Clamp plate
8. Flexible mounting strip
9. Setscrew
10. Clip
11. Mounting bracket
12. Clamp plate
13. Flexible mounting strip
14. Clamp plate
15. Setscrew
16. Bolt
17. Setscrew
18. Clip
19. Bracket
20. Front exhaust pipe
21. Gasket
22. Clip
23. Bolt
24. Nut
25. Front exhaust pipe
26. Gasket

Fig. E:37 Details of the exhaust system - Herald

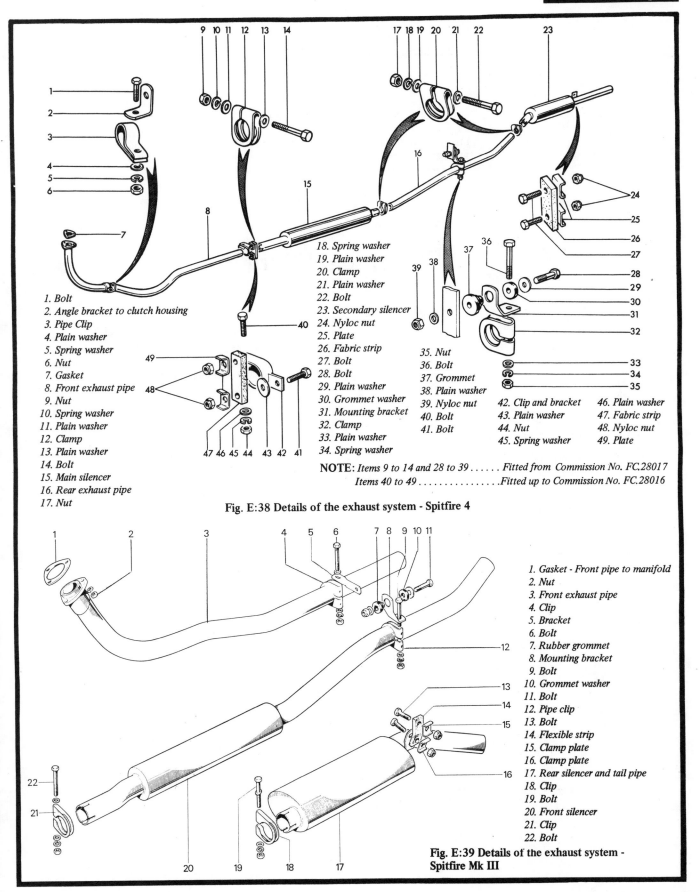

1. Bolt
2. Angle bracket to clutch housing
3. Pipe Clip
4. Plain washer
5. Spring washer
6. Nut
7. Gasket
8. Front exhaust pipe
9. Nut
10. Spring washer
11. Plain washer
12. Clamp
13. Plain washer
14. Bolt
15. Main silencer
16. Rear exhaust pipe
17. Nut

18. Spring washer
19. Plain washer
20. Clamp
21. Plain washer
22. Bolt
23. Secondary silencer
24. Nyloc nut
25. Plate
26. Fabric strip
27. Bolt
28. Bolt
29. Plain washer
30. Grommet washer
31. Mounting bracket
32. Clamp
33. Plain washer
34. Spring washer

35. Nut
36. Bolt
37. Grommet
38. Plain washer
39. Nyloc nut
40. Bolt
41. Bolt

42. Clip and bracket
43. Plain washer
44. Nut
45. Spring washer

46. Plain washer
47. Fabric strip
48. Nyloc nut
49. Plate

NOTE: Items 9 to 14 and 28 to 39 . . . . . . Fitted from Commission No. FC.28017
Items 40 to 49 . . . . Fitted up to Commission No. FC.28016

Fig. E:38 Details of the exhaust system - Spitfire 4

1. Gasket - Front pipe to manifold
2. Nut
3. Front exhaust pipe
4. Clip
5. Bracket
6. Bolt
7. Rubber grommet
8. Mounting bracket
9. Bolt
10. Grommet washer
11. Bolt
12. Pipe clip
13. Bolt
14. Flexible strip
15. Clamp plate
16. Clamp plate
17. Rear silencer and tail pipe
18. Clip
19. Bolt
20. Front silencer
21. Clip
22. Bolt

**Fig. E:39 Details of the exhaust system -
Spitfire Mk III**

47

D

1. Disconnect hoses clamping lower hose to prevent fuel loss.

2. Slacken bracket clamp bolt and remove filter.

3. Fit new filter, tighten clamp bolt and connect hoses.

MANIFOLD AND EXHAUST SYSTEMS

Figs. E:31 and E:39 give details and variants of the manifolds and exhaust systems and should be used for removal and installation operations.

Technical Data

Fuel Tank Capacity:-
Herald . . . . 6.5 Imp. gal.   (7.3 U.S. gal.; 32.0 litres)
Herald estate . . . . 9.0 Imp. gal.   (10.8 U.S. gal.; 41.0 litres)
Spitfire . . . . 8.25 Imp. gal. (10.0 U.S. gal.; 37.0 litres)
Pump:
Type . . . . A.C. mechanical diaphragm
Pressure . . . . 1.5 - 2.5 p.s.i. (0.1 - 0.18 kg/cm^2)
Carburettor:
Type:-
Herald 1200, 12/50 . . . . Solex B.30 P.S.E.I. downdraught
Herald 13/60 . . . . Stromberg 150 C.D. sidedraught
Spitfire . . . . Twin S.U. H.S.2. sidedraught
Spitfire Mk. III for U.S.A. market (N.A.D.A. Spec. AUD 285) . . Twin emission controlled S.U. H.S.2.
Spitfire Mk. III 1970 for U.S.A. market . . . . Single emission controlled Stromberg C.D.S.E. 150
Air Cleaner . . . . Paper or wire gauze element

TIGHTENING TORQUES

Fuel pump attachment . . . . 12 - 14 lbs./ft.   (1.66 - 1.94 kg./m.)
Manifold exhaust outlet . . . . 12 - 14 lbs./ft.   (1.66 - 1.94 kg./m.)
Manifold to cylinder head . . . . 24 - 26 lbs./ft.   (3.32 - 3.60 kg./m.)

Clutch

GENERAL

On earlier Herald 1200, 12/50 and Spitfire 4 and Mk. II models a coil spring clutch assembly was installed. This was replaced by a diaphragm spring type on later models which is also installed on the Herald 13/60 and Spitfire Mk. III and IV models. The release mechanism is hydraulically operated and is self-adjusting for wear. The clutch master cylinder with an integral hydraulic fluid reservoir is mounted on the engine compartment rear bulkhead immediately over the clutch pedal and the operating cylinder is located at the left hand side of the gearbox.

NOTE: During maintenance do not permit any dirt or other kind of fluid to enter the system. Clean around and blank all open ports and hoses. Use only fresh and unaereated fluid in system.

ROUTINE MAINTENANCE

Monthly

Check fluid level in master cylinder.

If necessary top up to bring level to mark on side of reservoir. Ensure breather hole is clear and investigate abnormal fluid loss.

Every 6,000 miles (10,000 km.)

1. Check flexible hose for damage, deterioration and evidence of chafing. Renew if necessary.

2. Check for excessive play in pedal pivot pin or bush, and push rod link pin. Renew parts as necessary.

RELEASE BEARING ASSEMBLY - Overhaul

(Figs. F:6 and F:7)

1. Remove gearbox as detailed in GEARBOX section.

2. Drive pin (17) out of housing and lever (23) and remove lever assembly. Retain spacers (19).

3. Drive out pins (21) and extract thrust plugs (16) to release bearing carrier.

4. Withdraw bearing from carrier.

5. Check pin (17) and housing bushes (18) for wear. Check attachment of push rod (22) for looseness. Examine release bearing for wear and scoring. Renew parts as necessary.

6. Reverse procedure for assembly and installation. Lightly peen ends of pins (17), (21) and (24) to secure.

CLUTCH UNIT - Removal and Installation

1. Remove gearbox as detailed in GEARBOX section.

2. Mark clutch and flywheel to maintain balance on re-assembly.

3. Progressively slacken the six setscrews and lift cover assembly and driven plate from the flywheel.

4. Inspect the flywheel friction face and skim or renew flywheel if necessary (see ENGINE section). Renew clutch plate if excessively worn.

5. With the longer hub boss towards the gearbox, centralise the clutch plate on the flywheel using a sawn-off input shaft or similar tool.

6. Locate the cover assembly on the three dowels and secure with the six setscrews tightened evenly and in turn to the correct torque. Remove centralising tool.

7. Install gearbox.

CLUTCH UNIT (COIL SPRING TYPE) - Overhaul

(Fig. F:2)

A faulty clutch cover assembly should be renewed complete but if dismantling should be decided upon proceed as detailed below using Churchill assembly fixture, Tool No. 99A (Fig. F:8) or a press and wooden blocks. (Fig. F:9).

Dismantling

1. Mark all parts to ensure re-assembly in original relative positions.

2. Place unit face down on tool kit baseplate with three spacers underneath at release lever positions.

3. Clamp unit to baseplate with tool operating handle and

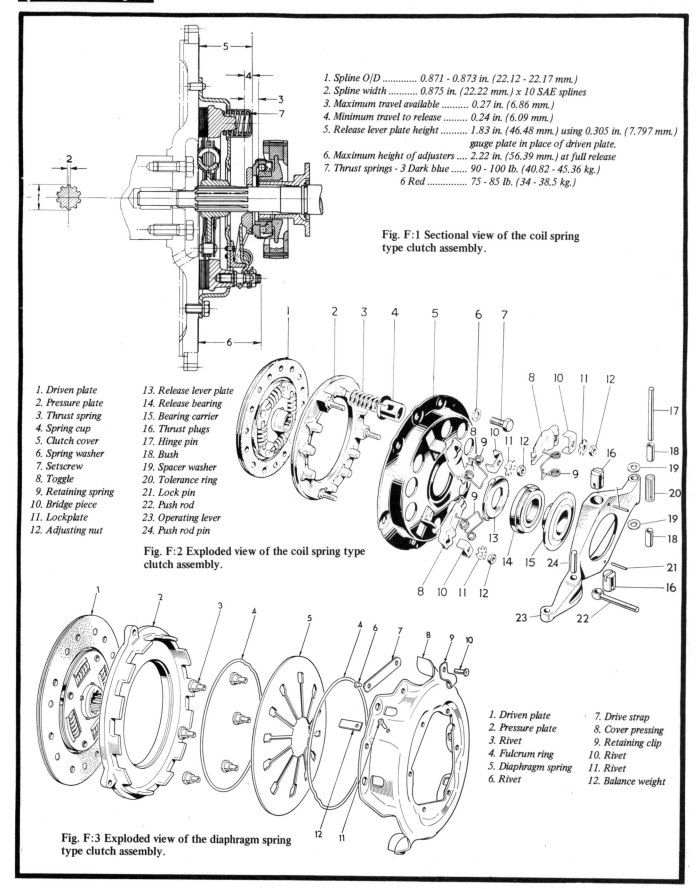

1. Spline O/D .... 0.871 - 0.873 in. (22.12 - 22.17 mm.)
2. Spline width .... 0.875 in. (22.22 mm.) x 10 SAE splines
3. Maximum travel available .... 0.27 in. (6.86 mm.)
4. Minimum travel to release .... 0.24 in. (6.09 mm.)
5. Release lever plate height .... 1.83 in. (46.48 mm.) using 0.305 in. (7.797 mm.)
   gauge plate in place of driven plate.
6. Maximum height of adjusters .... 2.22 in. (56.39 mm.) at full release
7. Thrust springs - 3 Dark blue ...... 90 - 100 lb. (40.82 - 45.36 kg.)
   6 Red .... 75 - 85 lb. (34 - 38.5 kg.)

Fig. F:1 Sectional view of the coil spring type clutch assembly.

1. Driven plate	13. Release lever plate
2. Pressure plate	14. Release bearing
3. Thrust spring	15. Bearing carrier
4. Spring cup	16. Thrust plugs
5. Clutch cover	17. Hinge pin
6. Spring washer	18. Bush
7. Setscrew	19. Spacer washer
8. Toggle	20. Tolerance ring
9. Retaining spring	21. Lock pin
10. Bridge piece	22. Push rod
11. Lockplate	23. Operating lever
12. Adjusting nut	24. Push rod pin

Fig. F:2 Exploded view of the coil spring type clutch assembly.

Fig. F:3 Exploded view of the diaphragm spring type clutch assembly.

1. Driven plate	7. Drive strap
2. Pressure plate	8. Cover pressing
3. Rivet	9. Retaining clip
4. Fulcrum ring	10. Rivet
5. Diaphragm spring	11. Rivet
6. Rivet	12. Balance weight

secure with six setscrews (Fig. F:10). Remove handle.

4. Press down release lever plate, detach retaining springs and remove plate.

5. Straighten tabs of lockplates (11) and remove nuts (12), lockplates, bridge pieces (10) and toggle levers (8).

6. Release holding down setscrews gradually and in turn and remove cover (5), retainers (4) springs (9) and pressure plate (2).

Inspection

1. Clean all parts and inspect for damage, cracks and scores. Renew parts as necessary.

2. Examine springs and renew if deformed.

3. Set up clutch plate on lathe or surface table and with plunger of dial indicator against friction lining face, check that run-out around face does not exceed 0.035 in. (0.23 mm.). Straighten plate if necessary.

4. Examine flywheel clutch face for scores and run-out (see ENGINE section).

Re-assembly

NOTE: Assemble items in original relative positions.

1. With tool kit distance pieces under release lever positions, position pressure plate (2) on baseplate and assemble springs (3), cups (4) and cover (5). Secure cover to baseplate with tool kit setscrews.

2. Assemble release levers (8), bridge pieces (10), lockplates (11) and lightly secure with nuts (12).

3. Fit tool kit items stud (3), adaptor (5) and gauge finger (4) to baseplate (Fig. F:8).

4. Adjust nuts until gauge finger just touches end of each release lever (Fig. F:11).

5. Remove finger gauge assembly, fit tool kit operating lever and operate clutch release several times. Re-check lever height and further adjust if necessary.

6. Secure nuts (12) with lockplate tabs, assemble release plate (13) and secure with springs (9).

7. With dial gauge on base plate check that release plate run-out does not exceed 0.015 in. (0.38 mm.). Re-adjust levers to correct excessive run-out (Fig. F:12).

8. Release clutch with tool kit operating lever, remove set-screws and remove clutch unit from baseplate.

NOTE: If press and wooden blocks are used release plate height must be 1.83 in. (46.48 mm.) measured from surface table with 0.305 in. (7.797 mm.) gauge plate or spacers in place of clutch plate. (Fig. F:1).

(DIAPHRAGM SPRING TYPE) - Overhaul (Fig. F:3)

CLUTCH UNIT

Due to specialised knowledge and equipment required, dismantling by unauthorised personnel is not allowed. If required, a replacement unit should be obtained.

MASTER CYLINDER - Removal and Installation

(Fig. F:13)

1. Attach hose from a receptacle to slave cylinder bleed plug, loosen plug and depress clutch pedal until system is drained.

2. Disconnect hydraulic pipe from master cylinder.

3. Pull back rubber (11) and remove pin (14).

4. Remove mounting bolts (16) and remove cylinder.

5. Reverse procedure to install.

6. Fill and bleed system.

MASTER CYLINDER - Overhaul (Fig. F:14)

1. Remove cylinder.

2. Remove circlip (11) to withdraw push rod (9) and stop (12).

3. Shake or gently blow out plunger and valve assemblies.

4. With small screwdriver lift tag of spring retainer (6) to permit withdrawal from plunger (7).

5. Remove spring retainer by aligning slot with valve shank head. Separate spring (5) distance cup (3) disc spring (2) and valve shank.

6. Ease seal (1) from shank and seals (8) and (13) from plunger with fingers.

7. Clean all parts ensuring feed and by-pass holes are clear. Renew seals. Check springs for damage, distortion or set, push rod and valve shank for straightness and cover for damage or deterioration, renew parts as necessary.

8. Assemble in reverse order lubricating seals with hydraulic oil and installing with lips facing forward. Position disc spring (2) with lip against distance cup as shown in Fig. F:15.

OPERATING CYLINDER - Removal and Installation

(Fig. F.5.)

1. Drain system and disconnect hydraulic pipe (26).

2. Remove bolt (34) and remove cylinder.

3. Reverse procedure to install ensuring that push rod is correctly engaged in piston cup. Fill and bleed system.

Fig. F:4 Clutch master cylinder

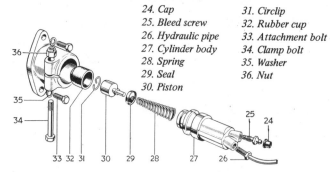

24. Cap	31. Circlip
25. Bleed screw	32. Rubber cup
26. Hydraulic pipe	33. Attachment bolt
27. Cylinder body	34. Clamp bolt
28. Spring	35. Washer
29. Seal	36. Nut
30. Piston	

Fig. F:5 Exploded view of the clutch operating cylinder.

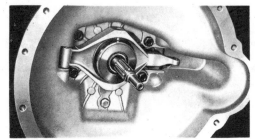

Fig. F:6 Clutch release mechanism

1. Spanner
2. Baseplate
3. Stud
4. Pointer gauge
5. Adaptor
6. Spacers
7. Attachment setscrews
8. Release handle.

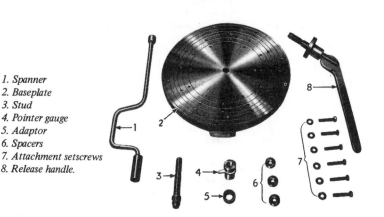

Fig. F:8 Churchill clutch assembly fixture, Tool, No. 99A.

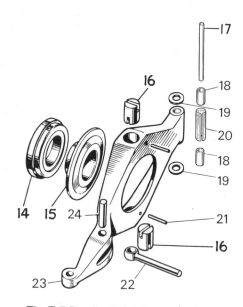

Fig. F:7 Details of the clutch release lever assembly (see Fig. F:2 for key).

Fig. F:9 Compressing the clutch unit with a press and wooden blocks.

Fig. F:10 Securing the clutch unit to the assembly fixture baseplate.

Fig. F:11 Setting the release lever height.

Fig. F:12 Checking the run-out at the release plate.

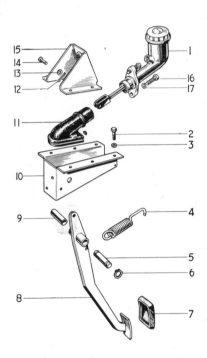

Fig. F:13 Details of the clutch pedal and bracket assembly.

1. Master cylinder	10. Pedal bracket
2. Bolt	11. Rubber dust excluder
3. Spring washer	12. Split pin
4. Return spring	13. Plain washer
5. Pivot pin	14. Clevis pin
6. Circlip	15. Master cylinder bracket
7. Pedal rubber	16. Bolt
8. Pedal	17. Spring washer
9. Pedal pivot bush	

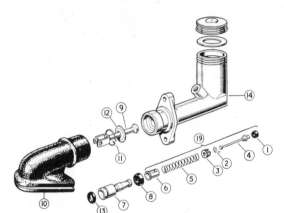

1. Valve seal
2. Spring (Valve seal)
3. Distance piece
4. Valve stem
5. Piston return spring
6. Spring retainer
7. Piston
8. Piston seal
9. Push rod
10. Dust cover
11. Circlip
12. Push rod stop
13. Piston seal
14. Fluid reservoir

Fig. F:14 Details of the clutch master cylinder components.

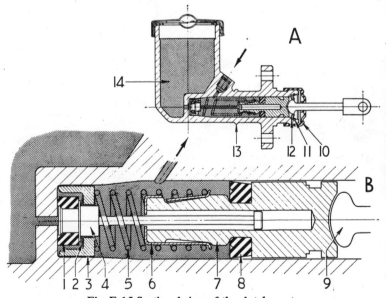

Fig. F:15 Sectional view of the clutch master cylinder (see Fig. F:14 for key).

OPERATING CYLINDER - Overhaul (Fig.F.5.)

1. Remove cylinder.

2. Remove cover (32) and circlip (31) and shake or gently blow out piston (30) and spring. Ease seal (29) from piston.

3. Check spring for distortion or set and cover for damage and deterioration. Renew parts as necessary and renew seal.

4. Lubricate parts and re-assemble in reverse order ensuring that seal lip is towards hydraulic pipe end. Install cylinder.

BLEEDING THE HYDRAULIC SYSTEM (Fig. F:5)

1. Clean the bleed nipple, attach a length of rubber hose and immerse the free end in a jar with hydraulic fluid.

2. Unscrew the bleed nipple half a turn, and, with the aid of a second person, depress the clutch pedal slowly. Tighten the nipple before the pedal reaches the end of its stroke, and allow the pedal to return unassisted.

   NOTE: During the operation do not allow the fluid in the master cylinder reservoir fall below half full to avoid the possibility of air being drawn into the system.

3. Continue bleeding until fluid entering the jar is free from air bubbles. Close the nipple, remove hose and check clutch operation.

Technical Data

Type . . . . Hydraulic, self-adjusting, single dry plate
Clutch Unit Type:-
   Early Herald 1200, 12/50 and early Spitfire 4 and Mk. II . . . . Borg and Beck, coil spring, 6 1/4 in. (15.87 mm.) dia.
   Late Herald 1200, 12/50 (from Eng. Nos. GA204020E and
   GB24121E), late Spitfire 4 and Mk. II (from Eng. Nos. FC17136E),
   Herald 13/60 and Spitfire Mk. III and IV . . . . Borg and Beck, diaphragm spring 6 1/2 in. (16.51 mm.) dia.
Hydraulic Fluid Specification . . . . SAE 70R3

TIGHTENING TORQUES

Clutch Unit Attachment . . . . 18 - 20 lbs./ft.   (2.49 - 2.77 kg./m.)
Clutch housing attachment . . . . 14 - 16 lbs./ft.   (1.94 - 2.12 kg./m.)

Gearbox

GENERAL
ROUTINE MAINTENANCE
GEARBOX - Removal and Installation
GEARBOX - Overhaul
OVERDRIVE
TECHNICAL DATA

GENERAL

The gearbox has four forward ratios and one reverse. Gear-shifting is achieved by means of a remote gear change mechanism with the lever centrally mounted on the floor. The gearbox is similar for all models with synchromesh on 2nd, 3rd and top gears, except for the Spitfire Mk. IV which has synchromesh on all forward gears and has a different 1st and reverse gear ratio. Optional overdrive, acting on 3rd and top gears, if available on the Spitfire range. The gearbox serial number is stamped on a flange at the right hand side of the gearbox.

ROUTINE MAINTENANCE

Every 6,000 miles (10,000 km.)

With vehicle on level ground remove filler plug (1, Fig. G:2) and check that oil is level with bottom of the filler plug threads. Top up, if necessary, with oil to S.A.E. 90 E.P. using a suitable pump type oil dispencer with flexible nozzle. Allow surplus oil to drain away before refitting filler plug and wiping clean.

NOTE: When an overdrive unit is fitted a common oil level is obtained through a transfer hole.

GEARBOX - Removal and Installation

1. Isolate battery and remove front seats and carpet.

2. Raise vehicle on ramp or on to axle stands.

3. Remove drain plug and drain gearbox (Fig. G:2).

4. On Spitfire models, remove bolts (1 and 3) and disconnect tachometer drive from instrument to remove support bracket (2) (Fig. G:3).

5. Release gear lever knob locknut, remove knob and remove rubber grommet.

6. Remove fixings (5 and 6), three screws from engine side of bulkhead and remove cover (7) (Fig. G:4).

7. Release clamp bolt (8), withdraw clutch operating cylinder (9) and leave suspended from pipeline (Fig. G:5).

8. Remove bolts (11) from front and rear of propeller shaft and remove shaft.

9. Release exhaust pipe from manifold down pipe and from clutch housing.

10. Remove starter motor and disconnect speedometer drive from right hand side of gearbox extension.

11. Remove nuts (13) and gearbox extension (14) and cover gearbox opening to exclude foreign matter.

12. Remove nuts (15), place wooden buffer block at rear of sump and jack up until gearbox extension clears mounting bracket. Remove mountings (16).

13. Remove clutch housing bolts (17) and manoeuvre gearbox from vehicle.

14. Install by reversing the removal procedure. Do not allow gearbox to hang on input shaft whilst re-installing. Renew gearbox extension gasket if damaged or distorted. With vehicle on level ground refill gearbox with oil.

GEARBOX - Overhaul

NOTE: The overhaul procedure is described below, but, because of the gearbox complexity, the procedure should only be attempted by competent personnel. If in doubt refer the work to an authorised dealer or transmission specialist.

Dismantling

Top Cover (Fig. G:6)

1. Remove bolts (17 & 47) (Fig. G:7) with washers and remove top cover (29) with gasket.

2. Remove nuts (27) with washers and remove extension piece (36) with gasket.

3. Remove bolt (38) at bottom of gear lever, release cover (4) and detach gear lever assembly. (Figs. G:8 and G:9).

4. Remove knob (1) with locknut and remove cover (4) cups (5 and 6) and outer spring (7) from gear lever. Remove snap ring (8), inner spring (9) and spherical bearing (10) and finally remove reverse stop pin (15) from gear lever and reverse stop plate (37) from top cover extension.

5. Release taper locking pin (43), withdraw remote control shaft assembly from cover extension and from selector (31) and ease out "O" ring (28) as shown in Fig. G:11.

6. Separate front and rear remote control shafts by removing bolt (32) and drifting out pin (41). Remove fibre washers (34) and rubber bush (35).

7. Drive out Welch plugs with a 1/8 in. (3.17 mm.) diameter pin punch as shown in Fig. G:10, ensuring selector shafts are clear of punch.

8. Remove locking pins from selectors (48, 49 and 52) push

Fig. G:1 Exploded view of the gearbox components

1. Knob
2. Locknut
3. Gear change lever
4. Cover
5. Shield
6. Plate
7. Spring
8. Circlip
9. Spring
10. Nylon sphere
11. Stepped nylon washer
12. Bush
13. Washer
14. Lever end
15. Reverse stop pin
16. Locknut
17. Bolt
18. Welch plug
19. Gasket
20. Spring
21. Plunger
22. Taper locking pin
23. 1st/2nd selector shaft
24. 3rd/top selector shaft
25. Reverse selector shaft
26. Interlock ball
27. Nut
28. Rubber "O" ring
29. Top cover
30. Gasket
31. Selector ball-end
32. Dowel
33. Dowel
34. Washer
35. Bonded rubber bush
36. Gear change extension
37. Reverse stop
38. Bolt
39. Dowel
40. Nyloc nut
41. Mills pin
42. Remote control shaft (front)
43. Taper locking pin
44. Fork
45. Nut
46. Remote control shaft (rear)
47. Bolt
48. 1st/2nd selector fork
49. Reverse selector
50. Interlock ball
51. Interlock plunger
52. Top/3rd selector fork
53. Taper locking pin
54. Clutch housing
55. Pin
56. Clutch release mechanism
57. Wedgelock bolt
58. Plain washer
59. Bolt
60. Gasket
61. Dowel
62. Rear extension
63. Rubber "O" ring
64. Peg bolt
65. Speedo drive gear housing
66. Speedo drive gear
67. Extension ball race
68. Oil seal
69. Gearbox mounting rubber
70. Mounting bracket
71. Bolt
72. Bolt
73. Gasket
74. Clutch slave cylinder bracket
75. Sump plug
76. Speedo driving gear
77. Circlip
78. Distance washer
79. Ball race
80. 1st speed gear
81. Shim
82. Shim
3. Synchromesh ball
84. Plunger
85. Ball
86. 2nd speed synchro hub
87. 2nd speed synchro cup
88. Thrust washer
89. 2nd speed mainshaft gear
90. Thrust washer
91. Bushes
92. 3rd speed mainshaft gear
93. Thrust washer
94. Circlip
95. 3rd/top synchro sleeve
96. 3rd speed synchro cup
97. 3rd/top inner synchro hub
98. Top synchro cup
99. Circlip
100. Distance washer
101. Circlip.
102. Ball race
103. Oil deflector
104. Input shaft
105. Torrington needle roller bearing
106. Mainshaft
107. Distance washer
108. Driving flange
109. Spring washer
110. Nut
112. Countershaft
113. Peg bolt
114. Spring washer
115. Rear fixed thrust washer
116. Rear rotating thrust washer
117. Countershaft gear cluster
118. Countershaft bush
119. Front fixed thrust washer (Vitesse has needle rollers and retaining rings)
120. Reverse gear bush
121. Reverse gear
122. Reverse gear actuator
123. Actuator pivot
124. Plain washer
125. Nyloc nut
126. Reverse gear shaft
127. Reverse shaft retaining bolt
128. Spring washer

56

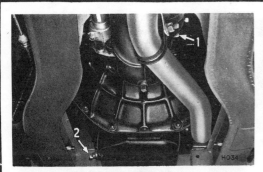

Fig. G:2 Gearbox filler/level and drain plugs

Fig. G:3 Fascia support bracket attachments - Spitfire.

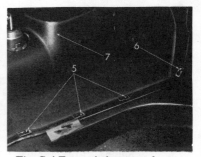

Fig. G:4 Transmission tunnel cover attachments.

Fig. G:5 Details of the gearbox attachments.

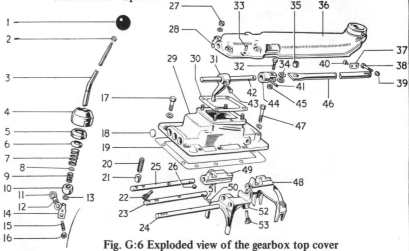

Fig. G:6 Exploded view of the gearbox top cover (see Fig. G:1 for key).

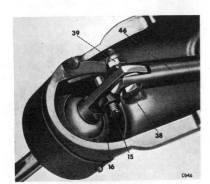

Fig. G:7 Removing the top cover.

Fig. G:9 Releasing the gear lever retaining cover.

Fig. G:10 Driving out the welch plugs at the selector shafts.

Fig. G:8 Details of the lower end of the gear lever.

Fig. G:11 Extracting the O-ring from the extension housing.

Fig. G:12 Removing the speedometer drive assembly

intereurope

57

Fig. G:13 Tapping the rear extension housing off the mainshaft.

Fig. G:14 Removing the countershaft.

Fig. G:16 Removing the bearing from the input shaft.

Fig. G:15 Extracting the input shaft assembly.

Fig. G:18 Removing the synchro unit from the mainshaft.

Fig. G:17 Driving the mainshaft rearwards

Fig. G:19 Removing the circlip from the mainshaft with Churchill Tool No. S.144.

Fig. G:20 Removing the components of the mainshaft

Fig. G:21 Removing the speedometer gear from the mainshaft.

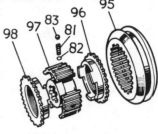

Fig. G:22 Details of the 3rd/4th gear synchro unit. (See Fig. G:1 for key).

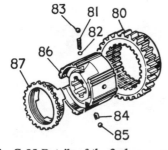

Fig. G:23 Details of the 2nd gear synchro unit (See Fig. G:1 for key).

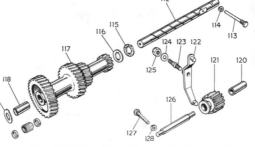

Fig. G:24 Details of the countershaft and reverse pinion (see Fig. G:1 for key).

Fig. G:25 Centralising the front thrust washer with the countershaft.

selector shafts (25, 23 and 24) from cover removing selectors, two interlock balls (26 and 50) with plunger (50) and three selector plungers (21) with springs (20).

Clutch Housing (Fig. G:1)

1. Remove clutch release gear as detailed in CLUTCH section.

2. Remove four bolts (59) and wedgelock bolt (57) to separate clutch housing from gearbox. Remove gasket (60).

Rear Extention

1. Release peg bolt (64) and withdraw speedometer drive assembly (Fig. G:12). Remove gear and "O" ring (63).

2. Remove nut (110) and washer and withdraw driving flange (108) from mainshaft.

3. Remove bolts (72) and, with hide hammer, tap extension from mainshaft as shown in Fig. G:13. Remove washer (107) and gasket.

4. Extract oil seal (68) and drive out ballrace (67) using tubular drift against outer race.

Main Gearbox Assembly

1. Remove countershaft securing bolt (113) and withdraw shaft (112) allowing countershaft gear cluster to drop away from mainshaft gears. (Fig. G:14).

2. Attach Churchill tool 4235A with adaptor 4235A-2 and withdraw input shaft assembly. (Fig. G:15).

3. Remove circlips (99) from shaft, circlip (101) from bearing and washer (100) and extract bearing (102) from shaft with Churchill press and adaptors. (Fig. G:16). Remove oil deflector (103).

4. With hollow drift of suitable size drive mainshaft (106) rearward until bearing (79) is clear of gearcase housing (Fig. G:17).

5. Raise end of mainshaft and remove synchro assembly (95 and 97) with synchro cups (96 and 98). (Fig. G:18).

6. Replace mainshaft in gearbox and remove circlip (94) with Churchill tool S144. (Fig. G:19).

7. Withdraw mainshaft from rear end, progressively removing component parts (Fig. G:20).

8. Use Churchill press and adaptors to remove speedometer drive gear from mainshaft. (Fig. G:21).

9. Remove circlips (77 and 101) washer (78) and draw bearing (79) from mainshaft.

10. Remove reverse idler gear (121), securing bolt (127) and withdraw shaft (126). Lift gear cluster (117) from gearcase with rear thrust washers (115 and 116) and front thrust washer (119) (Fig. G:22).

11. Remove nut (125) and remove reverse gear actuator (122)

and pin (123).

12. Dismantle synchro units by removing outer sleeves (80 and 95) with units enclosed in cloth or box to avoid losing balls, springs or shims. Figs. 22 and 23 give exploded views of units.

Inspection

Clean all parts and inspect for damage and wear. Examine gear teeth and bearing for cracks and check that bearings rotate freely. Check countershaft bushes for wear. Renew gaskets and other parts as necessary.

Assembly

Countershaft and reverse pinion (Fig. G:24)

1. Smear steel face of front countershaft thrust washer (119) with heavy grease as an adhesive and position in gearcase with tab in recess, bronze face towards gear and using shaft to align with hole (Fig. G:25).

2. Position rear rotating thrust washer (116) on gear cluster in same way and lower cluster into gearbox.

3. Move cluster forward to pinch front thrust washer apply grease to rear thrust washer and insert between casing and rotating thrust washer (116) with tab in recess (Fig. G:27).

4. Thread countershaft (112) through casing aperture, thrust washers and gear cluster to normal installed position.

5. Measure gear end float with a feeler blade or blades inserted between thrust washers (115 and 116) (Fig. G:26). Adjust by selective assembly of thrust washers to obtain specified end-float.

   NOTE: Permissible end-float is 0.0015 - 0.0125 in. (0.04 - 0.31 mm.) but an end-float of 0.006 in. (0.15 mm.) should be aimed at. If reduction of thrust washer thickness is necessary, metal must NOT be removed from bronze face.

6. Remove countershaft (112) and allow gear cluster to lie at bottom of gearcase.

7. Screw pivot pin (123) into reverse idler gear selector lever until one thread protrudes through boss on lever, install lever in gearcase and secure with nut and washer (125 and 124) (Fig. G:26).

8. Insert reverse idler gear shaft (126) into gearcase and secure with retaining bolt (127) and spring washer. Slide reverse idler gear onto shaft until annular groove engages pin at bottom of operating lever (122) (Fig. G:27).

Checking Release Loading of Synchro Units

1. Assemble spring (81) balls (83) and shims (82) to hub of 3rd/top synchro hub and position assembly inside sleeve (95) (Fig. G:22).

2. Similarly assemble hub and sleeve of 2nd speed synchro unit additionally assembling interlock plunger (84) and

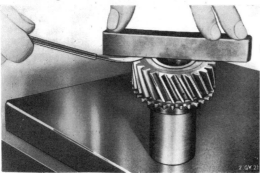

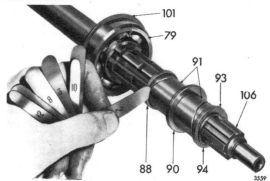

1. "Master" spline
2. Interlock ball
3. Synchro ball

Fig. G:28 Assembling the 2nd gear synchro unit.

Fig. G:27 Reverse pinion and countershaft rear thrust washer installation.

Fig. G:26 Measuring the countershaft end-float.

Fig. G:29 Measuring the gear end-float on the mainshaft bush.

Fig. G:30 Measuring the bush end-float on the mainshaft.

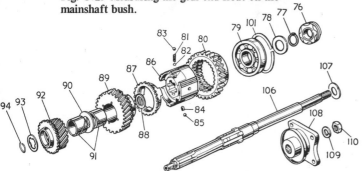

Fig. G:31 Details of the mainshaft assembly (see Fig. G:1 for key).

Fig. G:32 Refitting the mainshaft bearing.

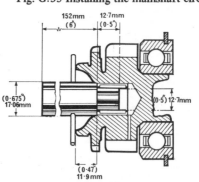

Fig. G:35 Installing the mainshaft circlip.

Fig. G:34 Assembling the components on the mainshaft.

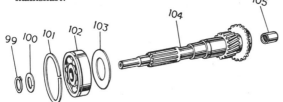

Fig. G:36 Details of the input shaft (see Fig. G:1 for key).

Fig. G:37 Dimensions of the drift required to drive the needle bearing into the input shaft.

152mm (6")
12·7mm (0·5")
(0·675") 17·06mm
(0·5") 12·7mm
(0·47") 11·9mm

Fig. G:33 Refitting the speedometer drive gear to the mainshaft.

ball (85) (Fig. G:28).

3. Check release loads of both synchro units as shown in Fig. G:29 with spring balance attached to loading hook.

Release load (both units) - 19-21 lbs. (8.62-9.53 kg.)

Adjust number of shims under synchro springs to correct loading if necessary.

End-Float of 2nd and 3rd Mainshaft Gears on Bushes

(Fig. G:29)

1. Measure end-float of each gear on its bush. This should be 0.002 - 0.006 in. (0.5 - 0.15 mm.). Fit new bush to increase float or shorten bush to decrease float.

CAUTION: Reduced bush length will increase bush end-float on shaft.

Overall End-Float of Mainshaft Bushes (Fig. G:30)

1. Assemble thrust washer (88) bush (91), washer (90) bush (91) and thrust washer (93) to mainshaft and secure with discarded half circlip (94).

2. Measure total end-float which should be 0.004 - 0.010 in. (0.10 - 0.25 mm.). Adjust by selective use of thrust washers (see TECHNICAL DATA for availability).

Mainshaft Assembly (Fig. G:31)

1. With circlip groove to rear, press bearing (79) on to shaft with Churchill tool and adaptor. (Fig. G:32).

2. Thread washer (78) on shaft and correctly position Seeger circlip (77) in groove. With Churchill press fit speedometer drive (76) on shaft. (Fig. G:33).

3. Locate circlip (10) into groove on bearing (79).

4. Thread mainshaft into gearbox and assemble components on to mainshaft, in following order.

   (a) Second gear synchro unit assembly with gear position forward. Ensure plunger (84) and ball (85) are correctly located.

   (b) Second speed synchro cup (87) with three lugs locating in synchro hub.

   (c) Rear thrust washer with scroll face to front of gearbox.

   (d) Second speed gear with bush (89 and 91), thrust washer (90) and third speed gear with bush (92 and 91).

   (e) Front thrust washer (93) with scroll face to rear of gearbox.

5. Using Churchill tool S145 fit circlip (94) (Fig. G:35).

6. Assemble top/third synchro unit with longer boss of inner

synchro hub (97) forward and cups (96 and 98) attached on to shaft.

7. With tubular drift against outer race drive rear bearing (79) into housing to complete mainshaft assembly.

Input Shaft (Fig. G:36)

NOTE: Replacement of needle bearing (105) in input shaft is not possible and if bearing is unserviceable a new bearing must be inserted in a new shaft using a drift to dimensions given in Fig. G:37 to ensure the bearing is correctly positioned.

1. Smear oil deflector (103) with grease, place on input shaft and press on bearing (102) using Churchill press (Fig. G:38).

2. Fit distance washer (100) and circlip (99) to shaft and circlip (101) to groove on bearing.

3. Install input shaft assembly in gearcase mating with mainshaft (Fig. G:39).

Countershaft

Align countershaft gear cluster and thrust washers in gearbox with 0.655 in. (16.64 mm.) dia. slave shaft with taper lead and follow through with countershaft. Remove slave shaft and lock countershaft in position with bolt (113) and spring washer (Fig. G:14).

Rear Extension

1. Drive bearing (67) into housing at rear of extension piece, then oil seal (68) with lip facing forward (Fig. G:40).

2. Lubricate and assemble speedometer drive gear assembly with new "O" ring (63) and install in rear extension. Secure with locking bolt (64) and washer (Fig. G:12).

3. Fit washer (107) over mainshaft, smear gasket (73) with grease and place against rear face of gearbox.

4. Place extension over mainshaft and with tubular drift against bearing outer race, drive bearing on to mainshaft. Secure rear extension tightening bolts evenly and in turn.

5. Fit driving flange (108) and secure with spring washer (109) and nut (110).

Clutch Housing

1. Smear gasket (60) with grease and secure housing to gearbox with four bolts (59) and Wedgelock bolt (57), with new copper plated washer (58).

2. Install clutch release gear.

Top Cover

1. Insert springs (20) and plungers (21) in top cover (Fig. G:41).

2. Slide 3rd/top selector shaft (24) into front end of top cover, depress plunger to permit passage of shaft, thread

Fig. G:38 Pressing the bearing onto the input shaft.

Fig. G:39 Installing the input shaft assembly

Fig. G:40 Installing the oil seal in the rear extension.

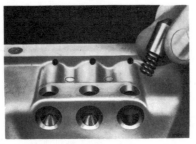

Fig. G:41 Installing the selector springs and plungers in the top cover.

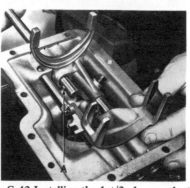

Fig. G:42 Installing the 1st/2nd gear selector shaft. Note position of interlock plunger (A).

Fig. G:43 Cut-away view of the top cover showing the interlock plunger and balls.

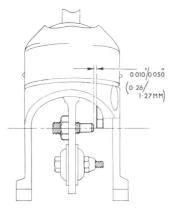

0.010"/0.050"
(0.26/
1.27MM)

Fig. G:44 Setting the reverse stop pin.

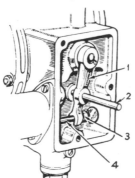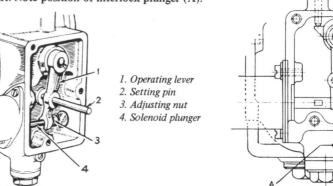

1. Operating lever
2. Setting pin
3. Adjusting nut
4. Solenoid plunger

Fig. G:45 Setting the solenoid operating lever position on the overdrive unit.

Fig. G:46 Checking dimension for the solenoid plunger.

Fig. G:47 Overdrive electrical circuit.

1. To "SW" terminal on ignition coil
2. Overdrive switch
3. To "No. 1" terminal on ignition switch
4. Overdrive operating solenoid
5. Solenoid relay
6. Gearbox isolator switch

Fig. G:48 Details of the mainshaft and adaptor plate with the overdrive unit.

7. Spring clip
79. Woodruff key
80. Spring ring
81. Cam

Fig. G:49 Checking the alignment of the splines on the planet carrier and the unidirectional clutch.

on selector fork (52) and continue insertion until plunger engages middle indent of shaft. This is neutral position.

3.   Insert reverse selector shaft (25) in same way to engage selector (49) and to reach neutral position.

4.   Enter 1st/2nd selector shaft into top cover with interlock plunger (51) in position, slide shaft into cover then through third/top fork and 1st/2nd selector fork (Fig. G:42).

5.   Before shaft reaches neutral position, insert both interlock balls (50 and 26) into the cross bore between shaft bores as shown in Fig. G:43, then push shaft to neutral position. Interlock balls and plunger are then retained by the shafts.

6.   Secure selector forks and reverse selector with locking pins (22).

7.   Apply jointing compound around edges of welch plugs (18) and tap them in the ends of the shaft bores.

8.   Ensure selectors and gears are in neutral position, smear gasket (19) with grease, position cover on gearbox and secure with bolts and spring washers tightened evenly and in turn placing longer bolts at rear.

9.   Assemble fork (44) to shaft (42) with new pin (41), renew bush (35) and secure shaft (46) to fork with bolt (32), and new fibre washers (34).

10.   Fit new "O" ring (28) into top cover extension and thread shaft (42) into cover extension and through selector (31). Secure selector with pin bolt (43).

11.   Assemble reverse stop pin (15) and spherical bearing (10) spring (9) and snap ring (8) to gear lever.

12.   Fit reverse stop plate (37) to cover.

13.   Position gear lever assembly into cover with two new stepped washers (11), fit bush (12) and bolt lever to shaft (46).

14.   Assemble spring (7) plate (6) shield (5) and secure with cover (4).

15.   Adjust reverse stop pin (15) to give clearance in neutral position of 1st/2nd gate as shown in Fig.44

16.   Assemble extension cover to top cover with new gasket (30).

OVERDRIVE

The overdrive is an additional gear unit, mounted on the rear face of the gearbox in place of the normal rear extension, to provide a higher overall gear ratio on third and top gears.

The overdrive is operated by an electric solenoid, controlled by a switch mounted on the steering column. When overdrive is selected, the solenoid actuates the operating valve, redirecting the flow of fluid under pressure and causing engagement of the epicyclic overdrive gears. Hydraulic pressure is developed by a plunger pump, cam operated from the input shaft. An inhibitor switch, fitted in the electrical circuit, prevents engagement of overdrive in reverse, 1st or 2nd gears.

NOTE: As specialised knowledge and equipment are required to overhaul the overdrive unit, any repair work should be entrusted to an authorised dealer or transmission specialist.

Lubrication

The gearbox and overdrive unit are interconnected and thus have a common oil level, which is maintained by topping up the gearbox. When draining, however, the separate drain plugs for the gearbox and overdrive unit must be removed. Removal of the overdrive drain plug will provide access to a gauze filter which should also be removed and cleaned, before refilling the unit with new oil.

Under normal circumstances, the special oil used for the initial fill of the gearbox and overdrive unit should NOT be changed - merely topped up with an approved oil. Where a new unit is fitted, or parts of the existing unit have been removed, the unit should be refilled with new special oil, available from Triumph dealers. If this oil is not available, an approved oil may be used as an alternative.

NOTE: Always use clean oil and take great care to avoid entry of dirt or lint from the wiping cloth into the unit whenever any part of the casing is opened.

After refilling the unit, run the car for a short distance and recheck the oil level. It will probably be necessary to top up the level to make up for the oil which has been distributed around the hydraulic system.

Adjustment of the Solenoid Operating Lever

When correctly set, with the solenoid engaged, a hole in the operating lever should align with a hole in the overdrive casing. This indicates that the operating valve is fully open. To check setting remove operating lever cover, energise solenoid and insert 3/16 in. (4.76 mm.) dia. pin through both holes (Fig. G:45). If holes are malaligned proceed as follows:

1.   Move lever until setting pin (2) enters both holes.

2.   With solenoid energised, screw adjusting nut (3) until it just contacts lever.

3.   Remove pin, de-energise and re-energise solenoid and re-check hole alignment.

4.   With solenoid de-energised, align holes and insert pin.

5.   Hole solenoid plunger against blanking plug and check that dimension "A" is 0.150 - 0.155 in. (3.81 - 3.94 mm.) (Fig. G:46). If necessary, vary thickness of washer under head of blanking plug. (On later units the plug is adjustable).

6.   Remove pin and refit cover.

Checking the Electrical Circuit (Fig. G:47)

If any operation failure of the overdrive unit occurs, first check the wiring and connections of the overdrive circuit, as in many cases failures are due to corroded terminals or faulty wiring.

E

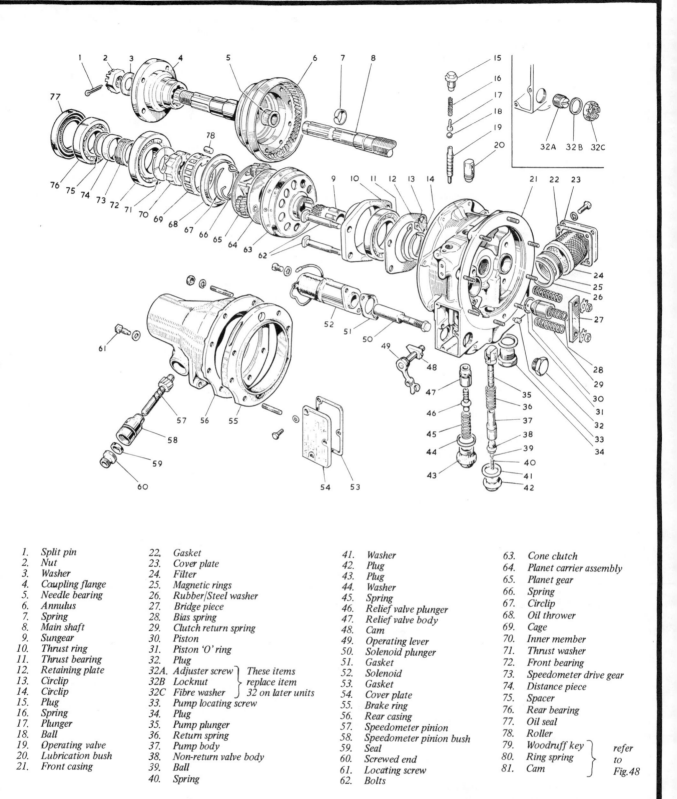

1.	Split pin	22.	Gasket
2.	Nut	23.	Cover plate
3.	Washer	24.	Filter
4.	Coupling flange	25.	Magnetic rings
5.	Needle bearing	26.	Rubber/Steel washer
6.	Annulus	27.	Bridge piece
7.	Spring	28.	Bias spring
8.	Main shaft	29.	Clutch return spring
9.	Sungear	30.	Piston
10.	Thrust ring	31.	Piston 'O' ring
11.	Thrust bearing	32.	Plug
12.	Retaining plate	32A.	Adjuster screw
13.	Circlip	32B	Locknut
14.	Circlip	32C	Fibre washer
15.	Plug	33.	Pump locating screw
16.	Spring	34.	Plug
17.	Plunger	35.	Pump plunger
18.	Ball	36.	Return spring
19.	Operating valve	37.	Pump body
20.	Lubrication bush	38.	Non-return valve body
21.	Front casing	39.	Ball
		40.	Spring

32A./32B./32C. — These items replace item 32 on later units

41.	Washer	63.	Cone clutch
42.	Plug	64.	Planet carrier assembly
43.	Plug	65.	Planet gear
44.	Washer	66.	Spring
45.	Spring	67.	Circlip
46.	Relief valve plunger	68.	Oil thrower
47.	Relief valve body	69.	Cage
48.	Cam	70.	Inner member
49.	Operating lever	71.	Thrust washer
50.	Solenoid plunger	72.	Front bearing
51.	Gasket	73.	Speedometer drive gear
52.	Solenoid	74.	Distance piece
53.	Gasket	75.	Spacer
54.	Cover plate	76.	Rear bearing
55.	Brake ring	77.	Oil seal
56.	Rear casing	78.	Roller
57.	Speedometer pinion	79.	Woodruff key
58.	Speedometer pinion bush	80.	Ring spring
59.	Seal	81.	Cam
60.	Screwed end		
61.	Locating screw		
62.	Bolts		

79./80./81. — refer to Fig.48

Fig.G.50 Exploded view of Overdrive (inset illustrates later condition of item 32)

If after checking all the electrical connections, the overdrive still fails to operate proceed as follows:

1. Switch on ignition and engage top gear. Set overdrive switch on steering column to overdrive position. Check that battery voltage is present at terminals "C1" and "W2".

2. Short out terminals "C1" and "C2" on relay unit. If overdrive solenoid operates, then relay unit, column switch and isolator switch are suspect. Remove shorting link from relay unit.

3. Earth terminal "W1" on relay unit. If solenoid now operates, column switch and isolator switch are suspect. If solenoid does not operate, replace relay unit.

4. Earth the yellow/green cable on the column switch. If solenoid now operates, replace isolator switch. If solenoid does not operate, replace the column switch.

Removal and Installation

The overdrive is removed in unit with the gearbox and apart from the disconnection of the solenoid and isolation switch leads, the removal procedure is the same as that described previously for the gearbox.

Separation from Gearbox

Remove attachment nuts and spring washers and carefully withdraw overdrive unit from gearbox.

Assembly to Gearbox

1. Align splines of planet carrier and uni-directional clutch with a long screwdriver and confirm by inserting dummy mainshaft (Churchill tool L210) (Fig. G:49).

2. Turn gearbox mainshaft until overdrive pump operating cam peak (81) is uppermost. Ensure spring clip (7) on mainshaft is located in groove and does not protrude above splines (Fig. G:48).

   NOTE: Do not rotate mainshaft or overdrive coupling until assembly is complete.

3. Remove dummy mainshaft and fit unit to gearbox tightening nuts evenly and in turn.

Technical Data

Type	Four forward speeds and one reverse with synchromesh on 2nd, 3rd and top gear (synchromesh on all forward gears on Spitfire Mk. IV). Overdrive optional on Spitfire models.

Ratios:

Top	1.00 : 1	
3rd	1.40 : 1	
2nd	2.16 : 1	
1st	3.75 : 1	(3.50 : 1 - Spitfire Mk. IV)
Reverse	3.75 : 1	(3.99 : 1 - Spitfire Mk. IV)
Top O/D	0.80 : 1	
3rd O/D	1.12 : 1	

Oil Capacity:

Gearbox	1.5 Imp. pints (1.8 U.S. pints: 0.85 litres)
Gearbox & Overdrive	2.38 Imp. pints (2.85 U.S. pints; 1.35 litres)
Lubricant Specification	SAE 90 EP

Dimension and Tolerences:

Input shaft spigot bush	- length	1.06 in. (26.92 mm.)
	- Bore in crankshaft	0.754 - 0.753 in. (19.15 - 19.13 mm.)
Mainshaft:		
Spigot dia.		0.5000 - 4.995 in. (12.7 - 12.687 mm.)
2nd/3rd gear bush journal dia.		0.8738 - 0.8733 in. (22.195 - 22.182 mm.)
Centre bearing journal dia.		1.0004 - 1.0000 in. (25.41 - 25.4 mm.)
Rear bearing journal dia.		0.7504 - 0.7501 in. (19.067 - 19.055 mm.)
Mainshaft gears and bushes		
2nd and 3rd gear inside dia.		1.0945 - 1.0935 in. (27.80 - 27.77 mm.)
2nd and 3rd speed bush	- inside dia.	0.876 - 0.875 in. (22.25 - 22.25 mm.)
	- outside dia.	1.0928 - 1.0908 in. (27.76 - 27.71 mm.)
3rd speed bush length		1.002 - 1.00 in. (25.45 - 25.40 mm.)
2nd speed bush length		1.127 - 1.125 in. (28.63 - 28.58 mm.)
2nd/3rd gear thrust washer thickness		0.154 - 0.152 in. (3.91 - 3.86 mm.)
2nd gear thrust washer thickness		0.124 - 0.122 in. (3.15 - 3.10 mm.)
3rd gear circlip washer thickness		0.124 - 0.122 in. (3.15 - 3.10 mm.)
2nd/3rd gear circlip thickness		0.072 - 0.069 in. (1.83 - 1.75 mm.)

Maximum overall end-float	. . . .	0.004 - 0.019 in.	(0.10 - 0.49 mm.)
Reverse gear pinion bush inside dia.	. . . .	0.658 - 0.6573 in.	(16.71 - 16.70 mm.)
Reverse gear spindle main dia.	. . . .	0.6555 - 0.6550 in.	(16.65 - 16.64 mm.)
Reverse gear end dia.	. . . .	0.5618 - 0.5613 in.	(14.27 - 14.26 mm.)
Countershaft Assembly:			
Countershaft outside dia.	. . . .	0.6555 - 0.6550 in.	(16.65 - 16.64 mm.)
Countershaft bushes - length	. . . .	1.385 - 1.365 in.	(35.18 - 34.67 mm.)
- inside dia.	. . . .	0.6580 - 0.6573 in.	(16.71 - 16.70 mm.)
Front thrust washer thickness	. . . .	0.125 - 0.123 in.	(3.18 - 3.12 mm.)
Rear thrust washer thickness	. . . .	0.068 - 0.066 in.	(1.73 - 1.68 mm.)
Rear rotating thrust washer thickness	. . . .	0.0665 - 0.0635 in.	(1.69 - 1.61 mm.)
Overall end-float	. . . .	0.0125 - 0.0015 in.	(0.31 - 0.04 mm.)
Ballraces			
Front & rear mainshaft	. . . .	Hoffman MS 10K	
Rear extension	. . . .	Hoffman LS 8	
Needle bearing	. . . .	Tonington B 810	

TIGHTENING TORQUES

Clutch housing to gearbox	. . . .	24 - 26 lbs./ft.	(3.32 - 3.60 kg./m.)
Countershaft location	. . . .	14 - 16 lbs./ft.	(1.93 - 2.21 kg./m.)
Operating shaft attachment	. . . .	6 - 8 lbs./ft.	(0.83 - 1.11 kg./m.)
Rear extension	. . . .	14 - 16 lbs./ft.	(1.93 - 2.21 kg./m.)
Top extension	. . . .	12 - 14 lbs./ft.	(1.66 - 1.94 kg./m.)
Driving flange	. . . .	70 - 80 lbs./ft.	(9.68 - 11.06 kg./m.)
Reverse lever fulcrum	. . . .	14 - 16 lbs./ft.	(1.93 - 2.21 kg./m.)
Mounting bracket	. . . .	18 - 20 lbs./ft.	(2.49 - 2.77 kg./m.)
Gear lever to shaft	. . . .	6 - 8 lbs./ft.	(0.83 - 1.11 kg./m.)
Reverse idler shaft	. . . .	14 - 16 lbs./ft.	(1.93 - 2.21 kg./m.)
Selector fork	. . . .	8 - 10 lbs./ft.	(1.11 - 1.38 kg./m.)
Speedometer sleeve	. . . .	14 - 16 lbs./ft.	(1.93 - 2.21 kg./m.)
Top cover	. . . .	6 - 8 lbs./ft.	(0.83 - 1.11 kg./m.)

Rear Axle

GENERAL

The hypoid bevel gear final drive unit is rubber mounted to the chassis at four points and incorporates right and left-hand short inner axle shafts which are universally jointed to the outer axle shafts. Each outer shaft is keyed to the wheel hub and is supported in a trunnion housing which is bolted to the vertical links of the rear suspension. The rear axle on both Herald and Spitfire is similar with a 4.11 : 1 axle ratio except for the Spitfire Mk. IV which has a 3.89 : 1 ratio.

NOTE: All illustration reference numbers apply to Fig. H:1.

ROUTINE MAINTENANCE

Every 6,000 miles (10,000 km.)

Top up with approved oil at filler/level plug (Fig. H:2). Allow surplus oil to drain before replacing plug and clean oil from exterior.

OUTER AXLE SHAFT AND HUB ASSEMBLY

Removal and Installation

(Figs. H:3, H:4, and H:5)

Removal

1. Raise rear of vehicle with jack and support on chassis stands.

2. Remove road wheel.

3. Disconnect brake hose (1) at bracket (2).

4. Disconnect handbrake cable from lever (4) and unhook spring.

5. Remove four attachment bolts (6) and nuts (7) from axle shaft coupling.

6. With jack locating at bottom of vertical links to relieve damper load, remove nut (8) with washer and pull damper clear of attachment pin and remove bolt (5) to disconnect radius rod.

7. Remove jack from beneath vertical links, support brake unit by hand and remove nut (9) and bolt to disconnect road spring from vertical links.

8. Remove shaft and hub assembly.

Installation

1. Place assembly in position and fit bolt to vertical link and road spring eye. Do not fully tighten nut (9).

2. Carefully jack vertical link and secure bottom of damper and radius rod to link.

3. Secure axle shaft coupling with four bolts and remove jack.

4. Load vehicle to "static laden" condition and fully tighten nut (9).

5. Reconnect handbrake cable and spring and flexible brake hose.

6. Replenish and bleed brake system and fit road wheel.

OUTER AXLE SHAFT - Overhaul

Dismantling

1. Remove brake drums.

2. Remove hub nut (31) and plain washer and withdraw hub with Churchill tool S109C. Retain key (Fig. H:7).

3. Remove trunnion bolt (73) and vertical links (75) and remove shims (25 and 28), seals (26), steel bush (38) and nylon inserts (27) from trunnion.

4. Straighten tabs of locking plate (71), remove bolt (70) and remove grease trap (32), backplate (72) seal housing (33) and gasket (36). Separate oil seal gasket (36). Separate oil seal (34) from housing.

5. Using Churchill tool S4221A with adaptor S4221A/14 remove trunnion (37) together with ballrace (35) and grease flinger (44).

6. Withdraw inner oil seal (41) and needle roller bearing (40) from trunnion.

Inspection

1. Clean all parts and inspect for wear or damage. Check needle and ball bearings for cracks and rough rotation. Renew if in doubt. Examine seals for deformation. Renew gasket and sealing rings and other parts as necessary.

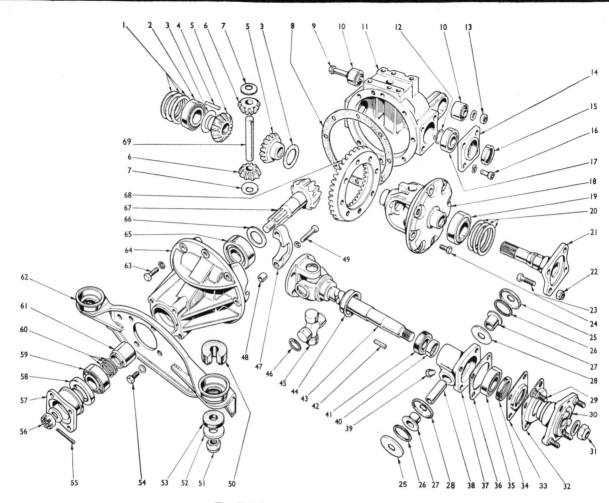

Fig. H:1 Exploded view of the rear axle components.

1. Shims
2. Differential side bearing
3. Thrust washer
4. Cross-shaft locking pin
5. Sun gear
6. Planet gear
7. Thrust washer
8. Joint washer
9. Rear mounting bolt
10. Metalastik bush
11. Hypoid rear casing
12. Circlip
13. Nyloc nut
14. Seal housing plate
15. Oil seal
16. Hexagon socket screw
17. Ball race
18. Differential carrier
19. Differential side bearing

20. Shims
21. Inner axle shaft
22. Nyloc nut
23. Bolt
24. Bolt
*25. Shim
*26. Rubber sealing ring
*27. Nylon bush
*28. Shim
29. Stud
30. Hub
31. Nyloc nut
32. Grease trap
33. Outer seal housing
34. Seal
35. Ballrace
36. Joint washer
37. Trunnion housing
38. Distance tube

39. Grease plug
40. Needle roller bearing
41. Inner oil seal
42. Key
43. Outer axle shaft
44. Grease flinger
45. Universal joint assembly
46. Circlip
47. Bearing cap
48. Tubular dowel
49. Bolt
50. Mounting rubber
51. Nyloc nut
52. Plain washer
53. Rubber pad
54. Bolt
55. Split pin
56. Slotted nut
57. Coupling flange

58. Oil seal
59. Pinion tail bearing
60. Shims
61. Spacer
62. Mounting plate
63. Bolt
64. Hypoid nose piece casing
65. Pinion head bearing
66. Spacer
67. Pinion
68. Crownwheel
69. Cross-shaft
70. Bolt
71. Lockplate
72. Brake backplate
73. Bolt
74. Nyloc nut
75. Vertical link

Note. *New trunnion sealing details introduced from Commission No. Herald 1200, GA184442 and GB36051; Herald 12/50, GD36956; Spitfire, FC62167; Vitesse 6, HB28055.*

Fig. H:2 Final drive unit filler/level plug

Fig. H:3 Vertical link and brake pipe attachments.

Fig. H:4 Handbrake cable, radius rod and damper attachments.

Fig. H:5 Axle shaft driving flange attachments

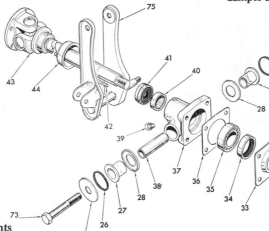

Fig. H:6 Exploded view of the outer axle shaft and hub assembly. (See Fig. H:1 for key).

Fig. H:7 Removing the rear hub.

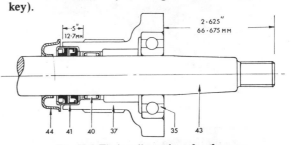

Fig. H:8 Fitting dimensions for the rear hub assembly (see Fig. H:1 for key).

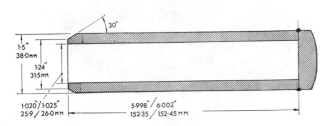

Fig. H:9 Dimension for the drift for fitting the flinger to the shaft.

Fig. H:10 Installing the needle roller bearing in the hub trunnion.

69

Fig. H:11 Pressing the axle shaft through the trunnion assembly.

Fig. H:12 Driving the ball race onto the shaft.

Fig. H:13 Axle shaft coupling attachments

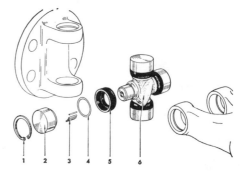

1. Circlip
2. Bearing cup
3. Needle rollers
4. Washer
5. Seal
6. Spider

Fig. H:14 Details of the axle shaft coupling

Fig. H:15 Extracting the circlips from the universal coupling

Fig. H:16 Tapping the coupling yoke to displace the bearing cup.

Fig. H:17 Extracting the needle roller cup.

Fig. H:18 Assembling the cup and needle rollers to the yoke.

Re-assembly

NOTE: Fig. H:8 shows correct position of needle roller bearing in trunnion and trunnion main bearing on shaft.

1. Press needle roller bearing (40) into trunnion to depth of 0.50 in. (12.7 mm.) with Churchill tool S300A. Press on lettered end of bearing (Fig. H:10).

2. Drive oil seal (41) into trunnion with lips trailing.

3. With tool shown at Fig. H:9 drive grease flinger (44) on to shaft.

4. Pack needle roller bearing with grease, carefully thread axle shaft through oil seal and bearing and press into position (Fig. H:11).

5. Pack ballrace with grease and drive on to shaft using Churchill tool S304. Secure and protect shaft in vice (Fig. H:12). Ensure trunnion and ballrace are positioned as shown in Fig. H:8.

6. Press seal (34) into housing (33) with lip trailing.

7. Assemble vertical links to trunnion.

8. Coat new gasket with grease, place against trunnion face and assemble seal housing, backplate (72) (with wheel cylinder at bottom in relation to vertical links) and grease trap (32) (with duct at bottom). Fit bolts (70) and secure with lockplates (71).

9. Fit and key hub (30) and secure with washer and new nyloc nut.

10. Assemble brake drum.

11. Assemble nylon inserts (27), sleeve (38), shims (28 and 25) and sealing rings (26).

OUTER AXLE SHAFT COUPLINGS

Inspection

1. Raise rear of vehicle with jack and support on chassis stands. Remove road wheels.

2. Raise vertical link on one side with trolley jack until in normal operating position.

3. Remove coupling attachment bolts (Fig. H:13).

4. Carefully lever flanges apart allowing vertical link to slide on trolley jack.

5. Hold shaft firmly and move flange yoke axially along spider journals. If end float exists, spider and cup assemblies must be renewed.

6. Repeat inspection procedure on opposite hand coupling.

NOTE: Needle rollers, cups, spiders, and circlip are supplied only as a complete replacement kit. Wear in yoke bore necessitates yoke renewal and the outer yoke is renewable only as part of shaft assembly.

Spider and Cup Assemblies Renewal (Fig. H:14)

1. Remove outer axle shaft.

2. Remove roller cup circlips (Fig. H:15).

3. Support yoke and tap with hide hammer to eject cup (Fig. H:16).

4. Complete removal of cup assembly using grips (Fig. H:17).

5. Remove opposite cup, separate flange yoke from spider and repeat procedure for outer yoke cups.

6. Clean bores of yokes.

7. Carefully fit seals (5) and washers (4) onto cups.

8. Position spider in outer yoke. Push cup assemblies squarely into yoke making sure needle rollers fit around yoke. (Fig. H:18).

9. Repeat with flange yoke and secure cups with circlips.

NOTE: Circlips are available in the following sizes to cater for varying spider lengths:

Part number	Width	
128651	0.058 - 0.059 in.	(1.47 - 1.50 mm.)
128652	0.059 - 0.060 in.	(1.50 - 1.52 mm.)
128653	0.060 - 0.061 in.	(1.52 - 1.55 mm.)
128654	0.061 - 0.062 in.	(1.55 - 1.57 mm.)

INNER AXLE SHAFT ASSEMBLY - Overhaul

(Fig. H:19) Removal

1. Remove hub and other shaft assembly.

2. Drain hypoid gear housing.

3. With hexagon key, 3/16 in. (6.76 mm.) remove socket screws from seal housing plate (14) (Fig. H:20).

4. Remove shaft assembly.

Dismantling (Fig. H:21)

1. Remove circlip (12).

2. Withdraw bearing (17) from shaft with Churchill tool and adaptor set S4221A-7B. (Fig. H:22).

3. Separate seal housing plate (14) and drive out oil seal (15).

Re-assembly

1. Drive seal with lip leading into housing plate (Fig. H:23).

2. With seal lip trailing slide housing carefully over serrations onto shaft.

3. Press shaft into housing and bearing (Fig. H:24).

Fig. H:19 Details of the inner axle shaft (see Fig. H:1 for key).

Fig. H:20 Removing the hexagon socket screws from the seal housing plate.

Fig. H:21 Inner axle shaft assembly (see Fig. H:1 for key).

Fig. H:22 Pressing the inner axle shaft out of the bearing race

Fig. H:23 Driving the inner axle shaft oil seal into its housing.

Fig. H:24 Pressing the inner axle shaft through the bearing and housing.

Fig. H:25 Installing the pinion shaft oil seal.

Fig. H:26 View of the inner axle shaft and prop shaft couplings.

Fig. H:27 Rear spring attachment.

4. Fit circlip (12) to shaft groove (Fig. H:21).

Installation

1. Install inner axle shaft in hypoid housing and secure with screws (16).

2. Refill hypoid housing with oil.

3. Install outer shaft and hub assembly.

PINION OIL SEAL - Replacement (Fig. H:25)

1. Drain final drive unit, remove exhaust tail pipe and disconnect propeller shaft.

2. Remove nut (56) and driving flange (57).

3. Lever out seal (58).

4. Drive new seal into nose casing (Fig. H:25).

5. Assemble driving flange to nose casing, connect propeller shaft and refit tail exhaust pipe.

6. Refill hypoid housing with oil.

FINAL DRIVE UNIT - Removal and Installation

1. Raise rear of vehicle with jack and support on chassis stands. Remove road wheels and drain unit.

2. Place jacks at bottom of vertical links to relieve damper load.

3. Disconnect bottom of damper and pull clear of mounting pins.

4. Remove exhaust silencer and tail pipe.

5. Disconnect inner shaft couplings and propeller shaft couplings (Fig. H:26).

6. Remove rear seat assembly and remove access panel over spring plate. Remove holding nuts and plate and remove three rear studs from axle casing. (Fig. H:27).

7. Remove bolts (9) from rear attachment, take the weight of unit and remove nuts (51), washers (52) and rubber pads (53) from nose mounting plate (62) (Fig. H:28).

8. Lower unit forward and down to clear vehicle.

9. Reverse procedure to install ensuring that rubber pads (53) are correctly located in nose mounting plate.

FINAL DRIVE UNIT - Overhaul

1. Clean unit with paraffin and overhaul on clean surface.

NOTE: Identify parts to avoid mixing and keep shim packs intact to assist in assembly.

Dismantling

2. Remove inner axle shafts (Fig. H:20).

3. Remove bolts (63) with spring washers and rotate pinion until two chamfered edges on differential carrier (18) permit withdrawal from rear casing (Fig. H:29).

4. Remove bearing caps (47) and attach Churchill spreading tool S101 to nose piece casing as shown in Fig. H:30. Open out tool by turning extension screw until hand tight then spread casing by giving a further HALF TURN ONLY with spanner.

   CAUTION: Do not spread more than this amount or housing will be irreparably damaged.

5. Remove differential carrier, identify bearings, caps and shim packs with their respective positions.

6. Remove crownwheel (Fig. H:31).

7. Re-assemble differential carrier in casing and secure with bearings and shims. Release spreading tool.

8. Mount dial indicator gauge on housing with plunger against carrier face, rotate carrier and check run out (Fig. H:32). Run out must not exceed 0.003 in. (0.076 mm.).

   NOTE: Excessive run out indicates distorted cage or defective bearings.

9. Spread casing to remove carrier, release and remove spreading tool.

10. Withdraw bearings (19) with Churchill tool S4221A-8C (Fig. H:33).

11. Drive out locking pin (4) as shown in Fig. H:34 and cross shaft (69) and rotate to remove differential gears (5 & 6) and thrust washers (3 & 7).

Pinion - Removal

1. Secure flange (57) against rotation and remove nut (56) and washer (Fig. H:35).

2. Drive pinion from casing with soft hammer to avoid damage to threads. Remove and retain shim pack complete and remove spacer (61).

3. Extract pinion head bearing with Churchill tool S4221A-4A as shown in Fig. H:36 and remove selective spacer (66).

4. Drive head and tail bearing outer races from casing (Fig. H:37).

5. Remove four bolts (54) and remove front mounting plate.

Inspection

1. Remove all traces of jointing material from joint faces. Clean all parts in trichlorethylene or paraffin and dry with air. Remove any burrs from bores, housings and joint faces.

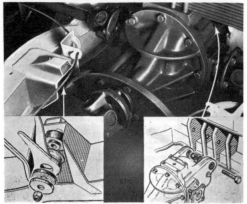

Fig. H:28 Final drive unit attachments

Fig. H:29 Removing the differential housing assembly from the final drive casing.

Fig. H:30 Removing the hypoid unit using the spreader tool.

Fig. H:31 Removing the crown wheel.

Fig. H:32 Checking the run-out on the differential carrier flange.

Fig. H:33 Removing the differential side bearings.

Fig. H:34 Driving out the cross-shaft locking pin.

Fig. H:35 Removing the pinion flange nut.

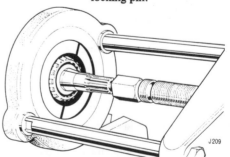

Fig. H:36 Pressing the pinion out of the head bearing.

Fig. H:37 Driving the outer races from the pinion casing.

Fig. H:38 Assembling the head bearing to the pinion.

Fig. H:39 Measuring the pinion height.

Fig. H:40 Identification markings on the crown wheel and pinion.

Fig. H:41 Torquing the pinion flange nut.

Fig. H:42 Measuring the pinion bearing pre-load.

Fig. H:43 Checking the run-out on the pinion flange.

Fig. H:44 Components of the differential assembly (see Fig. H:1 for key).

Fig. H:45 Measuring the planet gear backlash.

75

Fig. H:46 Assembling the side bearings to the differential carrier.

Fig. H:47 Measuring the total side float of the differential unit.

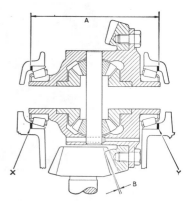

Fig. H:48 Determining the required shim pack thickness for the differential side gears.

Fig. H:49 Measuring the crown wheel "in and out" of mesh.

Fig. H:50 Assembling the bearing caps.

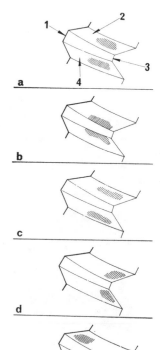

ADDENDUM — Pitch line to tooth tip.

DEDENDUM — Pitch line to tooth root.

Fig. H:53 Contact markings on the crownwheel teeth.

a. Correct marking
b. High contact
c. Low contact
d. Toe contact
e. Heel contact

1. Heel (Thick end)
2. Coast side (Concave)
3. Toe (Thin end)
4. Drive side (Convex)

Fig. H:51 Measuring the crownwheel backlash.

Fig. H:52 Applying marking compound to the crownwheel teeth to check the contact pattern.

Examine all parts for cracks or damage. Check for excessive wear against tolerances given in TECHNICAL DATA. Renew parts as necessary. Bearings must be renewed complete and crown wheels and pinions are identified matched pairs replaceable only by similarly identified matched pairs. Renew joint gasket and oil seals and use Hermetite or similar compound on gasket joint.

Re-assembly

Pinion

NOTE: Lightly oil bearings before assembly.

1. Using Churchill tool S124 assemble pinion bearing outer races in housing (64).

2. Assemble head bearing (65) to pinion without selective spacer (66) (Fig. H:38).

3. Install pinion in housing, assemble tail bearings flange (57), plain washer and nut (56) and tighten nut to specified torque. Do not assemble spacer (61) shims (60) and oil seal (58) at this stage.

    NOTE: Spin pinion during tightening process to "bed" bearing rollers.

4. Check pinion height with Churchill tool S108 as shown in Fig. H:39. Use ground button to fully depress gauge plunger and zero gauge before placing tool in casing with plunger on pinion head. When gauge is pressed downwards the dial indicates shim thickness required between normal pinion and head bearing.

    NOTE: Pinions of normal height are marked "N" on top face. Pinions varying from normal in height are marked with a plus or minus figure which indicates an amount to be added to, or subtracted from, gauge reading. With gauge reading of 0.013 in. and pinion marked as in Fig. H:40 shim thickness required is 0.013 + 0.001 in. = 0.014 in.

5. Remove flange, bearings and pinion from casing leaving outer races in position. Remove head bearing inner race from pinion, fit shims or spacer (66) and re-assemble head bearing.

6. Assemble spacer (61) and shim pack (60) to pinion shaft, install shaft in casing and fit bearing (59), flange (57) and washer and tighten nut (56) to specified torque (Fig. H:41).

7. With pre-load gauge (Churchill tool S98A) attached to driving flange, move weight along calibrated arm until pinion begins to turn (Fig. H:42).

    Gauge reading should be 12 - 14 lb./in. (0.014 - 0.185 kg/m).

    To increase loading subtract shims from shim pack (60) and to decrease loading add shims.

8. Remove flange and fit oil seal (58) then refit flange and washer and secure with nut (56) and split pin.

9. Attach dial gauge as shown in Fig. H:43 and check that flange run-out does not exceed 0.002 in. (0.05 mm.).

Differential Unit - Assembly (Fig. H:44)

1. Assemble thrust washers to both sun gears and insert into differential cage.

2. Attach thrust washers to planet wheels with grease, insert wheels from opposite sides to mesh with the sun gears.

3. Rotate sun gears together until planet gear and cage bores are aligned and insert cross shaft.

4. Check planet gear backlash by measuring sun gear end float (Fig. H:45).

5. Adjust for minimum backlash consistent with freedom of rotation by altering thickness of thrust washer fitted.

6. Align cross shaft, fit locking pin and retain by peening the edge of drilling in cage.

Differential - Total End - Float

1. Fit differential bearings (2 and 19) to carrier journals and assemble in casing without shims (1 and 20).

2. Mount dial gauge as shown in Fig. H:47 with plunger against crown wheel mounting flange.

3. Pressing both bearing outer races towards each other, lever differential away from indicator and zero gauge.

4. Lever differential towards indicator and note reading.

    This gives float "A" (Fig. H:48).

Crown Wheel - "In and Out" of Mesh

1. Ensure mating faces of differential carrier and crown wheel are clean and free from burrs and secure crown wheel to carrier using new bolts (24) and tightening evenly and in turn to specified torque.

    NOTE: Apply two drops of Loctite Studlock to each bolt before fitment.

2. Install differential assembly in casing without bearing caps and mount indicator with plunger against head of crown wheel attachment bolt (Fig. H:49).

3. Move differential assembly away from indicator to full mesh position and zero gauge.

4. Move assembly towards indicator and note dial reading. This gives float "B" (Fig. H:48).

5. Remove differential unit from housing retaining outer bearing race at its respective side.

Differential Bearing - pre-load (Fig. H:48).

The shim thickness required to give correct bearing pre-load is calculated as follows substituting actual float values for the hypothetical figures given:

EXAMPLE

Dimension A (Total end-float)	0.060 in.
Bearing pre-load	+ 0.003 in.
Total shim thickness required	0.063 in.
Dimension "B" (In and Out of Mesh)	0.025 in.
Specified backlash (0.004 - 0.006 in.)	- 0.005 in.
Shim thickness required at "Y"	0.020 in.
Total shim thickness required	0.063 in.
Shim thickness required at "Y"	- 0.020 in.
Shim thickness required at "X"	0.043 in.

Fit the appropriate shim packs and bearings to the differential cage trunnions.

Assembly of Differential Unit to Casing

1. Use spreading tool to assemble unit complete with shims into casing. Remove tool.

2. Fit bearing caps with new spring washers (Fig. H:50).

   Note identification markings.

Crownwheel backlash

1. Mount dial indicator with plunger on one of the crown wheel teeth (Fig. H:51).

2. Hold pinion firmly, rock crown wheel to fullest extent and note total indicator reading. Measure at several points and check that backlash is within 0.004 - 0.006 in. (0.01 - 0.15 mm.).

3. If backlash is excessive, transfer shims to equivalent value by which backlash is to be reduced from "X" to "Y". To increase backlash, transfer from "Y" to "X".

Tooth Contact (Fig. H:53)

With the backlash correctly set, coat eight to ten teeth on the crown wheel with engineers blue. Turn the pinion until all the marked teeth have been in contact with the pinion teeth. Check the tooth pattern on both sides of the gears.

a.   Correct marking: If the pinion bearing pre-load and crown wheel backlash have been set correctly, the margins above and below the area of contact should be the same. The marking should be lozenge shaped and nearer to the toe than the heel.

b.   High Contact: In this case the area of contact is above the centre-line of the tooth, due to the pinion being too far away from the crown wheel. To rectify, increase the shim thickness under the pinion head bearing outer ring to lower the contact area. The shim thickness between the tail bearing cone and the pinion bearing spacer must also be increased by the same amount to maintain correct bearing pre-load.

c.   Low Contact: In this case the area of contact is below the centre-line of the tooth, indicating that the pinion is too far in mesh. To rectify, decrease the shim thickness under the pinion head bearing outer ring. The pinion bearing pre-load shim pack must be decreased a corresponding amount to maintain the correct bearing pre-load.

NOTE: The above correction tends to move the tooth contact area towards the heel on "DRIVE" and the toe on "COAST". It may, therefore, be necessary to re-adjust the crown wheel "IN and OUT" of mesh and backlash.

d.   Toe Contact: When the area of contact is running off the toe of the tooth, this indicates insufficient backlash. Move the crown wheel away from the pinion by transferring shims from the crown wheel side of the differential carrier to the opposite side.

e.   Heel Contact: When the area of contact is concentrated at the large end of the tooth, this is an indication of excessive backlash. Move the crown wheel further into mesh with the pinion by transferring shims from the opposite side of the differential carrier to the crown wheel side.

NOTE: Backlash: Always move the crown wheel when adjusting to obtain the correct backlash as this has a more direct effect than moving the pinion.

Crown Wheel Movement: Moving the crown wheel out of mesh has the effect of moving the contact area up the tooth flank and towards the heel of the tooth.

Pinion Movement: Moving the pinion out of mesh has the effect of moving the contact area up the tooth and towards the heel on "DRIVE" and the toe on "COAST".

FINAL ASSEMBLY

1. Manoeuvre differential unit into rear casing using new gasket (8) and join casing sections tightening bolts evenly and in turn.

2. Assemble inner axle shafts and install final drive unit.

Technical Data

Crown Wheel:
Maximum Backlash . . . . 0.004 - 0.006 in. (0.10 - 0.15 mm.)

Pinion:
Journal Diameter   - Head Bearing . . . . 1.0006 - 1.0011 in. (25.415 - 25.428 mm.)
                           Tail Bearing . . . . 0.7504 - 0.7509 in. (19.06 - 19.073 mm.)
Bearing pre-load . . . . 12 - 16 lb./in. (0.014 - 0.19 kg./m.)
Bearing spacer length . . . . 1.450 - 1.455 in. (36.83 - 36.96 mm.)
           (Alternative) . . . . 1.544 - 1.549 in. (39.22 - 39.34 mm.)

Hypoid Housing:
Internal diameters:-
Pinion Head Bearing Housing . . . . 2.6860 - 2.6870 in. (68.224 - 68.250 mm.)
Pinion tail bearing housing . . . . 2.1235 - 2.1245 in. (53.937 - 53.962 mm.)
Differential bearing housing . . . . 2.4418 - 2.4428 in. (61.996 - 62.022 mm.)

Differential Carrier:
Bore for cross-shaft . . . . 0.4993 - 0.5000 in. (12.68 - 12.70 mm.)*
                           or 0.6245 - 0.6255 in. (15.86 - 15.89 mm.)**
Bore for sun gear spigot . . . . 1.126 - 1.128 in. (28.60 - 28.65 mm.)*
                           or 1.251 - 1.253 in. (31.78 - 31.83 mm.)**
Side bearing spigot dia. . . . . 1.251 in. (31.78 mm.)

Differential Gears:
Sun gear spigot dia. . . . . 1.1235 - 1.1243 in. (28.537 - 28.557 mm.)*
                           or 1.2485 in. (31.798 mm.)**
Planet gear bore dia. . . . . 0.5000 - 0.5015 in. (12.7 - 12.738 mm.)*
                           or 0.625 in. (15.815 mm.)**
Cross-shaft dia. . . . . 0.4990 - 0.4995 in. (12.60 - 12.61 mm.)*
                           or 0.6237 - 0.6242 in. (15.842 - 15.855 mm.)**

Inner Axle Shaft:
Bearing journal dia. . . . . 0.8754 - 0.8759 in. (22.215 - 22.228 mm.)*
                           or 0.9847 - 0.9852 in. (25.011 - 25.024 mm.)**

Rear Hub:
Needle roller bearing housing dia. . . . . 1.2508 - 1.2498 in. (31.775 - 31.750 mm.)
Main bearing housing dia. . . . . 2.2490 - 2.2495 in. (57.125 - 57.137 mm.)

Differential Bearing Shims:

Part No.	Thickness	
123813	0.0085 - 0.0095 in.	(0.216 - 0.241 mm.)
4	0.012 - 0.013 in.	(0.300 - 0.330 mm.)
5	0.014 - 0.015 in.	(0.350 - 0.381 mm.)
6	0.016 - 0.017 in.	(0.406 - 0.432 mm.)
7	0.019 - 0.021 in.	(0.483 - 0.533 mm.)

Planet Gear Thrust Washers*:

145282	0.033 - 0.035 in.	(0.838 - 0.889 mm.)
104572	0.035 - 0.037 in.	(0.839 - 0.939 mm.)
145262	0.037 - 0.039 in.	(0.939 - 0.990 mm.)
108935	0.039 - 0.041 in.	(0.990 - 1.041 mm.)
142167	0.041 - 0.043 in.	(1.041 - 1.092 mm.)
108963	0.043 - 0.045 in.	(1.092 - 1.143 mm.)
142168	0.045 - 0.047 in.	(1.143 - 1.193 mm.)
108937	0.047 - 0.049 in.	(1.193 - 1.244 mm.)
108938	0.051 - 0.052 in.	(1.295 - 1.320 mm.)
108939	0.055 - 0.057 in.	(1.397 - 1.447 mm.)

Planet Gear Thrust Washers**:

138440	0.026 - 0.028 in.	(0.660 - 0.711 mm.)
147249	0.028 - 0.030 in.	(0.711 - 0.762 mm.)
134076	0.030 - 0.032 in.	(0.762 - 0.812 mm.)
147250	0.032 - 0.034 in.	(0.812 - 0.863 mm.)
138441	0.034 - 0.036 in.	(0.863 - 0.914 mm.)
147251	0.036 - 0.038 in.	(0.914 - 0.965 mm.)
138442	0.038 - 0.040 in.	(0.965 - 1.016 mm.)
158805	0.040 - 0.042 in.	(1.016 - 1.066 mm.)
147252	0.042 - 0.044 in.	(1.066 - 1.117 mm.)

F

Pinion Bearing Shims:

Part No.	Thickness	
100562	0.003 in.	(0.076 mm.)
3	0.005 in.	(0.127 mm.)
4	0.010 in.	(0.254 mm.)

* Fitted to all 12/50 models, to 1200 models up to Commission No. GA237600 and GB57201 and Spitfire models up to FD22570.

** Fitted to all 13/60 models, to 1200 models from Commission No. GA237601 and Spitfire GB57202 models from FD22571.

Lubrication:
Oil Capacity . . . . 1.0 Imp. pts. (1.2 U.S. pints; 0.57 litres)
Oil Specification . . . . SAE 90 EP

TIGHTENING TORQUES

Bearing cap to housing	32 - 34 lbs./ft.	(4.5 - 4.7 kg./m.)
Crown wheel attachment	42 - 46 lbs./ft.	(5.8 - 6.4 kg./m.)
Front mounting plate to axle	26 - 28 lbs./ft.	(3.6 - 3.9 kg./m.)
Front mounting plate to chassis	26 - 28 lbs./ft.	(3.6 - 3.9 kg./m.)
Hypoid front casing to rear	18 - 20 lbs./ft.	(2.5 - 2.8 kg./m.)
Inner axle flange	24 - 28 lbs./ft.	(3.3 - 3.6 kg./m.)
Pinion flange	70 - 85 lbs./ft.	(9.7 - 11.8 kg./m.)
Road spring plate studs	28 - 30 lbs./ft.	(3.9 - 4.2 kg./m.)
Rear axle mounting	38 - 40 lbs./ft.	(5.3 - 5.5 kg./m.)
Damper lower attachment	30 - 32 lbs./ft.	(4.1 - 4.4 kg./m.)
Vertical link plates to hub	42 - 46 lbs./ft.	(5.8 - 6.4 kg./m.)
Hub nut	100 - 110 lbs./ft.	(13.8 - 15.2 kg./m.)
Pinion nut	90 - 100 lbs./ft.	(12.4 - 13.8 kg./m.)

Rear Suspension

GENERAL
REAR TRANSVERSE SPRING - Removal and Installation
DAMPER - Removal and Installation
RADIUS ARM - Removal and Installation
REAR WHEEL - Alignment
TRUNNION HOUSING - Overhaul
TECHNICAL DATA

GENERAL

The swing-axle type rear suspension is similar on all models, with a transverse leaf spring centrally clamped to the final drive unit casing and joined with vertical link plates to hub trunnions. Telescopic dampers connected from chassis to trunnion housing control the springing, and rear mounted radius arms connected to the vertical links control alignment. Rear suspension number references are as annotated in Fig. I:1.

REAR TRANSVERSE SPRING

Removal and Installation

Removal

1. Raise rear of vehicle with jack and place onto axle stands. Remove rear road wheels.

2. Disconnect each brake hose at chassis bracket, and disconnect handbrake cable and spring at backplate.

3. With jack under vertical link relieve damper load (Fig. I:2).

4. Remove bolts (47) to disconnect shaft couplings.

5. Slacken nut (8), remove nut (13) with washer and pull each damper off lower attachment (Fig. I:3). Remove jack from under link.

6. Supporting vertical links (10), remove spring eye bolt (46) from each side (Fig. I:4).

7. Remove rear passenger seat and spring centre attachment access cover. Remove nuts (4) with washers, plate (3) and extract three rear studs (42) (Fig. I:5).

8. Withdraw spring from under vehicle (Fig. I:5).

Installation

1. With spring "FRONT" marking in correct direction, pass spring over axle casing until centre bolt engages in locating hole. Turn shorter threaded lengths of studs (42) into axle casing, install spring plate and secure with nuts (4).

2. Apply "Prestik" sealer or similar at edge of access cover, secure cover, and coat joint with "Seelastik" or similar. Install passenger seat.

3. Assemble vertical links to spring eyes but do not fully tighten nuts (11).

4. Jack up vertical links to relieve damper load, attach bottom of dampers, and connect axle shaft couplings.

5. Connect handbrake cables and pull-off springs. Connect brake hoses and fill and bleed brake system.

6. Position trolley jack under axle casing, remove chassis stands, support vertical links at working height, load vehicle and lower trolley jack until axle shafts are at static laden position. (See TECHNICAL DATA section for specifications). Fully tighten nuts (11).

7. Install road wheels and remove jack.

DAMPER - Removal and Installation

Removal

1. Raise rear of vehicle with jack and place onto axle stands. Remove rear road wheels.

2. With jack under vertical link relieve damper load (Fig. I:2).

3. Remove bolt (44) and nut (13) with washer and remove damper (Fig. I:3).

4. Examine rubber bushes (6) for damage or deterioration and renew if necessary.

Installation

1. Remove air from damper by operating over full stroke whilst in vertical position.

2. Install damper and obtain "static load" condition before tightening attachment nuts.

3. Refit road wheels.

RADIUS ARM - Removal and Installation

1. Carry out damper removal procedure until jack is positioned under vertical links.

2. Adjust jack height until bolts (33 and 50) can readily be removed and radius arm withdrawn (Fig. I:7).

3. Examine rubber bushes (41) for damage or deterioration. If necessary remove with press, clean bores and press in new bushes.

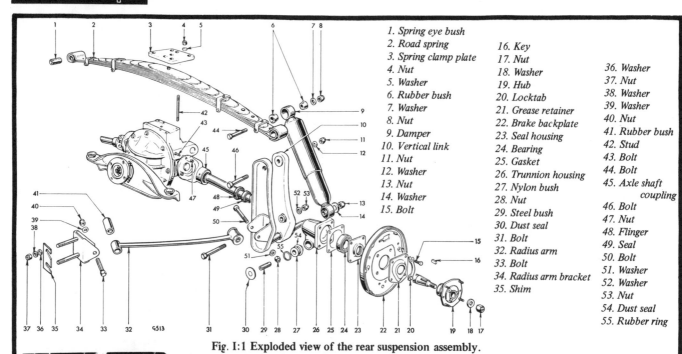

1. Spring eye bush
2. Road spring
3. Spring clamp plate
4. Nut
5. Washer
6. Rubber bush
7. Washer
8. Nut
9. Damper
10. Vertical link
11. Nut
12. Washer
13. Nut
14. Washer
15. Bolt
16. Key
17. Nut
18. Washer
19. Hub
20. Locktab
21. Grease retainer
22. Brake backplate
23. Seal housing
24. Bearing
25. Gasket
26. Trunnion housing
27. Nylon bush
28. Nut
29. Steel bush
30. Dust seal
31. Bolt
32. Radius arm
33. Bolt
34. Radius arm bracket
35. Shim
36. Washer
37. Nut
38. Washer
39. Washer
40. Nut
41. Rubber bush
42. Stud
43. Bolt
44. Bolt
45. Axle shaft coupling
46. Bolt
47. Nut
48. Flinger
49. Seal
50. Bolt
51. Washer
52. Washer
53. Nut
54. Dust seal
55. Rubber ring

Fig. I:1 Exploded view of the rear suspension assembly.

Fig. I:2 Jacking up the vertical link to relieve the load on the damper.

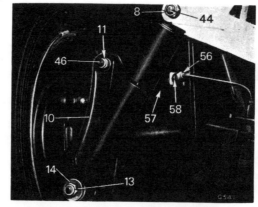

Fig. I:3 Rear suspension attachments.

Fig. I:4 Removing the pivot bolt from the vertical link and spring eye.

Fig. I:5 Rear spring clamp plate attachments.

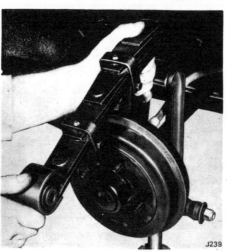

Fig. I:6 Withdrawing the rear spring.

Fig. I:7 Radius arm attachments.

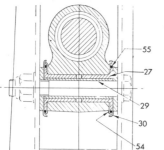

Fig. I:8 Sectional view of the trunnion assembly (see Fig. I:1 for key).

NOTE: If chassis mounting brackets are removed ensure the same number of shims (35) are replaced behind bracket.

4. Reverse procedure to install radius arms.

REAR WHEEL - Alignment

Check and, if necessary adjust rear wheel alignment by removing shims (35) to increase toe-in and adding shims to decrease toe-in.

NOTE: Toe-in should be checked with jigs or preferably with optical equipment which enables front and rear wheels to be aligned together.

This equipment projects a light beam at right angles to the axle on to a screen where dimensions and angles can be directly read off.

An approximate check may be made as follows.

1. Ensure tyres are evenly inflated and vehicle is on level ground.

2. Mark inside of each wheel rim in front of, and level with axle and measure distance between wheels:- distance "A".

3. Move vehicle until rim marking is behind and level with axle and again measure distance between wheels:- distance "B".

4. The difference when "A" is subtracted from "B" is approximate toe-in which should be zero to 1/16 in. (1.6 mm.).

TRUNNION HOUSING - Overhaul

1. Raise rear of vehicle onto chassis stands, remove rear road wheels and relieve damper load (Fig. I:2).

2. Disconnect brake hose at chassis bracket, handbrake cable and return spring from backplate axle shaft coupling and radius arm from vertical link.

3. Remove damper and remove jack from under vertical link.

4. Support brake drum, remove bolt (46) from road spring eye and remove brake/shaft assembly. Clean exterior of assembly and place on clean bench.

5. Detach links (10) from trunnion housing and remove dust seal (30), steel bush (29) flanged nylon bushes (27), "O" rings (55) and inner dust seals (54).

6. Clean and examine all parts for damage, deterioration or wear. Renew parts as necessary.

7. Apply grease (Shell Retinax "A" or similar) to bushes and assemble parts as shown in Fig. I:8.

8. Position brake/shaft assembly under vehicle and attach vertical link to road spring eye bush. Do not fully tighten bolt (44).

9. Place jack beneath vertical link and connect damper, radius arm and axle shaft coupling.

10. Position trolley jack under axle casing, remove chassis stands, support vertical links at working height, load vehicle and lower trolley jack until axle shafts are at static laden position. Fully tighten nut (11).

11. Connect brake hose and handbrake. Replenish and bleed brakes.

12. Fit road wheels and remove jack.

Technical Data

Road spring	Transverse leaf spring
Damper	Telescopic, hydraulic
Camber - Herald (Static laden*)	2° negative
- Spitfire	3° negative
Toe-in (Static laden*)	0 - 1/16 in. (1.6 mm.)

* Static laden:-
The condition when a weight of 150 lbs. (68 kg.) is placed on each front and rear seat.

TIGHTENING TORQUES

Backplate attachment	16 - 18 lbs./ft.	(2.21 - 2.44 kg./m.)
Radius arm brackets to frame	24 - 26 lbs./ft.	(3.32 - 3.60 kg./m.)
Damper lower attachment	30 - 32 lbs./ft.	(4.15 - 4.42 kg./m.)
Damper upper attachment	42 - 46 lbs./ft.	(5.81 - 6.36 kg./m.)
Hub nut	100 - 110 lbs./ft.	(13.83 - 15.21 kg./m.)
Road spring to axle unit	28 - 30 lbs./ft.	(3.87 - 4.18 kg./m.)
Spring end to vertical link	42 - 46 lbs./ft.	(5.81 - 6.36 kg./m.)
Vertical link to hub	42 - 46 lbs./ft.	(5.81 - 6.36 kg./m.)
Axle shaft coupling	24 - 28 lbs./ft.	(3.32 - 3.60 kg./m.)

1. Locknut
2. Nut
3. Washer
4. Rubber bush
5. Nyloc nut
6. Plain washer
7. Upper spring pan
8. Road spring
9. Damper
10. Front upper wishbone arm
11. Bolt
12. Rear upper wishbone arm
13. Rubber bush
14. Nyloc nut
15. Bolt
16. Ball joint
17. Rubber gaiter
18. Vertical link
19. Plain washer
20. Nyloc nut
21. Plain washer
22. Nyloc nut
23. Nyloc nut
24. Plain washer
25. Nyloc nut
26. Rubber bush
27. Plug
28. Steering arm
29. Nyloc nut
30. Plain washer
31. Shim
32. Inner fulcrum bracket
33. Fulcrum bolt
34. Nyloc nut
35. Lower wishbone assembly
36. Suspension unit fulcrum bolt
37. Nyloc nut
38. Plain washer
39. Steel bush
40. Rubber seal
41. Nylon bush

41A. Washer
41B. Washer
42. Lower trunnion
43. Rubber seal
44. Plain washer
45. Nyloc nut
46. Fulcrum bolt
47. Brake backplate
48. Locking plate

49. Spring washer
50. Setscrew
51. Bolt
52. Stub axle
53. Felt seal
54. Seal retainer
55. Taper roller bearing - inner
56. Roller bearing outer ring
57. Hub

58. Roller bearing outer ring
59. Taper roller bearing - outer
60. "D" washer
61. Slotted nut
62. Split pin
63. Spring retaining collet
64. Spring cup
65. Brake disc

66. Dust cap
67. Splash shield
68. Calliper mounting bracket
69. Bolt - disc attachment
70. Brake calliper
71. Spring washer
72. Bolt - Calliper attachment
73. O-ring

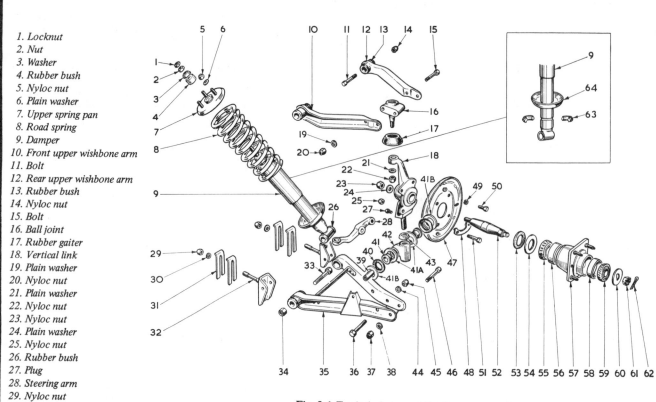

Fig. J:1 Exploded view of the front suspension unit.

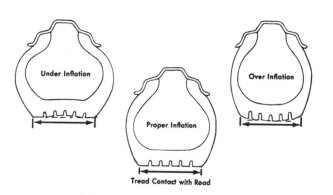

Fig. J:2 Effects of inflation pressure

Fig. J:3 Mounting bolts for the disc brake calliper

Front Suspension

GENERAL

The independent front suspension is of the double wish-bone type with coil springs and telescopic dampers. The unequal length wishbones are anchored through rubber-bushed fulcrum pivots at their inner ends and a cast vertical link is swivel mounted to their outer ends. The stub axle is a separate item attached to the vertical link. The hub assembly differs in detail dependent on whether drum or disc type brakes are fitted, but in either case is carried on tapered roller bearings. The suspension coil spring is mounted co-axially on the telescopic hydraulic damper, the unit acting on the lower wishbone. A transverse anti-roll bar also acts on the lower wishbones.

ROUTINE MAINTENANCE

Weekly

Check tyre pressures and adjust to correct pressures as necessary.

Every 6,000 miles (10,000 km.)

Check tightness of wheel nuts and examine tyres for wear.

Every 12,000 miles (20,000 km.)

Raise front of vehicle and check road wheels for freedom of rotation and front hub bearing end-float. Adjust end-float as necessary.

At overhaul periods strip, clean relubricate and adjust front hubs as described later in this section.

WHEELS AND TYRES

Wheel balancing

Imbalance of the road wheels may cause wheel tramp, vibration in the steering or abnormal tyre wear.

To obtain maximum ride comfort and tyre life, the balance of the road wheels should be checked periodically. Whenever any of the wheels are interchanged on the car, they should be rebalanced on the car. Since specialised knowledge and equipment are required to perform this operation, the work should be entrusted to an authorised dealer or tyre specialist.

Tyre Pressures

The tyre pressures should be checked and adjusted to the recommended pressure at least once a month. The recommended inflation pressures for the original equipment tyres are listed in the TECHNICAL DATA at the end of this section. Check the pressures when the tyres are cold as tyre pressure may increase by as much as 6 p.s.i. (0.4 kg./cm^2) when hot. Incorrect inflation pressure will result in abnormal wear, (Fig. J:2) and premature failure. There is an average loss of 13% tread mileage for every 10% reduction in inflation pressure below the recommended figure.

Tyre Wear

Abnormal tyre wear can be caused by improper inflation pressures, wheel imbalance, misaligned front suspension or mechanical irregularities. When rapid or uneven tyre wear becomes apparent, the fault should be sought and rectified.

Fins and feathers on the tread surface are an indication of severe wheel misalignment. The condition takes the form of a sharp "fin" on the edge of each pattern rib and the position of this indicates the direction of misalignment. Fins on the out-board edges are caused by excessive toe-out, whereas fins on the inboard edges of the pattern ribs are caused by excessive toe-in. Finning on the near-side front tyre only may be due to severe road camber conditions and cannot be eliminated by mechanical adjustment. In this event, frequent interchanging of the affected wheel is the only way to even out tyre wear.

Some mechanical defects which could be a cause of ab-normal tyre wear are:- loose wheel bearings, uneven brake adjustment, oval brake drum, distorted brake disc, excessive looseness or damage in the suspension, loose steering connections or bent steering arms.

Radial Ply and Cross Ply Tyres

It is dangerous to use a vehicle which is fitted with an unsuitable combination of tyres. Radial-ply and cross-ply tyres should not be used on the same axle. Radial-ply tyres should not be fitted to the front wheels when cross-ply tyres are fitted at the rear wheels. Radial-ply tyres may be fitted to the rear wheels when cross-ply tyres are fitted to the front wheels, but this is not recommended. It is far safer to fit radial-ply or cross-ply tyres in complete sets.

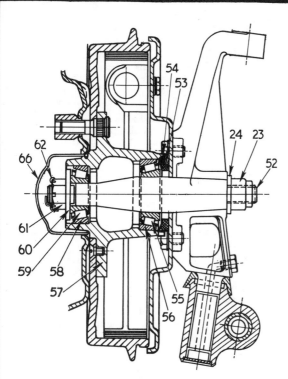

Fig. J:4 Cross-sectional view of the drum brake and hub assembly. (See Fig. J:1 for key).

Fig. J:5 Cross-sectional view of the disc brake and hub assembly. (See Fig. J:1 for key).

Fig. J:6 Details of the drum brake hub assembly (see Fig. J:1 for key).

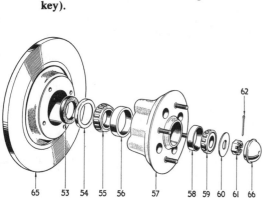

Fig. J:7 Details of the disc brake hub assembly (see Fig. J:1 for key).

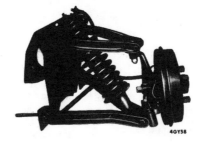

Fig. J:8 Disconnecting the brake hose.

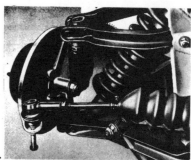

Fig J:9 Detaching the tie-rod from the steering arm.

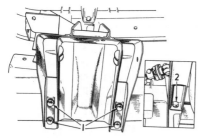

Fig. J:10 Suspension sub-frame attachment points.   1. Outer bolts   2. Inner bolts.

Fig. J:11 Suspension sub-assembly removed.

Fig. J:12 Anti-roll bar attachments at the lower wishbone.

SUSPENSION ALIGNMENT

The castor, camber, king pin inclination (K.P.I.) and turning angles of the front suspension are inherent in the design of the suspension and are not adjustable. However, they should be checked at regular intervals, particularly if the suspension has been subjected to heavy impact, as excessive wear or accidental damage may disturb one or more of the settings necessitating rectification. Specialised knowledge and equipment are necessary to check these dimensions satisfactorily and this operation should therefore be entrusted to an authorised dealer.

The above also applies in respect of the front wheel toe-in which must be correctly set to ensure parallel tracking when the vehicle is moving. A method of setting the toe-in is given in the STEERING section, but this should only be regarded as a temporary measure after the replacement of suspension or steering components. The toe-in should be re-checked as soon as possible afterwards with proper equipment.

FRONT HUB - Removal

1. Raise front of vehicle and place on chassis stands and remove road wheels.

2. Remove two counter sunk screws and brake drum or two bolts to remove disc brake calliper (Fig. J:3).

3. Support removed calliper with wire hook.

4. Remove grease cap (66), nut (61) and washer (60) and withdraw hub assembly from stub axle (Figs. J:4 or J:5).

Dismantling (Figs. J:6 or J:7)

1. Remove inner bearing race (55) from shaft and remove seal retainer (54) and seal (53) from stub axle.

2. With soft metal drifts drive outer bearing inner race (59) and both outer races (56 and 58) from the hub.

3. If required, remove disc (65) from hub.

Assembly

NOTE: Assemble bearings without grease initially to obtain correct adjustment. Re-assemble brake disc, if applicable.

1. Lightly oil stub axle and hub bearing housing.

2. Lubricate seal (53) squeeze out surplus oil and fit on to stub axle followed by seal retainer (54).

3. Press inner bearing inner race (55), onto axle and outer race (56) together with outer bearing (58 and 59) into hub.

4. Fit hub assembly onto axle with washer (60) and while rotating hub by hand, tighten nut until all slack is removed. Slacken nut to next split pin hole and mark position on nut and washer.

5. Remove hub assembly pack bearings with grease, re-assemble to axle shaft and secure with split pin in marked hole.

6. Assemble brake drum or brake calliper, as applicable, attach road wheels and remove chassis stands.

End Float Adjustment

(Road wheel and brake calliper removed)

1. Apply torque of not more than 5 lb./ft. (0.7 kg./m.) to hub nut whilst rotating by hand in same direction.

2. Slacken nut to nearest split pin hole and secure.

FRONT SUSPENSION UNIT

Removal and Installation

1. Raise front of vehicle and place on chassis stands just rear of front cross-member.

2. If drivers side unit is being removed withdraw steering column from coupling (see STEERING section).

3. Disconnect brake hose at bracket and drain system (Fig. J:8).

4. Remove nut and bolt securing valance to suspension sub frame (Herald 1200 Mk. II and 12/50 only).

5. Disconnect anti-roll bar from lower wishbone.

6. Remove nut and washer and detach steering tie-rod from steering arm (28) with Churchill tool No. S160 (Fig. J:9).

7. Remove two nuts (29) from lower wishbone fulcrum brackets and note number of shims at each bracket.

8. Remove four bolts (1) washers and tapping plates and one bolt (2) with washers (Fig. J:10).

9. Remove suspension unit complete (Fig. J:11).

10. Reverse procedure to install ensuring that shims (65) are in original position. Re-fill and bleed hydraulic system. Fit road wheels and check suspension geometry.

Dismantling

NOTE: The front suspension unit may be dismantled either on the vehicle as detailed or with unit removed as previously described. Follow applicable instructions.

1. Remove spring damper strut as described in separate instruction.

2. Detach brake drum or brake calliper (Fig. J;3).

3. Separate steering tie-rod from steering arm (Fig. J:9).

4. Remove front hub as earlier described.

5. Straighten tabs on lockwasher (48), remove bolts (50 and 51) and remove brake backplate or calliper mounting bracket, dust shield, and steering arm (28).

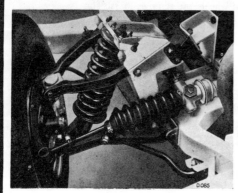

Fig. J:13 Details of the wishbone attachments.

Fig. J:14 Detaching the upper wishbone ball joint from the vertical link.

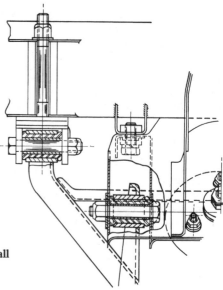

Fig. J:15 Sectional view of the upper and lower wishbone inner fulcrum pivots.

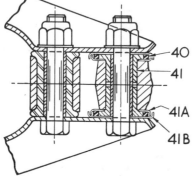

40
41
41A
41B

Fig. J:16 Sectional view of the lower wishbone outer fulcrum pivot.

Fig. J:17 Assembling the rubber seal to the vertical link.

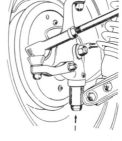

Fig. J:18 Right and left-hand lower trunnions, showing the reduced diameter on the R.H. one.

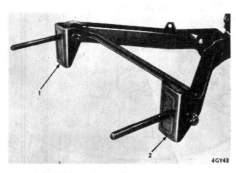

Fig. J:19 Lower wishbone fulcrum brackets. 1. Front 2. Rear.

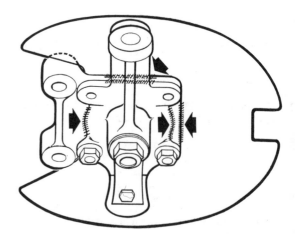

Fig. J:20 Positions of the sealing strip between the calliper mounting bracket and the vertical link.

6. Disconnect anti-roll bar at lower wishbone (Fig. J:12).

7. Remove bolts (11) from upper wishbone attachments and nuts (29) from lower wishbone bracket (32) (Fig. J:13). Note number and location of shims (31).

8. Remove vertical link and wishbone assembly.

9. Remove nut (22) and washer, and with Churchill tool S166A separate ball joint (16) from vertical link (Fig. J:14).

10. Remove bolts (15) to detach upper wishbone arms from ball joint (16).

11. Remove bolt (46) and remove lower wishbone assembly from lower trunnion (42).

12. Remove steel bush (39), flanged bushes (41) washers (41a) and dust seals (40) from trunnion.

13. Remove nut (23) and washer and press stub axle from vertical link.

Inspection

1. Examine rubber bushes at inner end of wishbone arms for deterioration cracks. If necessary press out old bushes and insert new items with press and pilot tool until bush protrudes equally at each side as shown in Fig. J:15.

2. Inspect all seals and nylon bushes and renew if damaged or deteriorated.

3. Examine all parts for wear and damage and renew as necessary.

Re-assembly

1. Insert stub axle in vertical link with split pin hole horizontal and secure with nut (23) and washer.

2. Fit flanged bushes (41) with washer (41a) under flange into trunnion (42), insert steel bush (39) and stretch rubber dust excluder (40) over bush flanges. (Fig. J:16).

3. With serviceable rubber seal (43) fitted as shown in Fig. J:17 screw vertical link into trunnion as far as possible then unscrew until 180° rotation in each direction is available.

   NOTE: The left-hand vertical link and trunnion has left-hand mating threads and the right hand assembly has right hand threads and has reduced diameter at the trunnion lower end for identification (Fig. J:18).

4. Fit washers (41b) and assemble lower wishbone arms to trunnion (Fig. J:16).

5. Assemble fulcrum brackets to lower wishbone arms located as shown in Fig. J:19.

6. Assemble ball joint unit (16) between upper wishbone arms and secure with bolts (15), washers and nuts.

7. With rubber gaiter (17) over shank assemble ball joint (16)

to vertical link and secure with nut (22) and washer.

8. Assemble steering arm (28) and brake backplate (47) to vertical link. On disc brake units, assemble dust shield and calliper bracket and apply Expandite Seal-a-Strip (105S) Pt. No. 554420 to joint of dust shield to vertical link and calliper bracket (Fig. J:20).

   NOTE: Later models have rubber seal (73) between recessed face of calliper bracket and vertical link (Fig. J:21).

   Secure with bolts (51), washers (49) nuts (25) and lock two lower bolt heads with lock washer (48).

9. Assemble and adjust hub assembly.

10. Attach upper and lower wishbone to sub-frame and chassis with original shim packs (31) behind lower fulcrum brackets (32). Do not fully tighten nuts (45), (14) and (34).

11. Install road spring assembly.

12. Attach steering tie-rod to steering arm.

13. Refit brake drum or calliper unit replacing any shims between calliper and bracket.

14. Lubricate lower trunnion with oil gun.

15. Refit road wheels and lower vehicle to ground, load to "static laden" condition and fully tighten nuts (45), (14) and (34).

16. Check castor, camber and front wheel alignment.

SPRING DAMPER STRUT - Removal and Installation

(Fig. J:22)

Removal

1. Raise front of vehicle, support on chassis stands and open bonnet.

2. Remove road wheel.

3. Disconnect anti-roll bar from lower wishbone.

4. Remove three nuts (4) and washers from upper spring pan attachments (Fig. J:23).

5. Remove bolt (14), support brake assembly and remove spring damper strut.

Installation

1. Reverse procedure to install unit.

   NOTE: A packing piece between upper spring pan and chassis is fitted to the left hand unit of left hand drive vehicles.

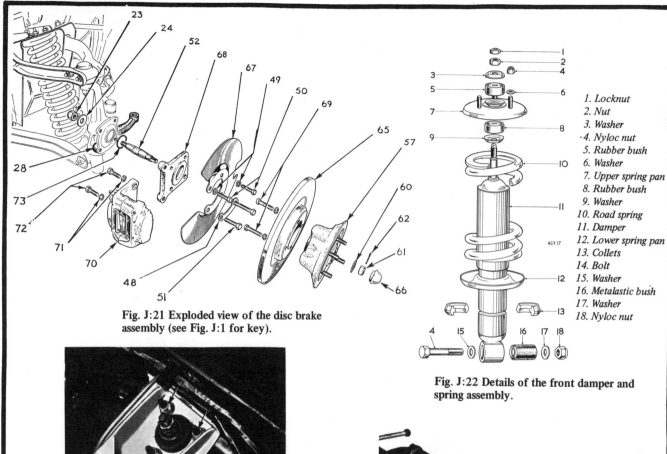

Fig. J:21 Exploded view of the disc brake assembly (see Fig. J:1 for key).

1. Locknut
2. Nut
3. Washer
4. Nyloc nut
5. Rubber bush
6. Washer
7. Upper spring pan
8. Rubber bush
9. Washer
10. Road spring
11. Damper
12. Lower spring pan
13. Collets
14. Bolt
15. Washer
16. Metalastic bush
17. Washer
18. Nyloc nut

Fig. J:22 Details of the front damper and spring assembly.

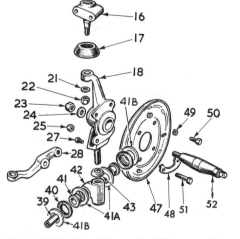

Fig. J:23 Spring/damper assembly attachment to the chassis sub-frame.

Fig. J:24 Compressing the coil spring.

Fig. J:25 Details of the vertical link assembly (see Fig. J:1 for key).

1. Nyloc nut
2. Link
3. Washer
4. Nyloc nut
5. Anti-roll bar
6. Nyloc nut
7. "U" bolt
8. Washer
9. Rubber bush
10. Clamp

Fig. J:26 Details of the anti-roll bar assembly

SPRING DAMPER STRUT - Overhaul (Fig. J:22)

Dismantling

1. Remove damper strut from vehicle.

2. Compress sufficient coils of road spring to relieve load from upper spring pan (7) using Churchill tool S4221A with adaptor S4221A-5 as shown in Fig. J:24.

3. Remove nuts (1 and 2), washer (3) and rubber bush (5) and gradually release load on spring.

4. Remove upper spring pan (7), rubber bush (8) washer (9) and road spring. On Woodhead-Monroe type remove lower spring pan (12) and collets (13).

Inspection

1. Examine rubber bushes for damage or deterioration. Renew if necessary.

2. Inspect lower Metalastic bush for distortion or deterioration cracks in rubber. If necessary press out old bush and insert new item with press and pilot tool.

3. Check coil spring for free length (see TECHNICAL DATA for specifications) and for deformation or cracks. Renew if necessary.

4. With damper in vertical position, slowly extend and compress it about ten times when resistance should be appreciable and constant. Renew if resistance is excessive, light, or irregular, or if damage, leakage or distortion is present.

Assembly

1. Fit washer (9) and rubber (8) to top of damper and, if applicable, collets (13) and lower spring pan (12).

2. Extend damper and insert in spring and upper spring pan (7).

3. Compress road spring sufficiently to fit rubber (5) washer (3) and nuts (2 and 1) (Fig. J:24).

4. Release spring and install spring damper strut.

VERTICAL LINK - Removal and Installation

(Fig. J:25)

Removal

1. Raise front of vehicle, support on chassis stands, open bonnet and remove road wheels.

2. Remove hub assembly.

3. Straighten tabs on lockwasher (48) remove bolts (50 and 51) remove backplate (47) and release steering arm (28) from vertical link. On disc brake models remove dust shield (67) and calliper bracket (68).

NOTE: Tie up backplate or brake calliper to avoid strain on brake hose.

4. Remove nut (22) and washer and detach ball joint from vertical link (Fig. J:14).

5. Unscrew vertical link from trunnion (42) and remove seal (43).

NOTE: Left hand vertical link has left hand thread and right hand link has right-hand thread.

6. Remove nut (23) and washer and press stub axle from vertical link.

Installation

1. Insert stub axle in vertical link with split pin hole horizontal and secure with nut (23) and washer.

2. With serviceable rubber seal (43) fitted as shown in Fig. J:17 screw vertical link into trunnion as far as possible then unscrew until 180° rotation in each direction is available.

3. With rubber gaiter (17) over shank assemble link to ball joint (16) and secure with nut (22) and washer.

4. Assemble steering arm (28) and brake backplate (47) to vertical link. On disc brake units, assemble dust shield and calliper bracket and apply Expandite seal-a-strip (105S) Pt. No. 554420 to vertical link and calliper bracket (Fig. J:20). Secure bolt heads with lockplate.

NOTE: Later models have rubber seal (73) between recessed face of calliper bracket and vertical link (Fig. J:21).

5. Install hub assemble and lubricate bottom trunnion with oil gun.

ANTI-ROLL BAR - Removal and Installation

Removal

1. Remove nuts (4) and washers.

2. Remove nuts (6) and washers and detach "U" bolts (7), and clamps (10) from each side of chassis. Withdraw anti-roll bar (5).

3. If required remove nuts (1) with washers and detach links (2).

Installation

1. Renew rubber sleeves (9) if damaged or deteriorated.

2. Secure anti-roll bar to chassis brackets with clamps and "U" bolts leaving nuts finger tight only.

3. Assemble links (2) onto adjustable ends and engage in lower wishbone brackets. Do not fully tighten nuts (1 and 4).

4. With vehicle in "static laden" condition tighten all nuts.

Technical Data

Type	. . . .		Independent coil spring with telescopic damper	

Spring:

Free length (approx.	- Herald	. . . .	12.08 in.	(306.8 mm.)
	- Herald (H.D.)	. . . .	10.97 in.	(278.6 mm.)
	- Spitfire	. . . .	12.59 in.	(319.8 mm.)
		or	12.21 in.	(310.2 mm.)
Fitted length	- Herald	. . . .	8.18 ± .09 in.	(207.8 ± 2.3 mm.)
	- Spitfire	. . . .	7.80 ± .09 in.	(198.1 ± 2.3 mm.)
		or	7.24 ± .09 in.	(188.5 ± 2.3 mm.)
Fitted load	- Herald	. . . .	790 lbs.	(358.7 kg.)
	- Spitfire	. . . . .	718 lbs.	(326 kg.)
Rate	- Herald	. . . .	203 lb./in.	(3624 kg./m.)
	- Herald (H.D.)	. . . .	284 lb./in.	(5071 kg./m.)
	- Spitfire	. . . .	150 lb./in.	(2875 kg./m.)
Toe-in (Static laden*)	. . . .		0 - 1/6 in.	(1.6 mm.)
Camber angle (Static laden*)	. . . .		2° positive	

* Static Laden

This condition is obtained when 150 lbs. (68 kg.) weight is placed on two front and two rear seats.

Wheels	. . . .		Steel disc. Wire type optional on Spitfire Mk. III & IV.	

Tyres and Pressures (2 up)

			Front	Rear
Herald	-	5.20 - 13	. . . . . . 21 p.s.i. (1.48 kg/cm²)	24 p.s.i. (1.7 kg/cm²)
Herald Estate		5.60 - 13	. . . . . . 21 p.s.i. (1.48 kg/cm²)	25 p.s.i. (1.75 kg/cm²)
Spitfire		5.20 S - 13 (Cross-ply)	. . . . 18 p.s.i. (1.26 kg/cm²)	24 p.s.i. (1.7 kg/cm²)
		1.45SR - 13 (Radial)	. . . 21 p.s.i. (1.48 kg/cm²)	26 p.s.i. (1.83 kg/cm²)

TIGHTENING TORQUES

Anti-roll bar link attachment	. . . . 38 - 42 lbs./ft.	(5.25 - 5.81 kg./m.)
Anti-roll bar link stud	. . . . 12 - 14 lbs./ft.	(1.66 - 1.94 kg./m.)
Anti-roll bar "U" bolts	. . . . 3 - 4 lbs./ft.	(0.42 - 0.28 kg./m.)
Vertical link, backplate and steering lever	. . . . 26 - 28 lbs./ft.	(3.60 - 3.87 kg./m.)
Vertical link and backplate	. . . . 16 - 18 lbs./ft.	(2.21 - 2.49 kg./m.)
Ball assemble to upper wishbone	. . . . 16 - 18 lbs./ft.	(2.21 - 2.49 kg./m.)
Ball assembly to vertical link	. . . . 38 - 42 lbs./ft.	(5.25 - 5.81 kg./m.)
Brake disc to hub	. . . . 32 - 35 lbs./ft.	(4.24 - 4.84 kg./m.)
Vertical link, calliper plate and steering lever	. . . . 32 - 35 lbs./ft.	(4.24 - 4.84 kg./m.)
Vertical link and calliper plate	. . . . 18 - 20 lbs./ft.	(2.49 - 2.77 kg./m.)
Brake calliper attachment	. . . . 50 - 55 lbs./ft.	(6.19 - 7.60 kg./m.)
Damper bottom attachment	. . . . 42 - 46 lbs./ft.	(5.81 - 6.36 kg./m.)
Suspension unit sub-frame	. . . . 26 - 28 lbs./ft.	(3.60 - 3.87 kg./m.)
Fulcrum bracket to lower wishbone	. . . . 26 - 28 lbs./ft.	(3.60 - 3.87 kg./m.)
Stub axle to vertical link	. . . . 55 - 60 lbs./ft.	(7.60 - 8.30 kg./m.)
Steering tie-rod ball joint	. . . . 26 - 28 lbs./ft.	(3.60 - 3.87 kg./m.)
Top wishbone attachment	. . . . 26 - 28 lbs./ft.	(3.60 - 3.87 kg./m.)
Trunnion to wishbone	. . . . 35 - 38 lbs./ft.	(4.84 - 5.25 kg./m.)
Wishbone assemble to frame	. . . . 22 - 24 lbs./ft.	(3.04 - 3.32 kg./m.)

Steering

GENERAL

The steering gear is of the rack and pinion type, rubber mounted on two front suspension crossmember brackets with the pinion shaft connected to the steering column and wheel through a flexible coupling. The rack ends are connected to the steering arm at each wheel by a tie-rod. The tie-rods are fitted with ball joints at each end and are adjustable. The steering column is designed to telescope on impact as a safety feature and this also provides a limited column length adjustment.

ROUTINE MAINTENANCE

Every 6,000 miles (10,000 km.)

Raise front wheels clear of ground, remove plug (arrowed in Fig. K:3), fit screwed grease nipple and with an oil gun pump hypoid oil until oil exudes from lower swivel. Remove nipple and refit plug. Repeat on other side.

Every 12,000 miles (20,000 km.)

1. Remove plug on steering unit (arrowed on Fig. K:4), fit screwed grease nipple and apply five strokes only with grease gun. Remove nipple and replace plug.

2. Check tightness of steering unit attachments and retaining bolts.

TOE-IN

The following methods of setting the toe-in should be used only as a temporary measure after replacement of steering or suspension components. It is highly recommended that the toe-in be rechecked as soon as possible using proper equipment so that the toe-out on turns can also be checked.

Roll the car straight forward on level ground and stop it without using the brakes. Take a reading "A" of the distance between the inside edges of the front wheel rims at a point level with, and in front of the wheel axis. Mark the measurement points with chalk. Roll the car forwards until the chalk marks are level with, but behind, the wheel axis and take a second reading "B". The toe-in is the difference by which "B" is greater than "A". This should be 0 - 1/6 in. (0 - 1.6 mm.).

If adjustment is necessary, first check the distance between the centre lines of the tie-rod inner and outer ball joints in both tie-rods (Dimension "1", Fig. K:5) this should be the same for both tie-rods. If otherwise, both tie-rods should be set initially to 8.715 in. (221.36 mm.) and toe-in rechecked.

To adjust the tie-rod length, release the locking nut at the tie-rod outer end and the clip securing the rack bellows to the tie-rod (see Fig. K:6). Twist the tie-rod in the appropriate direction, using a pair of plier grips if necessary, until the correct setting is obtained.

NOTE: Adjustment made to correct the toe-in setting should be made equally to both tie-rods, except in the case above to obtain the initial setting.

When the correct toe-in setting is obtained, tighten the tie-rod end locknut and the bellows clip.

TIE-ROD OUTER END - Replacement

Wear in the tie-rod outer ends cannot be removed by adjustment and thus renewal of the complete tie-rod end is necessary. The tie-rod outer ends should be renewed in pairs.

1. Apply handbrake, jack up front end of vehicle and support on stands.

2. Remove road wheels.

3. Scribe a line on one flat of locknut (43) and tie-rod outer end (44) and corresponding line on tie-rod. Slacken locknut.

4. Remove ball stud retaining nut (19) and disconnect tie-rod end from steering arm using Churchill tool S160 (Fig. K:7).

5. Unscrew tie-rod outer end from tie-rod, noting number of turns required to release it.

6. Screw on new tie-rod end the same number of turns as was required to remove old end. Tie-rod should now be located in original position on tie-rod, thus ensuring that distance between centre lines of inner and outer ball joints on tie-rod is the same as previously.

7. Connect tie-rod end to steering arm and secure with retaining nut.

8. Tighten tie-rod end locknut. Scribed lines made previously should be aligned.

9. Repeat for tie-rod end on the other side of vehicle.

10. Mount road wheels and check toe-in as described above, adjusting as necessary.

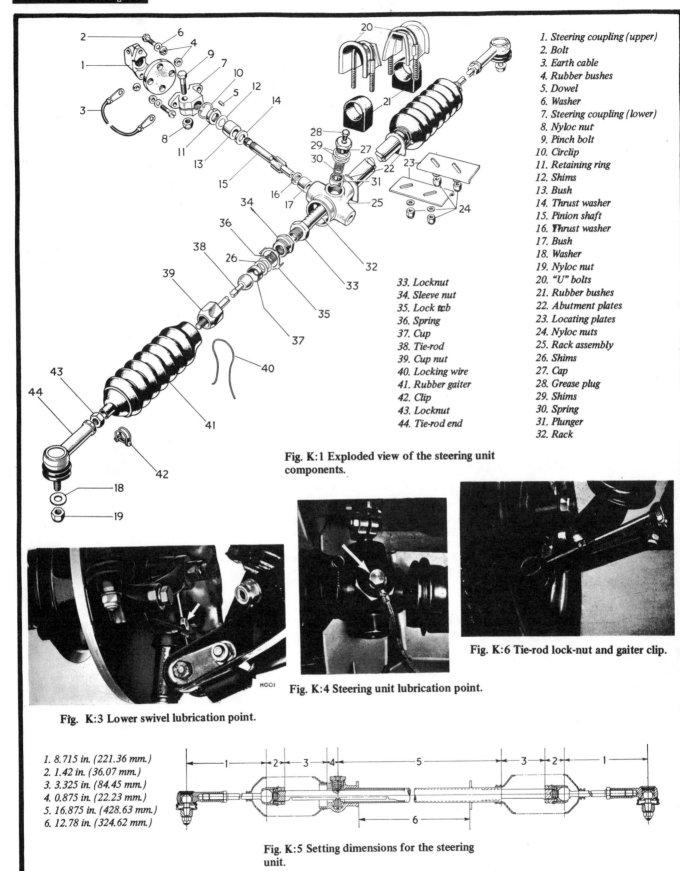

1. Steering coupling (upper)
2. Bolt
3. Earth cable
4. Rubber bushes
5. Dowel
6. Washer
7. Steering coupling (lower)
8. Nyloc nut
9. Pinch bolt
10. Circlip
11. Retaining ring
12. Shims
13. Bush
14. Thrust washer
15. Pinion shaft
16. Thrust washer
17. Bush
18. Washer
19. Nyloc nut
20. "U" bolts
21. Rubber bushes
22. Abutment plates
23. Locating plates
24. Nyloc nuts
25. Rack assembly
26. Shims
27. Cap
28. Grease plug
29. Shims
30. Spring
31. Plunger
32. Rack

33. Locknut
34. Sleeve nut
35. Lock tab
36. Spring
37. Cup
38. Tie-rod
39. Cup nut
40. Locking wire
41. Rubber gaiter
42. Clip
43. Locknut
44. Tie-rod end

Fig. K:1 Exploded view of the steering unit components.

Fig. K:6 Tie-rod lock-nut and gaiter clip.

Fig. K:4 Steering unit lubrication point.

Fig. K:3 Lower swivel lubrication point.

1. 8.715 in. (221.36 mm.)
2. 1.42 in. (36.07 mm.)
3. 3.325 in. (84.45 mm.)
4. 0.875 in. (22.23 mm.)
5. 16.875 in. (428.63 mm.)
6. 12.78 in. (324.62 mm.)

Fig. K:5 Setting dimensions for the steering unit.

STEERING RACK - (Fig. K:1)

Removal

1. Raise and support front of vehicle on chassis stands. Remove road wheels.

2. Remove pinch bolt (9, Fig. K:8).

3. Disconnect tie-rod end from steering arm using Churchill tool S160 (Fig. K:7).

4. Remove nuts (24) and washers and remove "U" bolt assemblies (20) and locating plates (23).

5. Move rack forward to disengage from coupling and remove from vehicle through valance aperture on drivers side.

Installation

1. Ensure steering rack is assembled to dimensions given in Fig. K:5.

2. Centralise rack on pinion by counting number of revolutions from lock to lock and turning pinion back half this number.

3. Position steering wheel with spokes horizontal and beneath wheel boss centre.

4. Position rack onto cross member brackets and engage pinion shaft in coupling. Loosely assemble "U" bolt assemblies (20) and locating plates (23). Attach earthing cable to one "U" bolt.

5. Use Churchill tool S341 or similar to push "U" bolt assemblies outwards until 1/8 in. (3.17 mm.) clearance remains between "U" bolt bracket flange "A" and tube flange plate "A". Slide plates (23) inboard until edge "B" is against frame flange "B". Elongate slots further if necessary. Tighten "U" bolt nuts and remove spreading tool (Fig. K:9).

6. Fit and secure pinch bolt (9, Fig. K:8).

7. Connect tie-rod ends to steering arms.

8. Mount road wheels and lower vehicle

9. Check wheel alignment.

Dismantling (Fig. K:1)

1. Release clips (42) and (40), move gaiters outwards, slacken locknuts (33) and remove both tie-rod assemblies from the rack. Remove springs (36).

2. Remove sleeve nut (34), tabwasher, shims (26) and thrust cup (37). Detach both tie-rod ends (44).

3. Remove locknut (43), gaiters, clips and cup nut (39) from each tie-rod. Remove locknut (33).

4. Remove cap nut (27), shims, spring and pressure pad (31) from housing.

5. Remove circlip (10) and withdraw pinion assembly with dowel (5). Remove items (11), (12), (13) and (14). Remove "O" ring from (11).

6. Remove rack from the tube and items (16) and (17) from the housing.

Inspection

1. Clean and check all parts for wear, damage and deterioration. Renew parts as necessary.

2. Renew "O" ring.

3. If worn, drift out the bush in the end of the rack tube and press in a new item.

Assembly

1. Insert the rack into tube and place bush (17) and thrust washer (16) into pinion housing.

2. Adjust pinion end-float as follows:-

   (a) Assemble thrust washer (14), bush (13) and retainer (11) to pinion. Insert assemble into housing and secure with circlip (10).

   (b) Mount dial gauge as shown in Fig. K:10. Push pinion down and zero the gauge. Lift rack until retaining ring contacts circlip and note total end-float. Remove assemble and fit new "O" ring in retainer (11).

   (c) Shim to give minimum end-float consistent with free rotation. Maximum end-float 0.010 in. (.254 mm.).

   NOTE: Shims are available in 0.004 in. (0.10 mm.) and 0.010 in. (0.25 mm.) thickness.

   (d) Re-insert assembly and secure with dowel and circlip.

3. Adjust pinion pressure pad end-float as follows:

   (a) Fit pressure pad and cap nut (27). Tighten cap nut to just eliminate all end-float and measure clearance under cap nut head (Fig. K:11). Remove pressure pad.

   (b) Make shim pack equal to clearance plus 0.004 in. (0.1 mm.) nominal end-float.

   (c) Pack unit with grease and assemble pad, spring, shim pack and cap nut with grease plug (Fig. K:12).

   (d) When correctly adjusted, a 2 lb. (0.91 kg.) on an 8 in. (20.3 cm.) arm should turn the pinion shaft 3/4 of a turn either side of mid position, and must not exceed 3 lb. (1.36 kg.) for the remainder of rack travel. (Fig. K:13. Adjust shimming if necessary.

4. Assemble and adjust inner ball joints as follows (Fig. K:14).

   (a) Position cup nut over tie-rod ball end, fit thrust cup (37) and attach sleeve nut (34) with tab washer.

G

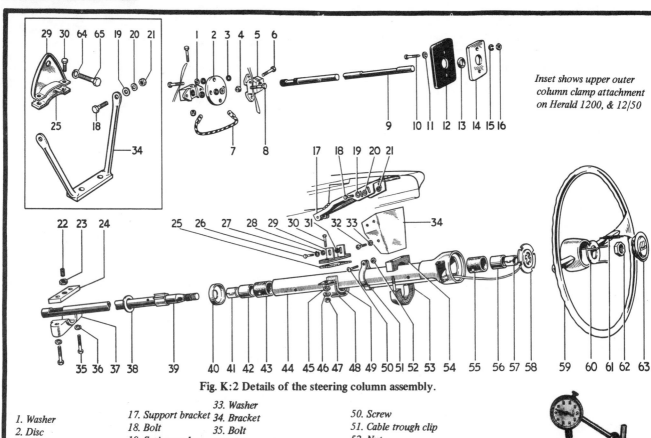

Inset shows upper outer
column clamp attachment
on Herald 1200, & 12/50

Fig. K:2 Details of the steering column assembly.

1. Washer
2. Disc
3. Rubber washer
4. Nyloc nut
5. Adaptor
6. Pinch bolt
7. Earth cable
8. Bolt
9. Lower steering column
10. Bolt
11. Washer
12. Rubber seal
13. Washer
14. Retaining plate
15. Spring washer
16. Nut

17. Support bracket
18. Bolt
19. Spring washer
20. Washer
21. Nut
22. Socket screw
23. Nut
24. Clamp plate
25. Felt pad
26. Bolt
27. Spring washer
28. Washer
29. Bracket
30. Bolt
31. Nut
32. Screw

33. Washer
34. Bracket
35. Bolt
36. Spring washer
37. Clamp
38. Nylon washer
39. Upper inner steering column
40. End cap
41. Nylon bush
42. Steel bush
43. Rubber bush
44. Outer upper column
45. Washer
46. Spring washer
47. Nut
48. Lower outer column clamp
49. Felt pad

50. Screw
51. Cable trough clip
52. Nut
53. Upper clamp (lower half)
54. Upper clamp (upper half)
55. Rubber bush
56. Steel bush
57. Nylon bush
58. Horn contact ring
59. Steering wheel
60. Clip
61. Horn contact brush
62. Nut
63. Horn push
64. Spring washer
65. Bolt

Fig. K:10 Measuring the pinion end-float.

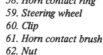

Fig. K:11 Determining the shim thickness
required under the cap nut.

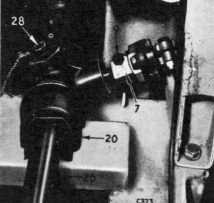

Fig. K:7 Disconnecting the tie-rod end from
the steering arm.

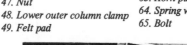

Fig. K:8 Details of the steering unit attachments.

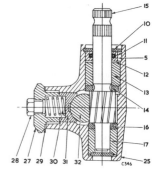

Fig. K:12 Cross-sectional view of the
steering unit (see Fig. K:1 for key).

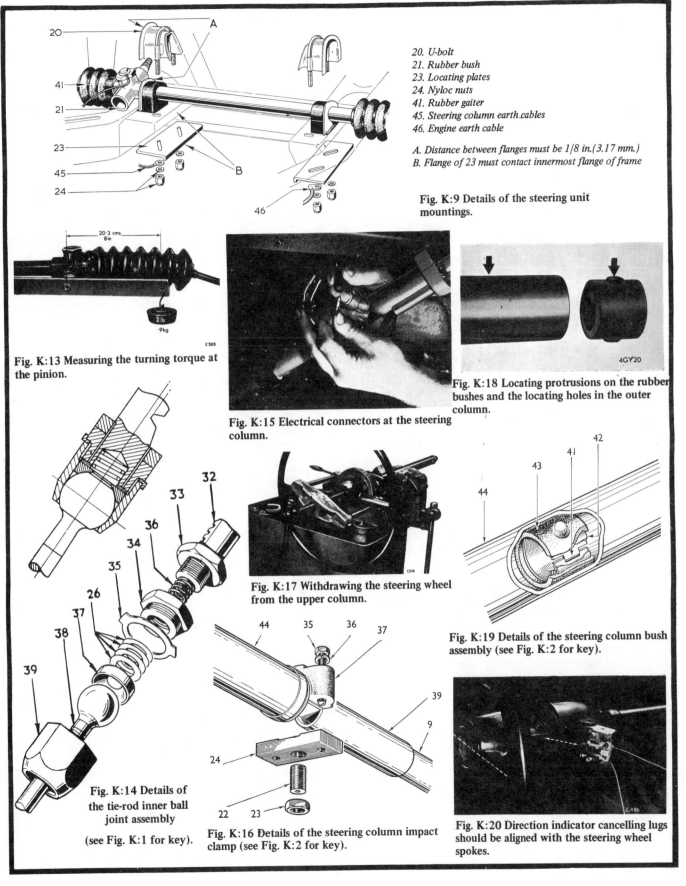

20. U-bolt
21. Rubber bush
23. Locating plates
24. Nyloc nuts
41. Rubber gaiter
45. Steering column earth cables
46. Engine earth cable

A. Distance between flanges must be 1/8 in.(3.17 mm.)
B. Flange of 23 must contact innermost flange of frame

Fig. K:9 Details of the steering unit mountings.

Fig. K:13 Measuring the turning torque at the pinion.

Fig. K:15 Electrical connectors at the steering column.

Fig. K:18 Locating protrusions on the rubber bushes and the locating holes in the outer column.

Fig. K:17 Withdrawing the steering wheel from the upper column.

Fig. K:19 Details of the steering column bush assembly (see Fig. K:2 for key).

Fig. K:14 Details of the tie-rod inner ball joint assembly

(see Fig. K:1 for key).

Fig. K:16 Details of the steering column impact clamp (see Fig. K:2 for key).

Fig. K:20 Direction indicator cancelling lugs should be aligned with the steering wheel spokes.

(b) With the fully tightened cup nut held in vice, pull and push the tie-rod to estimate end-float. Fit shims to provide 0.002 in. (0.05 mm.) end-float when the cup nut is fully screwed onto the sleeve nut. Ensure ball moves freely in the joints. Lock with tab washer.

NOTE: Shims are obtainable in 0.002 in. (0.05 mm.) and 0.010 in. (0.25 mm.) thickness.

5. Assemble locknut (33) and spring (36) to each end of rack and screw on tie-rod assemblies. Adjust to dimensions in Fig. K:5 and secure with locknuts.

6. Fit gaiters (41), pack with grease (1/2 oz. Retinax "A" from dry), and secure with clip (42) and wire (40).

STEERING COLUMN (Fig. K:2)

Removal

1. Isolate battery and disconnect electrical leads under fascia (Fig. K:15).

2. Remove bottom halves of clamps (53 and 48).
    NOTE: Remove driver side glove box on Spitfire to gain access to clamp nuts.

3. Remove pinch bolt (9) from bottom coupling (7) (Fig. K:8).

4. Withdraw steering column from vehicle.

Dismantling

1. Remove bolt (50) and remove cable trough (51).

2. Lever horn button assembly (63) from steering wheel boss and remove horn contact.

3. Remove switch covers and detach switches.

4. Remove impact clamp sections (37 and 24) (Fig. K:16).

5. Withdraw lower column (9) and washer (38).

6. Grip column (39) in vice with jaws protected, remove nut (69) and clip (60), and with Churchill tool S3600 remove steering wheel (Fig. K:17).

7. Remove end cap (40) and push out rubber bushes (43 and 55) with a bar after depressing protrusions as shown in Fig. K:18. Remove steel sleeve (42 and 55) and nylon

inserts (41 and 57) from rubber bushes.

8. Inspect all parts for damage and wear and renew as necessary. Renew rubber bushes if deteriorated.

Re-assemble and Installation

1. Assemble steel sleeves and nylon inserts into bushes (43 and 55) and insert in column until locating protrusions engage in holes in column (Fig. K:19). Metal reinforcement rings at end of bush must be towards lower end of column. Fit end cap (40).

2. Assemble horn contact ring (58) then steering wheel to column with direction indicator cancelling lugs in line with steering wheel spokes as shown in Fig. K:20. Fit clip (60) secure wheel with nut (62), and lock nut by peening.
    NOTE: If new direction indicator switch is being fitted the cancellation clip and screw must also be renewed.

3. Thread inner column into outer column.

4. Insert direction indicator and lighting switches through holes at top of column, and fit switches and covers.

5. Fit horn contact plunger (61) in boss and fit horn button assemble (63).

6. Assemble lower column to upper column and secure with impact clamp (37 and 24) leaving attachment nuts loose at this stage (Fig. K:15).

7. Pass column into position through bulkhead grommet, attach cable trough (51) and assemble bottom halves of clamps (53 and 48) placing felt (49) in lower clamp. Position steering wheel at required height before tightening clamp bolts.

8. With steering wheel and road wheels in straight ahead position engage lower column in steering coupling and secure with pinch bolt (6).

9. Tighten bolts (35) on impact clamp, and tighten friction screw (22).
    NOTE: If column is adjusted to lowest position telescoping will not be possible.

10. Connect electrical leads under fascia (Fig. K:15).

11. On Spitfire models install glove box on driver's side.

12. Connect battery.

Technical Data

Type	Rack and pinion (Limited collapsible column)
Lubricant	Energrease L2 or equivalent
Pinion end float	0.010 in. (0.25 mm.) maximum
Pinion pressure pad end-float	0.004 in. (0.1 mm.) nominal

TIGHTENING TORQUES

Coupling pinch bolt	18 - 20 lbs./ft.	(2.49 - 2.77 kg./m.)
Column clamps	6 - 8 lbs./ft.	(0.83 - 1.11 kg./m.)
Safety clamp friction screw	18 - 20 lbs./ft.	(2.49 - 2.77 kg./m.)
Safety clamp attachments	6 - 8 lbs./ft.	(0.83 - 1.11 kg./m.)
Steering unit to frame	18 - 20 lbs./ft.	(2.49 - 2.77 kg./m.)

Braking System

GENERAL

The foot brake operates hydraulically through a conventional single line system on all four wheels with disc type brakes at the front and drum type at the rear on all models except the Herald 1200 which has drum type on all wheels. The handbrake operates mechanically on the rear wheels only.

The front brake callipers are of the twin opposed type and are self-adjusting.

The rear drum brakes are of the leading and trailing shoe type with one double acting wheel cylinder and one adjuster while the front drum brakes on the "1200" have two leading shoes with individual cylinders and adjusters.

The handbrake is floor-mounted and operates through a two cable linkage.

The brake master cylinder with integral hydraulic fluid reservoir is mounted on the engine compartment rear bulkhead immediately over the brake pedal.

On the Spitfire Mk. III model for the U.S.A. market, a dual circuit braking system is used in which pressure is transmitted to separate front and rear hydraulic circuits from the master cylinder. A pressure differential valve between the two circuits operates a warning light if pressure drops in one of the circuits.

ROUTINE MAINTENANCE

Every Month

Check the fluid level in the brake master cylinder and top up to the bottom of the filler neck if required. If fluid loss is excessive, this should be investigated.

Every 6,000 miles (10,000 km.)

Check the front brake pads for wear and renew if reduced to 1/8 in. (3.0 mm.) or less in thickness. Adjust the drum brake shoes if necessary as described under brake adjustment. Check all pipes and hoses for damage, deterioration, leakage or chafing, and renew as necessary.

Every 12,000 miles (20,000 km.)

Smear the handbrake compensator and cable guides with grease.

BRAKE ADJUSTMENT

Front Brakes

Disc Type

These are self-adjusting and do not require adjustment.

Drum Type

1. With wheel clear of ground rotate it to ensure shoes are free.

2. Screw in one adjuster as far as possible then release one notch at a time until wheel is just free to turn (Fig. L:3).

3. Repeat with other adjuster.

4. Lower vehicle to ground.

Rear Brakes

1. With wheel clear of ground, fully release handbrake and check wheel is free to rotate.

2. Screw in adjuster as far as possible then release one notch at a time until it is just free to turn (Fig. L:4).

3. Lower vehicle to ground.

Handbrake

Adjustment of the handbrake is normally effected automatically by shoe adjustment at the rear wheels. However after considerable mileage, stretching of the cables may necessitate adjustment as follows: (Fig. L:5).

1. Raise rear wheels, release handbrake and turn adjuster on rear wheel backplates fully in.

2. Disconnect pull-off spring (12) and remove clevis pin (17) at each wheel.

3. Release locknuts (18) and turn each fork end (16) by equal amounts until cable slack is taken up, yet pin (17) can be easily inserted. Tighten locknuts.

4. Secure clevis pins with split pins, connect springs and adjust spring bracket (20), on cables to provide slight spring tension.

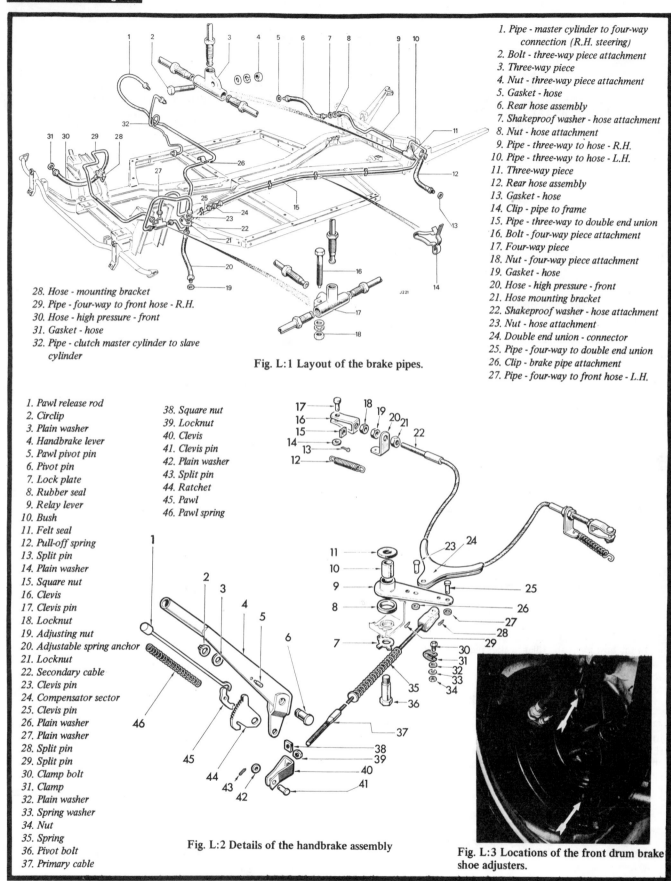

1. Pipe - master cylinder to four-way
   connection (R.H. steering)
2. Bolt - three-way piece attachment
3. Three-way piece
4. Nut - three-way piece attachment
5. Gasket - hose
6. Rear hose assembly
7. Shakeproof washer - hose attachment
8. Nut - hose attachment
9. Pipe - three-way to hose - R.H.
10. Pipe - three-way to hose - L.H.
11. Three-way piece
12. Rear hose assembly
13. Gasket - hose
14. Clip - pipe to frame
15. Pipe - three-way to double end union
16. Bolt - four-way piece attachment
17. Four-way piece
18. Nut - four-way piece attachment
19. Gasket - hose
20. Hose - high pressure - front
21. Hose mounting bracket
22. Shakeproof washer - hose attachment
23. Nut - hose attachment
24. Double end union - connector
25. Pipe - four-way to double end union
26. Clip - brake pipe attachment
27. Pipe - four-way to front hose - L.H.

28. Hose - mounting bracket
29. Pipe - four-way to front hose - R.H.
30. Hose - high pressure - front
31. Gasket - hose
32. Pipe - clutch master cylinder to slave
    cylinder

Fig. L:1 Layout of the brake pipes.

1. Pawl release rod
2. Circlip
3. Plain washer
4. Handbrake lever
5. Pawl pivot pin
6. Pivot pin
7. Lock plate
8. Rubber seal
9. Relay lever
10. Bush
11. Felt seal
12. Pull-off spring
13. Split pin
14. Plain washer
15. Square nut
16. Clevis
17. Clevis pin
18. Locknut
19. Adjusting nut
20. Adjustable spring anchor
21. Locknut
22. Secondary cable
23. Clevis pin
24. Compensator sector
25. Clevis pin
26. Plain washer
27. Plain washer
28. Split pin
29. Split pin
30. Clamp bolt
31. Clamp
32. Plain washer
33. Spring washer
34. Nut
35. Spring
36. Pivot bolt
37. Primary cable

38. Square nut
39. Locknut
40. Clevis
41. Clevis pin
42. Plain washer
43. Split pin
44. Ratchet
45. Pawl
46. Pawl spring

Fig. L:2 Details of the handbrake assembly

Fig. L:3 Locations of the front drum brake
shoe adjusters.

Fig. L:4 Rear brake shoe adjusters.

1. Rubber O-ring
2. Fluid transfer channels
3. Calliper body
4. Brake pad
5. Anti-squeal plate
6. Piston
7. Piston sealing ring
8. Dust cover
9. Retaining clip
10. Pad retaining pin
11. Fluid hose connection
12. Bleed nipple

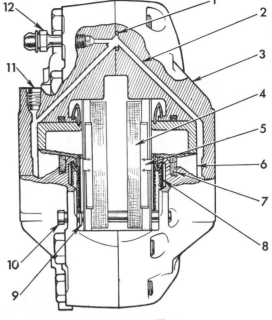

Fig. L:6 Sectional view of the disc brake calliper

Fig. L:5 Details of the handbrake secondary cable at the rear wheel.

Fig. L:7 Details of the brake calliper installation (see Fig. L:8 for key).

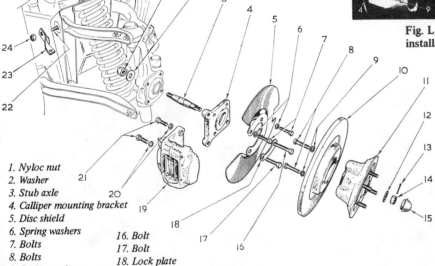

1. Nyloc nut
2. Washer
3. Stub axle
4. Calliper mounting bracket
5. Disc shield
6. Spring washers
7. Bolts
8. Bolts
9. Spring washers
10. Disc
11. Hub
12. Washer
13. Split pin
14. Slotted nut
15. Dust cap

16. Bolt
17. Bolt
18. Lock plate
19. Calliper assembly
20. Spring washer
21. Bolts
22. Bolt
23. Bracket
24. Nyloc nut

Fig. L:8 Exploded view of the disc brake assembly

Fig. L:11 General view of the front drum brake assembly (R.H. shown).

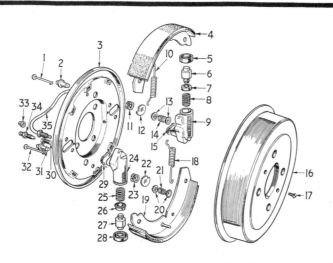

1. Shoe steady pin
2. Adjuster shank
3. Backplate
4. Brake shoe
5. Dust excluder
6. Piston
7. Piston seal
8. Piston return spring
9. Wheel cylinder
10. Shoe retracting spring
11. Spring
12. Adjuster cam
13. Steady pin cups
14. Spring
15. Rubber seal
16. Brake drum
17. Countersunk screw
18. Shoe retracting spring

19. Brake shoe
20. Steady pin cups
21. Spring
22. Adjuster cam
23. Spring
24. Wheel cylinder
25. Piston return spring
26. Piston seal
27. Piston
28. Dust excluder
29. Rubber seal
30. Screw - wheel cylinder attachment
31. Adjuster shank
32. Shoe steady pin
33. Dust cap
34. Bleed valve
35. Bridge pipe

Fig. L:9 Exploded view of the front drum brake assembly (L.H. shown)

1. Handbrake lever
2. Split pin
3. Dust cap
4. Bleed nipple
5. Dust excluder
6. Retaining clip
7. Retaining clip
8. Steady pins
9. Backplate
10. Dust excluder
11. Clip
12. Steady pin cups
13. Springs
14. Steady pin cups
15. Piston

16. Seal
17. Wheel cylinder
18. Return spring
19. Brake shoe
20. Countersunk screw
21. Brake drum
22. Adjuster tappet
23. Adjuster wedge and body
24. Adjuster tappet
25. Return spring
26. Brake shoe
27. Shakeproof washers
28. Nuts

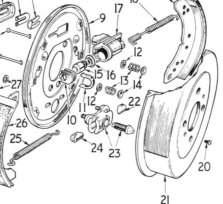
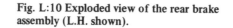

Fig. L:10 Exploded view of the rear brake assembly (L.H. shown).

Fig. L:12 General view of the rear brake assembly (R.H. shown).

Fig. L:13 Removing the retaining plate from the rear wheel cylinder.

Fig. L:14 Removing the rear wheel cylinder and handbrake lever.

5. Turn each brake shoe adjuster back one notch at a time until wheels are free to rotate.

6. Lower vehicle and remove jack.

FRONT BRAKE PADS - Replacement (Fig. L:6)

1. Remove front wheel, withdraw spring clips (9) and remove retaining pins (10).

2. Remove friction pads (4) and damping shims (5) where fitted.

   CAUTION: Do not depress pedal while pads are removed.

3. Clean exposed faces of pistons and pad recesses and force pistons back into cylinders.

   NOTE: This will displace fluid back to master cylinder. Avoid overflowing by temporarily opening bleed screw.

4. Install new friction pads and shims (where fitted) insert pins (10) and secure with clips (9).

   NOTE: Shims must be fitted with engraved arrow in direction of wheel forward rotation.

5. Pump brake pedal several times to bed down pads and spin discs to ensure brakes do not drag.

6. Refit wheel and road test vehicle.

FRONT BRAKE CALLIPER - Removal and Installation

(Fig. L:7)

Removal

1. Drain system and remove road wheels.

2. Remove friction pads.

3. Disconnect brake pipe at bracket and unscrew hose from calliper.

4. Remove two bolts (21) and remove calliper unit.

   NOTE: If calliper is being removed to gain access to another component only, the hydraulic pipe need not be disconnected and unit should be suspended from frame with string or wire. In this case, bleeding after installation is not necessary.

Installation

1. Assemble to hub and connect hose from calliper to pipe.

2. Install friction pads and refit road wheels.

3. Fill and bleed system. Check for leaks.

4. Road test vehicle.

FRONT BRAKE CALLIPER - Overhaul (Fig. L:6).

Dismantling

1. Clean unit with brake fluid or methylated spirits. Do NOT use paraffin or other mineral based solvents.

2. Remove pistons (6) and bleed screw (12).

3. Lever dust seal and retainer (8) from mouth of cylinder and with blunt-ended wire pick seal (7) from inner groove in cylinder wall.

   NOTE: Do not separate calliper halves.

Inspection

Clean and dry all parts and examine for cracks and damage. Renew seals.

Assembly

1. Apply Lockheed disc brake fluid or methylated spirits to seal (7) and work into inner groove in cylinder, with fingers.

2. Locate lip of dust seal and retainer (8) in its recess in the cylinder.

3. Square piston at mouth of cylinder with closed end leading and press into cylinder. Push cylinder fully home and engage outer lip of dust exluder with recess in piston.

4. Refit bleed screw.

BRAKE DISCS

Normally the front brake discs require no maintenance but should be checked for scores and distortion on overhaul. With dial indicator set up as shown in Fig. L:8, the maximum run-out on the friction faces is 0.004 in. (0.10 mm.).

Removal and Installation

1. Remove front hub (see FRONT SUSPENSION section).

2. Remove four bolts (8, Fig. L:8) and separate disc from hub.

3. Install by reversing removal procedure.

FRONT BRAKE SHOES (Herald 1200 only)

Replacement (Figs. L:9 and L:11)

Removal

1. Remove wheel and brake drum and turn adjusters fully anti-clockwise.

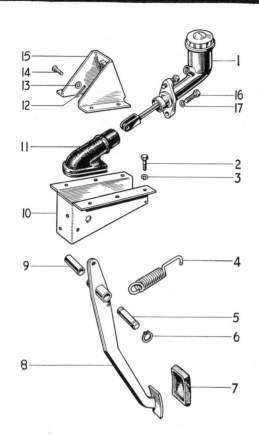

1. Brake master cylinder
2. Bolt
3. Spring washer
4. Pedal return spring
5. Pivot pin
6. Circlip
7. Pedal rubber
8. Brake pedal
9. Pedal pivot bush
10. Pedal bracket
11. Rubber dust excluder
12. Split pin
13. Plain washer
14. Clevis pin
15. Master cylinder bracket
16. Bolt
17. Spring washer

Fig. L:15 Details for the brake pedal assembly

Fig. L:17 Bleeding the disc brake calliper.

1. Valve seal
2. Spring (valve seal)
3. Distance piece
4. Valve stem
5. Piston return spring
6. Spring retainer
7. Piston
8. Piston seal
9. Push rod
10. Dust cover
11. Circlip
12. Push rod stop
13. Identification ring(s)
14. Fluid reservoir

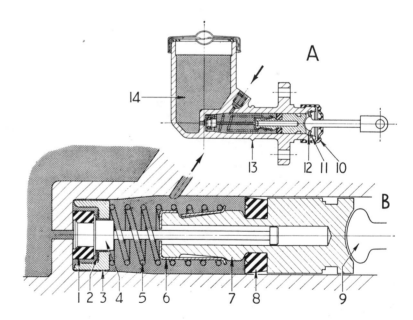

Fig. L:16 Sectional view of the brake master cylinder

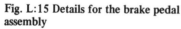

2. Release steady pins (1), cups (13) and springs (14).

3. Lift shoes (4 and 19) from abutments and detach return springs (10 and 18) from backplate.

4. Remove shoes and springs and place rubber band or string around bottom cylinder to retain piston in cylinder.

Inspection

1. Wire brush shoes and examine for cracks. Renew shoes if linings are worn to one third of original thickness, contaminated with oil or grease or are damaged.

2. Clean adjusters and ensure free rotation. Renew cam if teeth are worn.

3. Renew springs if stretched or distorted.

Installation

1. Apply zinc base grease sparingly to adjuster cams and shoe abutment ends. Keep grease from linings.

2. Attach spring to shoe, engage in backplate then lift each shoe onto cylinder and piston. Remove restrainer as shown in Fig. L:11 from bottom cylinder.

3. Fit anti-rattle springs (14) on shoes and secure with steady pin (1) passed through cups (13) and rotated 90° to engage groove in cup.

4. Refit brake drum and adjust brake.

5. Mount road wheel and road test vehicle.

REAR BRAKE SHOES - Replacement

(Figs. L:10 and L:12)

Removal

1. Remove wheel and brake drum and turn adjuster fully anti-clockwise.

2. Release steady pins (8), cups (12 and 14) and springs (13).

3. Pull one shoe out of slots in adjuster (31) and piston (15) move away from backplate and release towards other shoe. Release springs and remove shoes.

Inspection

1. Wire brush shoes and examine for cracks. Renew shoes if linings are worn to below one third original thickness, contaminated with oil or are damaged.

2. Clean adjuster and ensure screw turns freely.

3. Renew springs if distorted or stretched.

Installation

1. Apply zinc base grease sparingly to adjuster and shoe abutment ends.

2. Assemble brake shoes and springs (18 and 25) with exposed position of each lining surface against direction of rotation. Locate one shoe in slots on adjuster and piston and pull other shoe to engage opposite slots. Ensure handbrake lever enters slotted shoe web and fit split pin to handbrake lever (Fig. L:12).

3. Fit anti-rattle springs (13) on shoes and secure with steady pins (8) passed through cups (12 and 14) and rotated 90° to engage groove in cup.

4. Fit brake drum and adjust brakes.

5. Mount road wheel and road test vehicle.

FRONT WHEEL CYLINDER - Removal and Installation

Removal

1. Remove brake shoes as described under relevant heading.

2. Drain hydraulic system through bleed screw and disconnect hose from pipe and unscrew from cylinder.

3. Detach bridge pipe from both wheel cylinders, remove attachment screws and remove cylinders from backplate.

Installation

Reverse removal procedure, adjust brakes and bleed hydraulic system.

REAR WHEEL CYLINDER - Removal and Installation

1. Carry out operation 1 and 2 as above.

2. Disconnect handbrake cable from lever.

3. Remove dust excluder and retaining plates (Fig. L:13).

4. Withdraw cylinder and handbrake lever from backplate (Fig. L:14).

Installation

Reverse removal procedure, adjust brakes and bleed hydraulic system.

PISTON SEALS - Replacement

1. Remove cylinder.

2. Remove dust excluder and extract piston.

3. Remove old seal from piston.

4. Clean cylinder and piston with methylated spirits or brake fluid. Examine contact surfaces for scores or pitting and renew if necessary.

5. Using fingers only, fit new seal on piston with lip towards bottom of cylinder.

6. Lubricate seal with brake fluid, insert piston in cylinder and fit dust excluder.

7. Install cylinder.

MASTER CYLINDER - Removal and Installation

(Fig. L:15)

Removal

1. Drain system at any wheel unit, bleed screw.

2. Pull back rubber dust excluder (11) and remove clevis pin (14).

3. Disconnect pipe line at cylinder.

4. Remove two bolts (16) and remove cylinder.

Installation

1. Secure master cylinder to mounting bracket.

2. Connect push rod to pedal with clevis pin and refit dust excluder.

3. Connect pipe line and fill and bleed system.

4. Road test vehicle.

MASTER CYLINDER - Overhaul (Fig. L:16)

Dismantling

1. Pull back dust cover (10), depress push rod (9), remove circlip (11) and remove push rod with dust cover and stop plate (12).

2. Shake or gently blow out plunger (7) with attached parts.

3. Lift securing clip on spring retainer (6) and remove retainer with valve assembly from plunger.

4. Guide valve shank (4) through offset hole in retainer.

Remove spring (5), distance piece (3) and spring (2) from valve shank.

5. Remove seal (1) from shank with fingers and remove distance cup (3).

6. Remove seal (8) from plunger.

Inspection

1. Clean all parts in methylated spirits or brake fluid and inspect for damage. Renew all rubber parts.

Re-assembly

NOTE: Observe strict cleanliness during assembly.

1. Lubricate all interior parts with brake fluid.

2. Fit seals (1 and 8) to valve shank (4) and plunger (7).

3. Fit disc spring (2), distance piece (3) and spring (5) to valve shank (4) attach spring retainer (6) and locate assembly on plunger (7).

   NOTE: Disc spring (2) must be assembled as shown in Fig. L:16 with periphery against distance piece (3).

4. Insert plunger assembly in cylinder, fit push rod (9) with stop plate (12) and secure with circlip (11). Assemble dust cover (10).

BLEEDING THE HYDRAULIC SYSTEM

1. Attach hose to bleed nipple on brake unit nearest to master cylinder and immerse other end in brake fluid (Fig. L:17).

2. Unscrew nipple approximately one turn and have an assistant slowly depress and hold down pedal.

3. Repeat until fluid is free from bubbles and emerges from the hose.

4. Finally tighten nipple and remove hose.

5. Repeat for other three brake units working progressively away from the master cylinder.

6. When bleeding operation is completed, adjust rear brake shoes.

Technical Data

System	Girling hydraulic
Front - Herald 1200	Drum 8 in. x 1 1/4 in. (20.32 cm. x 3.17)
- 12/50, 13/60, Spitfire	Disc 9 in. (22.86 cm.) dia.
Rear	Drum 7 in. x 1 1/4 in. (17.78 x 3.17 cm.)
Adjustment - Drum	Front - two adjusters;
	Rear - one adjuster
- Disc	Self-adjusting
Shoe lining material - Front	Ferodo M.S.I.
- Rear	Ferodo M.S.I. (with 12P callipers)
	or Don 242 (with 14LF callipers)
Disc pad material	Don 55 (with 12P callipers)
	or Don 212 (with 14LF callipers)
Disc maximum run-out	0.004 in.
Fluid type	Girling Crimson (SAE 70R 3)

TIGHTENING TORQUES

Rear backplate attachment	16 - 18 lbs./ft.	(2.21 - 2.49 kg./m.)
Brake disc to hub	32 - 35 lbs./ft.	(4.42 - 4.84 kg./m.)
Callipers to mounting plate	50 - 55 lbs./ft.	(6.91 - 7.60 kg./m.)
Master cylinder attachments	16 - 20 lbs./ft.	(2.21 - 2.77 kg./m.)
Pipe attachments	6 - 8 lbs./ft.	(0.83 - 1.11 kg./m.)

Fig. M:1 Lubricating the generator rear bearing.

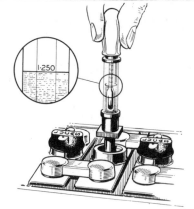

Fig. M:2 Checking the specific gravity of the battery electrolyte.

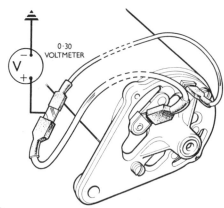

Fig. M:3 Generator output test.

Fig. M:4 Voltage regulator and cut-out - Herald

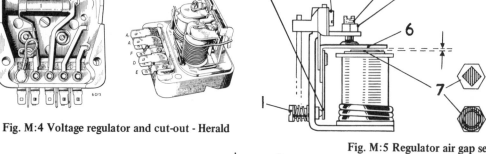

1. Voltage adjusting screw
2. Armature tension spring
3. Armature securing screws
4. Fixed contact adjustment screw
5. Locknut
6. Armature
7. Core face and shim

Fig. M:5 Regulator air gap settings - Herald.

1. Follow-through - 0.010 - 0.020 in. (0,254 - 0,508 mm.)
2. Stop arm
3. Armature securing screws
4. Cut-out adjusting screw
5. Armature tension spring
6. Fixed contact blade
7. Armature tongue and moving contact

Fig. M:6 Cut-out air gap settings - Herald

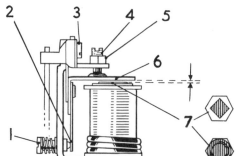

1. Cut-out
2. Current regulator
3. Voltage regulator

Fig. M:7 Control box - Spitfire

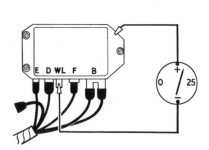

Fig. M:8 Checking the open-circuit setting and the cut-out cut-in voltage - Spitfire.

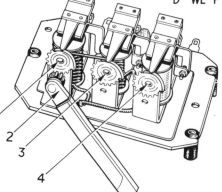

Fig. M:9 Adjusting the cut-out cut-in voltage - Spitfire

1. Cut-out   3. Current regulator
2. Cam adjusting tool   4. Voltage regulator

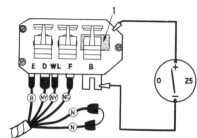

Fig. M:10 Checking the drop-off voltage setting - Spitfire.

Electrical Equipment

GENERAL

This section deals primarily with the charging and starting systems, the ignition system having been dealt with previously in the IGNITION SYSTEM section. On Herald 1200 models produced up to Commission numbers GA238107 and GB57263, the Herald 12/50 and Spitfire 4 Mk. I and Mk. II models, the 12 volt electrical system is of positive ground polarity. Later Herald 1200 models, the 13/60 model and Spitfire Mk. III and IV models all have negative ground polarity. Care should be taken, therefore, when reconnecting the battery to ensure the correct polarity is observed.

The charging system comprises the battery, the generator, (or alternator on the Spitfire Mk. IV), and the charging system control unit. The lead-acid type battery has a capacity of 43 ampere hours at the 20 hour rate. The generator output on the Herald series is regulated by a two bobbin type control unit - voltage regulator and cut-out - while the Spitfire series has a three bobbin unit, voltage regulator current regulator and cut-out.

The Spitfire Mk. IV is equipped with an alternator with the control unit incorporated.

The alternator has an output of 36 amps. Only the charging circuit voltage is regulated by the alternator control unit as the inherent self-regulating properties of the alternator limit the output current, obviating the need for a current regulator. The need for a cut-out is also eliminated by the effect of the diodes incorporated in the alternator which prevents reverse current from flowing.

The starter motor is an inertia-engagement type, operated by a separate solenoid switch.

Front lighting comprises sealed beam headlamps with left and right hand parking and flasher filaments combined in one bulb. At the rear the tail/stop and flasher lamp bulbs are incorporated in the same housing.

ROUTINE MAINTENANCE

Monthly

Check the level of the electrolyte in the battery and if required add distilled water to bring the level above the tops of the separators.

Every 6,000 miles (10,000 km.)

Check the operation of all the electrical circuits.

Every 12,000 miles (20,000 km.)

Apply a few drops of engine oil to the generator rear bearing (Fig. M:1). Clean the exterior of the battery, remove any corrosion from the battery terminal posts and coat the posts with vaseline before securing the leads. Check the earth lead for security and condition.

BATTERY

Check and maintain the battery at regular intervals as the quick starting of the engine depends to a great extent on the state of charge of the battery.

Electrolyte Level

The level of the electrolyte in the battery should be checked periodically and replenished with distilled water as required. In an emergency, it is permissable to use melted snow, rain water or plain drinking water free of high mineral content. Add water as required to each cell so that the electrolyte level is approx 1/4 in. (6.0 mm.) above the separators. DO NOT OVERFILL. The engine should be operated immediately after adding water, particularly in cold weather, to assure proper mixing of the water and acid.

Sulphuric acid of the correct concentration should be added only if the specific gravity of the electrolyte needs to be corrected as a result of drainage or leakage from the battery.

Exterior

The external condition of the battery, the terminal posts and the cable terminals should be checked periodically. If the top of the battery is contaminated by acid film or dirt between the terminal posts, wash with a diluted ammonia or soda solution to neutralise any acid present and then flush with water. Care must be taken to keep the vent plugs tight so that the neutralising solution does not enter the cells.

To ensure good contact, the battery cables should be tight

109

on the terminal posts. If the battery posts or cable terminals are corroded, the cables should be disconnected and the terminals and posts cleaned with a soda solution and a wire brush. Apply a thin film of petroleum jelly to the posts before reconnecting the cables. The battery ground cable and the engine unit ground strap should also be inspected for proper connection and condition.

Specific Gravity

The specific gravity of the electrolyte is a good indication of the state of charge of the battery. Prior to testing, inspect the battery for any damage, such as a broken casing or cover, loose terminal posts, etc., which would make the battery unserviceable. Check the specific gravity of each cell with a hydrometer, drawing enough electrolyte into the hydrometer to make the scale float (Fig. M:2). If the electrolyte level is less than 1/4 in. (6.0 mm.) above the separators, distilled water should be added and the battery charged for at least one hour before carrying out the check.

The following table relates the specific gravity to the battery condition at $16^{O}C$ ($60^{O}F$).

HYDROMETER READING	BATTERY CONDITION
1.280	Fully charged
1.240	75% charged
1.200	50% charged
1.160	25% charged
1.120	Discharged

If the electrolyte temperature varies from $16^{O}C$ ($60^{O}F$), adjust the reading obtained by adding 0.004 for every 5 1/2^{O}C ($10^{O}F$) above $16^{O}C$ and by subtracting the same amount for every 5 1/2^{O}C below $16^{O}C$.

If the readings are reasonably uniform, the battery is probably healthy, although low readings indicate that charging is required. If one cell is about 0.030 lower than the rest, it is probably failing. An extended charge may revive it. If the readings are irregular, with one or more cells 0.050 lower than the rest, the battery is not fit for further use and should be replaced.

Charging

Slow charging is the preferred method of re-charging a battery as it may safely be used regardless of the condition of the battery provided that the electrolyte is at the proper level in all the cells. The normal charging rate is 1 amp. per positive plate per cell (i.e. 3.0 amps for 40 amp/hr. battery with 7 plates per cell, since there is always one more negative plate per cell than positive). A minimum of 24 hours is required when using this method. The vent plugs must be removed while charging takes place as the electrolyte boils due to the decomposition of the water. Where an auto-fill type cover is fitted, the cover should be left on as this displaces the vent hole ball plugs. A battery is in a fully charged condition when all cells are gassing freely and three corrected specific gravity readings, taken at hourly intervals, indicate no increase in specific gravity.

If fast charging the battery, the precautions given above for slow charging are even more important. A battery may be charged at any rate which does not cause the electrolyte temperature to exceed $52^{O}C$ ($125^{O}F$) and which does not cause excessive gassing and loss of electrolyte.

DO NOT ATTEMPT TO CHARGE A BATTERY WITH FROZEN ELECTROLYTE AS IT MAY CAUSE THE BATTERY TO EXPLODE.

FAULTS IN THE CHARGING SYSTEM

The ignition warning light on the instrument panel can give a reasonable indication of the operation of the charging system and it may be of general interest to name a few of the faults which can be indicated by the functioning of the lamp.

When the charging system is operating correctly, the lamp should be out when the ignition is switched off, on when the ignition is switched on and should go out again once the engine is running at speed.

Should the warning light still be illuminated with the engine running at speed (above the cut-in speed of the generator/alterator) this indicates that the generator/alternator is not supplying current to the battery. First check the condition and the adjustment of the generator/alternator drive belt and, if satisfactory, check all wiring connections between the generator/alternator, control unit (where separate) and the ignition switch. If the warning light now functions correctly, test the state of the battery and recharge as required. However, persistent illumination of the light indicates a fault in the generator/alternator or the control unit and the tests described below should be carried out on the individual components to isolate the fault.

If the warning light glows only slightly with the engine at speed, a high resistance in the circuit is indicated. Check for loose or corroded terminals or damaged wires.

If the warning light does not illuminate under any conditions, a blown bulb or broken connection to the warning light are indicated. Check the wiring or replace the bulb as necessary.

GENERATOR OUTPUT TEST

Disconnect the leads from the "D" and "F" terminals at the control unit and join the leads together. Connect a 0 - 30 voltmeter between their junction and a good earthing point. Run the engine at approximately 1,000 rev./min.

NOTE: Do not exceed this speed otherwise the generator may be damaged.

The voltmeter reading should rise rapidly without fluctuation to more than 24 volts. Should the reading be incorrect, connect a jumper lead between the "D" and "F" terminals on the generator and connect the voltmeter between this wire and a good earthing point (Fig. M:3). If the reading if still incorrect, there is a fault in the generator. A cure may be effected by replacing the generator brushes.

GENERATOR CONTROL UNIT (HERALD)

(Fig. M:4)

NOTE: Before disturbing electrical or mechanical settings ensure that any suspected fault is not due to defective battery. slack generator drive belt, defective wiring or connections or poor earth.

Clean regulator contacts with carborundum stone or silicon carbide paper followed by methylated spirits and cut-out contacts with fine glass paper followed by methylated spirits.

Voltage Regulator Open Circuit Setting

1. Insert thin piece of cardboard between armature and core of cut-out.

2. Connect 0.20 volt moving coil voltmeter between terminal and good earth point.

3. Start engine and slowly increase speed up to 2,700 r.p.m. and check voltmeter reading against following table:

Ambient Temperature	Voltage Setting
10°C (50°F)	16.1 - 16.7
20°C (68°F)	16.0 - 16.6
30°C (86°F)	15.9 - 16.5
40°C (104°F)	15.8 - 16.4

NOTE: A reading fluctuation of more than 0.3 volts may be due to dirty contacts.

4. To bring a steady reading inside limits where necessary turn adjusting screw (1, Fig. M:5) clockwise to increase voltage and counter clockwise to decrease.

5. Remove voltmeter and cardboard and replace cover.

Cut-out Voltage Setting

1. Connect voltmeter between terminals "D" and "E".

2. Start engine, slowly increase speed, voltage should rise steadily then drop slightly when voltage is 12.7 - 13.3 volts and contacts close.

3. If operation is outside limits adjust by turning adjusting screw (4, Fig. M:6) clockwise to raise voltage setting or counter clockwise to lower voltage.

NOTE: Turn the screw in small increments only and check closing voltage after each adjustment.

4. Remove voltmeter and refit cover.

Air Gap Settings

Voltage Regulator (Fig. M:5)

1. Release locknut (5) and turn adjusting screw (4) until well clear of moving contact.

2. Slacken voltage adjusting screw (1) until spring is free from tension.

3. Slacken screws (3).

4. Insert setting gauge between armature and copper separator (7).

NOTE: Where separator is square, the air gap and gauge thickness should be 0.021 in. (0.53 mm.) and where

separator is round, dimension is 0.015 in. (0.38 mm.).

5. Press armature down against gauge, tighten screws (3) and screw in (4) until just touching moving contact and tighten locking nut.

6. Recheck open circuit setting.

Cut-out Relay (Fig. M:6)

1. Slacken adjustment (4) until clear of spring (5) and slacken armature securing screws (3).

2. Press armature down squarely onto core face and retighten screws (3).

3. With armature still held against core face, set gap between armature stop arm (2) and armature tongue (7) to 0.032 in. (0.81 mm.) by bending stop arm.

4. Adjust fixed contact blade (6) so that it is deflected to 0.015 in. (0.38 mm.) by moving contact (7) when armature is pressed against core face.

5. Re-check electrical setting.

GENERATOR CONTROL UNIT (SPITFIRE)

NOTE: Before disturbing the electrical or mechanical settings of the control unit, ensure that any suspected fault is not due to a defective battery, slack generator drive belt, defective wiring or connections, or poor earth.

Items (1), (2) and (3) in Fig. M:7 indicate cut-out, current regulator and voltage regulator.

Clean regulator contacts with carborundum stone or silicon carbide paper followed by methylated spirits and cut-out contacts with fine glass paper followed by methylated spirits.

Voltage Regulator Open-Circuit Setting

1. Insert a piece of cardboard between armature and core of cut-out. Connect 0 - 20 volt moving coil voltmeter between "WL" terminal and good earth point as shown in Fig. M:8.

2. Run engine at 2,700 r.p.m. Check voltmeter reading against following table.

Ambient Temperature	Voltage Setting
10°C (50°F)	14.9 - 15.5
20°C (68°F)	14.7 - 15.3
30°C (86°F)	14.5 - 15.1
40°C (104°F)	14.3 - 14.9

NOTE: A reading fluctuation of more than ± 0.3 volt may be due to dirty contacts.

3. To bring a steady reading inside limits when necessary, rotate the voltage regulator cam with the special tool clockwise to raise setting or counter clockwise to lower it. Check the setting by stopping the engine then again bringing the engine speed to 2.700 r.p.m.

H

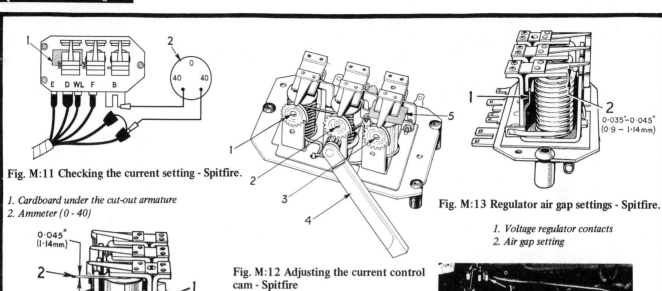

Fig. M:11 Checking the current setting - Spitfire.

1. Cardboard under the cut-out armature
2. Ammeter (0 - 40)

Fig. M:12 Adjusting the current control cam - Spitfire

1. Cut-out cam
2. Current control cam
3. Voltage regulator cam
4. Cam adjusting tool
5. Cardboard under the voltage regulator

Fig. M:13 Regulator air gap settings - Spitfire.

1. Voltage regulator contacts
2. Air gap setting

0.045" (1.14mm.)

Fig. M:14 Cut-out air gap settings - Spitfire

1. Backstop adjustment
2. Air gap settings

Fig. M:15 Generator adjusting and mounting points.

1. Bolts
2. Brush
3. Felt ring and aluminium sealing disc
4. Brush spring
5. Bearing bush
6. Commutator end bracket
7. Field coils
8. Rivet
9. Bearing retainer plate
10. Corrugated washer
11. Felt washer
12. Driving end bracket
13. Pulley retainer nut
14. Bearing
15. Woodruff key
16. Armature

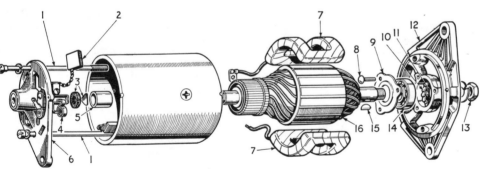

Fig. M:16 Exploded view of the generator

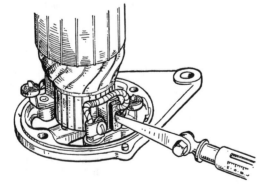

Fig. M:17 Checking the generator brush tension.

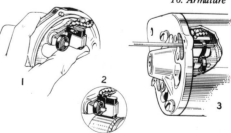

Fig. M:18 Assembling the end bracket to the generator.

1. Method of trapping brush in raised position with spring
2. Normal working position
3. Method of releasing brush onto commutator

4. Remove cardboard and voltmeter and replace cover.

Cut-out Cut-in Voltage Setting

1. Disconnect cables from terminal "B" at control box and connect together with jumper lead. Connect a moving coil volt meter between terminal "B" and earth (Fig. M:10).

2. Switch on headlamps.

3. Start engine and slowly increase speed. Voltage should rise steadily then drop slightly when voltage is 12.6 to 13.4 volts and contacts close.

4. If necessary, bring cut-in within limits by turning the cut-out relay adjustment cam clockwise to raise setting and counter clockwise to lower it (Fig. M:9).

5. Remove voltmeter, restore connections and refit cover.

Cut-out Drop-off Voltage Setting

1. Disconnect cables from terminal "B" at control box and connect together with jumper lead.

   Connect a moving coil voltmeter between terminal "B" and earth (Fig. M:10).

2. Start engine and run up to 2,700 r.p.m. Slowly decelerate and check that voltmeter pointer drops to zero (contacts open) between 9.3 and 11.2 volts.

3. If drop-off outside limits, stop engine and adjust cut-out contact gap by bending fixed contact. Reducing gap increases voltage and increasing gap decreases voltage.

4. Repeat test until correct result is obtained.

5. Remove voltmeter, restore connections and refit cover.

Current Regular On-load Setting

1. Arrange ammeter and cardboard as shown in Fig. M:11.

   NOTE: Ensure terminal "B" carries only this connection.

2. Switch on all lights, run engine at about 2,700 r.p.m. and check maximum rated output on ammeter. A reading fluctuating more than one amp indicates possible dirty contacts.

   CAUTION. Do not switch on all lights after engine has been started.

3. If necessary bring output within limits by rotating current adjustments cam (Fig. M:12).

4. Switch off engine, restore connections, remove cardboard and fit cover.

Air Gaps Settings

NOTE: The air gaps should normally require no attention. If setting has been lost reset as described.

1. On voltage and current regulators turn cam to minimum lift (Fig. M:13). Slacken contact screw and insert a suitable feeler gauge as far as the two rivet heads. Press down on armature and set adjustable contact to just touch armature contact. Remove feeler and adjust voltage or current setting.

2. On cut-out relay insert 0.015 in. feeler gauge between armature and core, press down armature, bend cut-out fixed contacts until contacts just touch, release armature and remove feeler gauge. Adjust armature back stop to give core gap of 0.035 - 0.045 in. (0.9 - 1.14 mm.) (Fig. M:14). Check cut-in and drop-off voltage settings.

GENERATOR - Removal and Installation (Fig. M:15)

Removal

1. Isolate battery and disconnect the leads from the generator terminals.

2. Slacken bolts (1) and (2), pivot generator towards engine and remove fan belt.

3. Remove bolts and remove generator.

Installation

1. Reverse the removal procedure, tensioning the fan belt to give 0.75 - 1.00 in. (19.00 - 25.00 mm.) side movements at the mid point on the longest run.

GENERATOR BRUSHES - Inspection and/or Replacement

1. Remove generator from car as described above.

2. Remove two through bolts at rear of generator and withdraw commutator end bracket.

3. Lift up brush springs and withdraw brushes from holders.

4. Check brushes for wear. Renew if less than 11/32 in. (8.7 mm.) in length.

5. Check commutator for oil contamination. If present, brushes must be renewed.

   Clean commutator surface with cloth moistened in white spirit, drying carefully afterwards. Contact surface of commuatator should be smooth and dark grey in colour.

6. To renew brushes, remove screw and lock washer securing each brush lead to holder and detach brushes. Ensure replacement brushes are of correct length and type.

   Secure leads of new brushes to holders.

7. Check brushes for freedom of movement in holders. If necessary, clean brush and holder with cloth moistened in white spirit or petrol, drying carefully.

8. Check brushes spring tension, using a spring scale (Fig. M:17). If tension is below 15 oz., fit new springs.

9. Locate brush springs on side of brush as shown in item Fig. M:18.

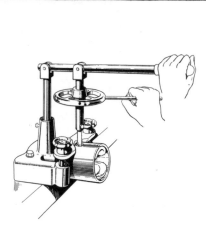

Fig. M:19 Removing/tightening the pole shoe screws.

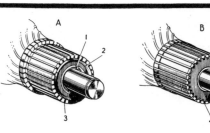

A. Fabricated type
B. Moulded type

1. Metal roll-over
2. Insulating cone
3. Slot depth 0.032 in. (0.81 mm.) max.
4. Slot depth 0.020 - 0.035 in.
   (0.508 - 0.890 mm.)

Fig. M:20 Details of the commutator.

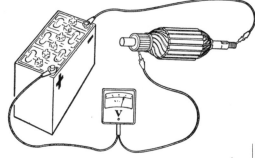

Fig. M:22 Armature insulation test.

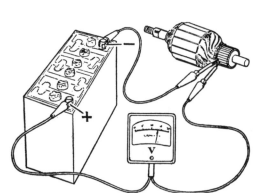

Fig. M:21 Armature open-circuit test.

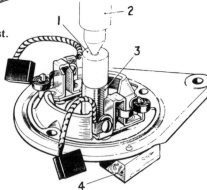

1. Mandrel
2. Press
3. Bush
4. Wooden blocks

Fig. M:23 Pressing a new bush into the commutator end bracket.

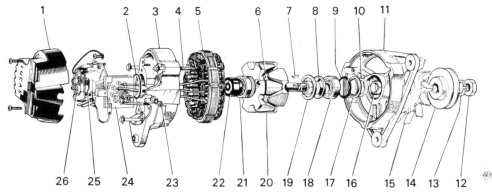

1. Moulded cover	6. Field windings	11. Drive end bracket
2. Rubber O-ring	7. Key	12. Nut
3. Slip ring end bracket	8. Bearing retaining plate	13. Spring washer
4. Through-bolt	9. Pressure ring	14. Pulley
5. Stator windings	10. Felt ring	15. Fan
		16. Spacer

17. Pressure ring and felt ring
    retaining plate
18. Drive end bearing
19. Circlip
20. Rotor
21. Slip ring end bearing

22. Slip ring moulding
23. Nut
24. Rectifier pack
25. Brushbox assembly
26. Control unit

Fig. M:24 Exploded view of the Lucas 15 ACR alternator.

10.	Ensure fibre washer is fitted on armature shaft and assemble end bracket. Fit and secure through bolts.

11.	Insert thin screwdriver through ventilation hole in commutator bracket, adjacent to brush holders (3, Fig. M:18). Gently lever up spring ends, press down brush onto commutator and position spring end on top of brush (2, Fig. M:18). Repeat for other brush.

12.	Install generator on car as described above.

GENERATOR - Overhaul (Fig. M:16)

Disassembly

1.	Remove shaft nut (13) and washer and draw off drive pulley.

2.	Remove two through-bolts at rear of generator and withdraw commutator end bracket. Remove fibre thrust washer from armature shaft and retain.

3.	Withdraw armature complete with drive end bracket (12) from generator yoke.

4.	If necessary, press armature shaft out of drive end bracket after removing Woodruff key from shaft.

5.	Clean yoke, field coils, armature and end brackets with a brush or air line. Wash all other parts in solvent and dry thoroughly.

Field Coils

Inspect field coils for burned or broken insulation and for broken or loose connections. With field coils still installed in yoke, measure resistance by connecting an ohmmeter between field terminal post and yoke. Field resistance should be 6 ohms. If an ohmmeter is not available, a 12 volt D.C. supply with an ammeter in series can be used instead. Ammeter reading should be approx. 2 amps. Zero reading on ammeter or "infinity" reading on ohmmeter indicates open circuit in field coils. If current reading is much more than 2 amps. or ohmmeter reading is much below 6 ohms., this indicates insulation of one coil has broken down. In either case coils must be renewed. Replace coils as follows:-

1.	Drill out rivet securing field terminal assembly to yoke. Unsolder field coil connections from terminal post, marking relative positions of wires. Inner wire (yellow) is insulated and outer wire (red) connects to earth.

2.	If original field coils are to be refitted, mark yoke and pole pieces to ensure each pole piece is refitted in exactly the same position, otherwise residual magnetic polarity of the generator will be altered.

3.	Remove insulation piece.

4.	Remove pole shoe screws (Fig. M:19), remove pole shoes and withdraw field coils.

5.	Fit new field coils to shoes. If original shoes are being refitted, ensure they are installed in exactly the same positions as before.

6.	Fully tighten pole screws (Fig. M:19) and centre punch into

screw slots to lock.

7.	Fit insulation piece.

8.	Solder field coil connections to terminal post, ensuring that wires are correctly fitted.

9.	Before finally peening over rivet end to secure field terminal assembly to yoke, temporarily fit commutator end bracket to ensure correct alignment of post.

Armature

Clean armature with petrol soaked rag. Inspect commutator surface for pits or burned spots. If commutator is in good condition, the surface will be smooth and dark grey in colour. If pits or burned spots are present, carefully polish the surface of the commutator with strip of glass paper while rotating armature. NEVER use emery cloth. If commutator is badly worn or scored, it should be reskimmed and the segments undercut or the armature exchanged. The reskimming operation should be entrusted to an electrical specialist. The segments should be undercut to a depth of 1/32 in. (0.8 mm.), using a hacksaw blade ground to the thickness of the insulator (Fig. M:20).

NOTE: If the commutator is of the moulded type (B, Fig. M:20) the segments do NOT require undercutting. However, the insulation slots should be kept clear of copper and carbon residue.

Indications of a short circuit are discolouration of any one or two coils and a blackening of two or more commutator segments. An open circuit will cause burned spots between the commutator segments.

To test for open circuit in the commutator segments or in the armature windings, connect a 12 volt battery and voltmeter in series with a pair of test prods. Place prods on each pair of adjacent segments in turn and note volt meter readings. If armature is in good order, all readings will be similar. If a low zero reading is obtained between any pair of segments, one or more adjacent coils are open-circuited.

To check if armature is grounded, using same circuit as above, place one of prods in contact with end of armature shaft and other on each commutator segment in turn (Fig. M:22). There should be no voltmeter readings. If reading is obtained, one of the armature coils is grounded. A test lamp may be used instead of voltmeter, in which case lamp will glow if there is a ground.

Bearings

If worn or damaged, the armature shaft bearings can be replaced as follows:-

Commutator end bracket

a).	Remove old brush from bracket by screwing 5/8 in. tap a few turns squarely into bush and withdrawing.

b).	Remove felt ring and retainer and clean housing. Renew felt washer if necessary.

c).	Install felt ring and retainer in bore and press in bush until

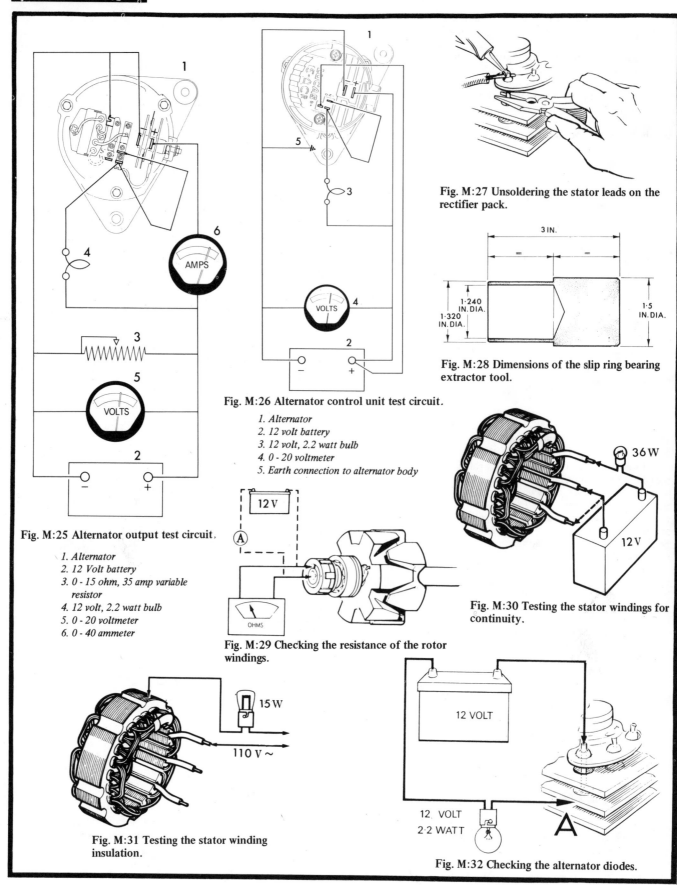

Fig. M:27 Unsoldering the stator leads on the rectifier pack.

Fig. M:28 Dimensions of the slip ring bearing extractor tool.

Fig. M:26 Alternator control unit test circuit.

1. Alternator
2. 12 volt battery
3. 12 volt, 2.2 watt bulb
4. 0 - 20 voltmeter
5. Earth connection to alternator body

Fig. M:30 Testing the stator windings for continuity.

Fig. M:25 Alternator output test circuit.

1. Alternator
2. 12 Volt battery
3. 0 - 15 ohm, 35 amp variable resistor
4. 12 volt, 2.2 watt bulb
5. 0 - 20 voltmeter
6. 0 - 40 ammeter

Fig. M:29 Checking the resistance of the rotor windings.

Fig. M:31 Testing the stator winding insulation.

Fig. M:32 Checking the alternator diodes.

flush (Fig. M:23). New bush should be soaked in engine oil for 24 hours before fitting.

Drive end bracket

a). Drill out rivets (8) and remove plate (9). Press bearing (14) from bracket and remove corrugated washer (10) felt washer (11) and oil retaining washer.

b). Clean all items. Check ball race for cracks and wear and renew if necessary.

c). Install items in reverse order of removal. Pack bearing with high melting point grease before installation.

Re-assembly

1. Support inner journal of drive end bracket bearing and press bracket onto armature shaft.

2. Assemble armature and end bracket to yoke, ensure that locating dowel on bracket correctly engages groove in yoke.

3. Fit thrust washer to end of armature shaft and refit commutator end bracket as described in "GENERATOR BRUSHES - Inspection and/or Replacement".

4. Refit Woodruff key to armature shaft and secure the drive pulley with the nut and washer.

5. It may be necessary to provide residual megnetism in the field coils after the generator has been installed in the car. With the leads disconnected from the "D" and "F" terminals on the generator, connect a jumper lead to the battery negative terminal and flick the other end of the jumper lead several times against the "F" terminal on the generator.

ALTERNATOR - PRECAUTIONARY SERVICE NOTES

(Spitfire Mk. IV only) (Fig. M:24)

It is essential that the following notes be observed when carrying out the maintenance or repairs on a charging system which includes an alternator.

1. Never remove alternator without first disconnecting battery.

2. Never disconnect or reconnect battery while alternator is running, otherwise damage to control box may occur.

3. Never run alternator with battery disconnected and field windings energised, otherwise control unit may be damaged.

4. When installing battery or reconnecting battery leads, always ensure that correct polarity is observed. Reversal of battery connections may damage alternator diodes.

5. Never allow alternator output cable to ground if it is disconnected at alternator. If this cable grounds with ignition switched on, control unit and associated wiring may be damaged.

6. Never allow alternator output cable or terminal to ground as damage to alternator and/or alternator circuit may result, even when ignition is switched off.

7. Never allow field terminal of alternator or connecting lead to ground.

8. No attempt should be made to polarise alternator. This is not necessary and any attempt to do so may result in damage to alternator, control unit or associated wiring.

9. Never use regulator terminal on alternator as a source for running lights or other accessories otherwise the control unit will be adversely affected.

10. Never use an ohmmeter of the type incorporating a hand-driven generator to check the alternator diodes. Only D.C. current, not exceeding 24 volts should be used when testing.

11. If arc welding is to be carried out on vehicle, disconnect alternator and control unit to avoid possible damage.

12. Always disconnect positive lead from battery before using a fast charger. Charger must always be connected in parallel with battery, positive to positive, negative to negative.

13. When using a starting unit, voltage must not exceed charging system voltage or damage to battery, alternator and starter may result. Fast charger must never be used as a booster unit for starting because of accompanying high voltage. After engine has started, always disconnect negative cable.

14. To avoid damaging alternator bearings when adjusting drive belt tension, apply leverage only on drive end bracket of alternator, not on any other part.

ALTERNATOR OUTPUT TEST

SPECIAL NOTE:- Polarity sensitive components in the alternator may be damaged if subjected to incorrect polarity. Check polarity of alternator and battery terminals.

NOTE: When alternator is cold, the stated output may be exceeded slightly. To avoid misleading results, the check should be performed with the unit as near to its normal operating temperature as possible.

Disconnect the multi-socket connector from the rear of the alternator. Remove the moulded cover from the rear of the unit. Connect a test circuit as shown in Fig. M:25.

NOTE: The variable resistor should only be connected across the battery for as long as is necessary to carry out the check.

Start engine and gradually increase the speed. The test light should go out at 720 rev/min.

Further increase the engine speed to 2.870 rev/min. With the engine held at this speed, adjust the variable resistor until the voltmeter reads 14 volts. The ammeter reading should now be approximately 28 amps.

If the ammeter reading is incorrect, the alternator should be overhauled or exchanged.

TESTING THE ALTERNATOR CONTROL UNIT

(Fig. M:26)

CAUTION. DO NOT SUBJECT UNIT TO INCORRECT POLARITY.

1. Disconnect leads at alternator and provide test circuit as shown in illustration.

2. Run engine at gradually increasing speed. At 1500 alternator R.P.M. (720 engine R.P.M.) light should go out.

3. Hold speed at approx. 6,000 alternator R.P.M. (2,870 engine R.P.M.) Voltmeter should now read steady 14.0 - 14.4 volts.

4. If a steady 14.0 - 14.4 volts is not obtained and alternator functional check is satisfactory, the control unit should be replaced.

ALTERNATOR - Removal and Installation

Refer to ALTERNATOR - PRECAUTIONARY SERVICE NOTES before attempting removal of the alternator.

Disconnect the battery, Disconnect the multi-socket connector from the rear of the alternator. Slacken the alternator mounting bolts and the bolts of the tensioning strap. Push the alternator towards the engine and lift off the drive belt. Completely remove the mounting bolts and detach the alternator from the engine.

Installation is the reverse of the removal procedure.

Tighten the mounting bolts so that the drive belt has a total free movement of 0.75 - 1.00 in. (19.0 - 25.0 mm.) at the midpoint on the longest run.

If the alternator has been overhauled or an exchange unit fitted, check the alternator output once installed.

ALTERNATOR - Overhaul (Fig. M:24)

Dismantling

1. Remove moulded cover.

2. Disconnect brushbox connector, using longnosed pliers if necessary, remove two screws and brushbox.

3. Identify three stator wires on rectifier pack and unsolder wire connections as quickly as possible using longnosed pliers as heat sink (Fig. M:27). Slacken nut and remove rectifier pack.

4. Remove through bolts.

5. Using tool detailed on Fig. M:28 against bearing (21) outer journal, support slip ring end bracket by hand and tap out bearing. Carefully file out surplus solder on slip ring moulding if necessary to accommodate tool. Remove "O" ring from bearing housing.

6. Remove stator from end bracket.

7. Remove pulley and fan. Retain key.

8. Press rotor from drive end bracket.

Inspection

Brushes

Clean the brushes with a cloth moistened in petrol or white spirit. Check brushes for wear. Renew if less than 0.2 in. (5 mm.) protrudes from the brushbox when free. Check brushes for freedom of movement in the brushbox. If necessary, lightly polish the brush sides with a fine file. Check the brush spring pressure, using a push type spring scale. The specified tension is 7 - 10 oz. If the tension is low, renew the brushbox assembly.

Slip Rings

Clean the slip rings with a cloth moistened in petrol or white spirit. Inspect the contact faces of the rings. These should be smooth and clean. If necessary, polish the faces with very fine glass paper. Never attempt to machine the rings.

Rotor

Check the resistance of the rotor windings by connecting an ohmmeter between the slip rings (Fig. M:29). The resistance should be 4.3 ohms. If an ohmmeter is not available, an ammeter and a 12 volt battery can be used instead. The ammeter reading should be 2.8 amps.

Test the rotor insulation, using a 110 volts A.C. power supply and a 15 watt test lamp. Connect the lamp between one of the slip rings and one of the rotor poles. The lamp must not light up. If it does, the rotor should be replaced.

The stator leads must be disconnected before carrying out the following tests.

Test the stator windings for continuity, using a 12 volt battery and a test lamp of at least 36 watts. Connect the lamp and battery in series with any two of the three stator leads (Fig. M:30). Repeat the test with the two other combinations of leads. The test lamp must light during all three test. Replace the stator if this is not the case.

Using a 110 volt A.C. power supply and a 15 watt test lamp connected in series, connect one lead to one of the stator cables and the other to the stator casing (Fig. M:31). If the lamp lights up, the stator windings are grounded and the stator must be replaced.

Diodes

The diode leads must be completely detached from the phase terminals before performing the following tests. Use a pair of longnose pliers as a heat sink when unsoldering the connections, as the diodes are heat sensitive and can be easily damaged (Fig. M:27). Release the connections quickly with a hot soldering iron.

Connect each of the diodes in turn in series with a 2.2 watt test lamp and a 12 volt battery. Connect one of the test leads to one of the diode leads and the other test lead to the diode heat sink (Fig. M:32). Note the behaviour of the test lamp. Reverse the connections and repeat the test. The test lamp should light up in one direction only. A diode that passses current in both directions has probably been subjected to excessive voltage and the rectifier pack must be replaced.

Rotor Bearings

The rotor bearings are "unit-life" items and it is therefore unlikely that replacement will become necessary. However, if replacement is required proceed as follows:-

Slip Ring End Bearing (Fig. M:33)

1. Unsolder the two field winding connections from the slip ring moulding and pull the moulding from the shaft. Extract bearing and remove grease retainer.

2. Pack bearing with Shell Alvania R.A. grease or equivalent, fit serviceable grease retainer to shaft, press bearing on to shaft with shielded face outwards and fit slip ring mouldings on to shaft. Solder two connections to slip ring moulding.

Drive End Bearing (Fig. M:34)

1. Remove the circlip and retaining plate, push out the bearing and remove the "O" ring, retaining plate, felt ring and spacer.

2. Fit the retaining plate, felt ring, pressure ring and serviceable "O" ring, pack bearing with Shell Alvania R.A. grease or equivalent and press the bearing into the housing. Fit the retainer and circlip.

Re-assembly

1. Using spacer (16) and suitable size tube against bearing inner journal press rotor into drive end bracket.

2. Locate key and fit fan and pulley. Torque load nut to 25 - 30 lb./ft.

3. Position stator windings in correct attitude to drive end bracket.

4. Fit serviceable "O" ring in bearing housing and carefully press slip ring end bracket over bearing.

5. Fit through bolts.

6. Position rectifier pack with rubber locating piece and secure with nut.

7. Correctly position three stator wires on rectifier pack and quickly solder with "M" grade 45 - 55 tin lead solder (Fig. M:27). Do not overheat or bend diode pins.

8. With brushes correctly entered secure brushbox to rectifier pack with connector and two screws.

9. Fit moulded cover.

STARTER MOTOR - Removal and Installation

The starter motor is mounted on the rear right-hand side of the engine.

Removal

1. Disconnect cable from battery and starter motor.

2. Remove two attachment bolts and remove starter motor upwards.

Installation

1. Reverse removal procedure ensuring that the mounting face shoulder correctly registers on the engine bearer plate face.

2. Reconnect cables.

    NOTE: A clearance of 3/32 in. to 5/32 in. is required between end of pinion and starter ring gear. Packing pieces and shims in thickness of 0.4 in., 0.5 in. and 0.016 in. are available.

STARTER MOTOR (Fig. M:35)

Inspection and/or Replacement of the Brushes

1. Remove starter motor from car.

2. Slacken clamp screw and slide brush cover (8) away from brush apertures. Lift brush springs using piece of hooked wire and withdraw brushes from holders.

    NOTE: If the original brushes are to be re-used, they MUST be refitted in their ORIGINAL positions.

3. Check brushes for wear. If brushes are so worn that they do not bear on the commutator, or if the flexible lead is visible on the brush contact face, new brushes must be fitted. Minimum brush length is 5/16 in. (8 mm.).

4. Check brush spring tension, using a spring scale (Fig. M:36). If tension is below 32 oz., fit new springs.

5. If brushes are to be renewed, remove nuts and washer (1), insulating washer (2) and insulating bush (3) from field terminal post. Unscrew two through-bolts (24) and withdraw end plate (4) from starter yoke.

6. Check commutator for oil contamination. If present, brushes must be renewed. If commutator is blackened or dirty, clean with cloth moistened in white spirit or petrol, drying thoroughly, or clean with very fine glass paper. NEVER use emery cloth and NEVER attempt to undercut the mica insulation between the segments.

7. To renew earthed brushes (5) on end plate, unsolder brush leads from clip beneath brush box. Open clip, insert replacement brush lead, squeeze clip and resolder.

8. To renew insulated brushes (21) on field coils, cut off brush leads 1/8 in. (3 mm.) from aluminium. Clean and

I

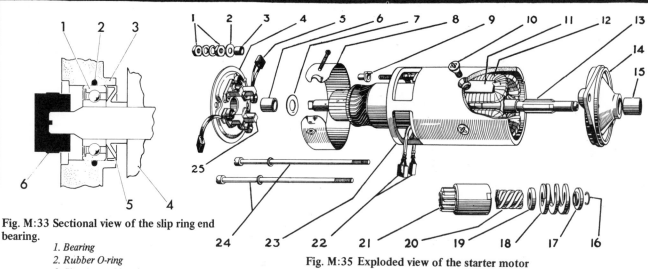

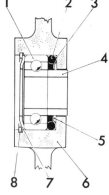

Fig. M:33 Sectional view of the slip ring end bearing.

1. Bearing
2. Rubber O-ring
3. Slip ring end bracket
4. Rotor
5. Grease retainer
6. Slip ring moulding

Fig. M:35 Exploded view of the starter motor

1. Terminal nuts and washers
2. Insulating washer
3. Insulating bush
4. End plate
5. Brush
6. Bush
7. Thrust washer
8. Cover band
9. Insulating bush
10. Pole shoe securing screw
11. Pole shoe
12. Field coil
13. Commutator shaft
14. End bracket Bush
16. Jump ring
17. Retainer
18. Main spring
19. Thrust washer
20. Sleeve
21. Pinion and barrel assembly
22. Brushes
23. Yoke
24. Through-bolts
25. Brush box

Fig. M:34 Sectional view of the drive end bearing.

1. Bearing
2. Pressure ring
3. Pressure ring and felt ring retaining plate
4. Spacer
5. Felt ring
6. Drive end bracket
7. Bearing retaining plate
8. Circlip

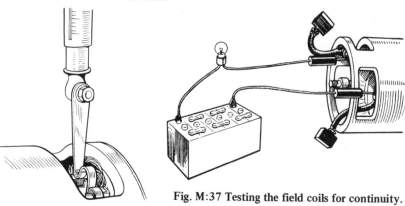

Fig. M:36 Checking the brush spring tension.

Fig. M:37 Testing the field coils for continuity.

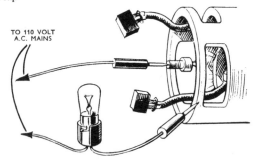

TO 110 VOLT
A.C. MAINS

Fig. M:38 Testing the field coil insulation.

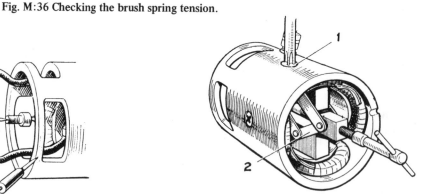

Fig. M:39 Removing/installing the starter motor field coils.

1. Pole shoe retaining screw. 2. Pole shoe expander.

tin original brazed joint at field coil connection. Open loop of replacement brush lead and tin loop, taking care not to allow solder to run towards brush. Place brazed joint within loop, squeeze loop and resolder.

9. Check brushes for freedom of movement in holders. If necessary, clean brush and holder with cloth moistened in white spirit or petrol, drying carefully. Sides of brushes can be eased by lightly polishing with a fine file.

10. Check that insulator band is fitted between yoke and end of field coils and insulating bush (9) is fitted to filed terminal post.

11. Pass insulated brushes out through apertures in yoke.

12. Check that thrust washer (7) is fitted on armature shaft.

13. Fit earthed brushes in their holders and assemble end plate to starter yoke, ensuring that dowel on plate correctly engages notch in yoke. Fit through-bolts and tighten securely.

14. Refit insulating bush (3), insulating washer (2) and nuts and washers (1) on field terminal post. Tighten inner nut securely.

15. Fit insulated brushes in insulated holders.

16. Press brushes down onto commutator and lift brush springs into position on top of brushes.

17. Refit brush cover (8) over brush apertures and tighten clamp screw.

18. Refit starter on car.

Replacement of the Drive Pinion

NOTE: If difficulty is experienced with the starter motor not meshing correctly with the ring gear, it may be that the drive assembly requires cleaning. The pinion and barrel assembly should move freely on the screwed sleeve. If there is any dirt or other foreign matter on the sleeve, it must be washed off with paraffin. Do NOT use grease on the drive assembly as this would attract dirt.

1. Remove starter motor from car.

2. Compress drive spring (18) and retainer (17), using a suitable clamping device, and release jump ring (16). Remove clamping device and withdraw retainer (17), drive spring (18), thrust washer (19), screwed sleeve (20) and pinion and barrel assembly (21).

NOTE: The pinion and barrel assembly cannot be dismantled, it is serviced as a complete assembly with the screwed sleeve.

3. Assemble in the reverse order of removal.

Overhaul

Disassembly

1. Remove end plate as described above for replacing brushes.

2. Withdraw armature and end bracket assembly.

3. Remove drive pinion assembly as described above and withdraw front plate from armature shaft.

4. Clean yoke, field coils, armature, drive assembly and end plate with a brush or air line. Wash all other parts in solvent and dry thoroughly.

Field Coils

Inspect the field coils for burned or broken insulation and for broken or loose connections. Check the field brush connections and brush lead insulation.

Test the field coils for continuity by connecting a 12 volt battery and test lamp between the brush tappings on the field coils (Fig. M:37). If the lamp fails to light, an open circuit in the field coils is indicated and the coils must be replaced. Lighting of the lamp does not necessarily indicate that the field coils are in order. It is possible that a field coil may be grounded to a pole shoe or the starter yoke.

Test the insulation of the field coils by connecting a 110 volt A.C. supply and a test lamp between the field terminal and the starter yoke (Fig. M:38). If the lamp lights, this indicates that the field coils are grounded to the starter yoke and must be replaced. Replace the coils as follows.

1. If original field coils are to be refitted, mark yoke and pole pieces to ensure each pole piece is fitted in exactly the same position as before.

2. Fit pole expander and remove pole screws (Fig. M:39). Remove pole pieces and withdraw field coils.

3. Unsolder coil tappings from terminal post.

4. If required, new insulated brushes should be soldered to field coil tappings before installing the coils in the starter yoke. See brush replacement for details.

5. Fit pole pieces and field coils in starter yoke, ensuring that the pole pieces are installed in exactly the same positions as before.

6. Fit pole shoe expander and fully tighten pole screws (Fig. M:39). Centre punch into screw slots to lock.

7. Fit insulator band between yoke and end of field coils (Fig. M:35).

8. If a new field terminal post is being fitted, temporarily fit end plate to ensure correct alignment of the post before finally soldering.

Armature

The armature and commutator should be inspected and tested as described previously for the generator.

NOTE: The mica insulation between the commutator segments must NOT be undercut on the starter armature.

Bearings

Bearings which are worn to such an extent that they allow

excessive side play of the armature shaft must be renewed.

NOTE: New bushes must be soaked in engine oil for 24 hours prior to fitting.

1. Press old bearing bush out of end bracket.

2. Using a shouldered mandrel diameter as armature shaft, press new bush into end bracket.

NOTE: Bush is made of porous bronze and must NOT be reamed out after fitting as this may impair the porosity of the bush.

Re-assembly

Assemble in the reverse order of dismantling.

Technical Data

BATTERY

Type	Lead/acid: BT.7A (HOME) or BTZ - 7A (EXPORT)
Voltage	12 volts
Capacity	43 amp./hr. at 20 hr. rate
Plates per cell	7

GENERATOR

Model	Lucas C40 - 1
Type	Two brush, two pole compensated voltage control
Rotation	Clockwise
Max. output at 13.5 volts	22 amperes at 2.050 - 2.250 r.p.m. (connected to load of 0.61 ohms

CONTROL BOX (Herald)

Type	Lucas RB106/2
Cut-in voltage	12.7 - 13.3
Drop-off voltage	11.0 - 8.5

CONTROL BOX (Spitfire)

Type	Lucas RB 340
Cut-in voltage	12.6 - 13.4
Drop-off voltage	11.2 - 9.3

ALTERNATOR (Spitfire IV)

Type	Lucas 15 ACR
Rectifier pack-output	6 diodes (3 live side - 3 earth side)
- field winding supply	3 diodes
Stator windings	3 phase - star connected
Drive ratio - engine r.p.m.; generator r.p.m.	19:46
Output	28 amp.
Control unit	Incorporated in alternator

STARTER MOTOR

Model	Lucas M35G
Type	Four pole, four brush, series wound

TIGHTENING TORQUES

Alternator Attachment	18 - 20 lbs./ft.	(2.49 - 2.77 kg./m.)
Generator attachment	16 - 18 lbs./ft.	(2.77 - 3.05 kg./m.)
Starter motor attachment	26 - 32 lbs./ft.	(3.60 - 4.40 kg./m.)
Generator pulley attachment	10 - 12 lbs./ft.	(1.38 - 1.66 kg/m.)

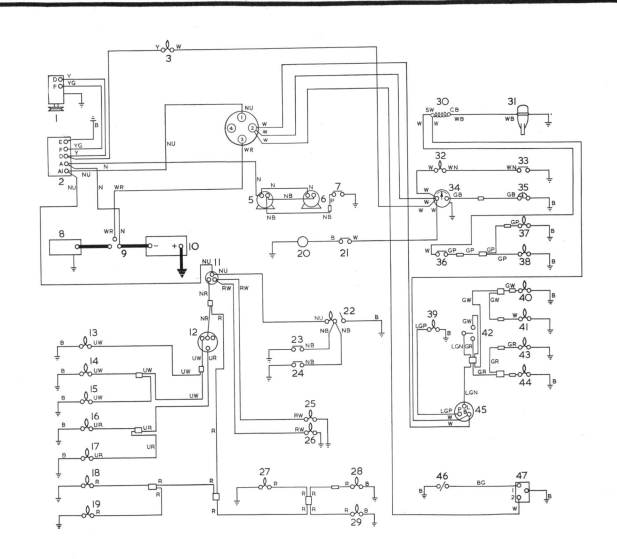

Fig. N:1 Wiring Diagram - Herald positive earth.

1. Generator
2. Control box
3. Ignition warning light
4. Ignition/start switch
5. Horn
6. Horn
7. Horn push
8. Starter motor
9. Starter solenoid switch
10. Battery
11. Master lighting switch
12. Column switch
13. Main beam warning light
14. R.H. headlamp main beam
15. L.H. headlamp main beam
16. R.H. headlamp dip beam
17. L.H. headlamp dip beam
18. L.H. side lamp
19. R.H. side lamp
20. Heater motor
21. Heater switch
22. Interior light and switch
23. R.H. courtesy light switch
24. L.H. courtesy light switch
25. Panel illumination
26. Panel illumination
27. Number plate lamp
28. R.H. tail lamp
29. L.H. tail lamp
30. Ignition coil
31. Distributor
32. Oil pressure warning light
33. Oil pressure switch
34. Fuel gauge
35. Fuel tank unit
36. Stop lamp switch
37. R.H. stop lamp
38. L.H. stop lamp
39. Flasher warning light
40. R.H. rear flasher
41. R.H. front flasher
42. Flasher switch
43. L.H. front flasher
44. L.H. rear flasher
45. Flasher unit
46. Screen wiper switch
47. Screen wiper motor

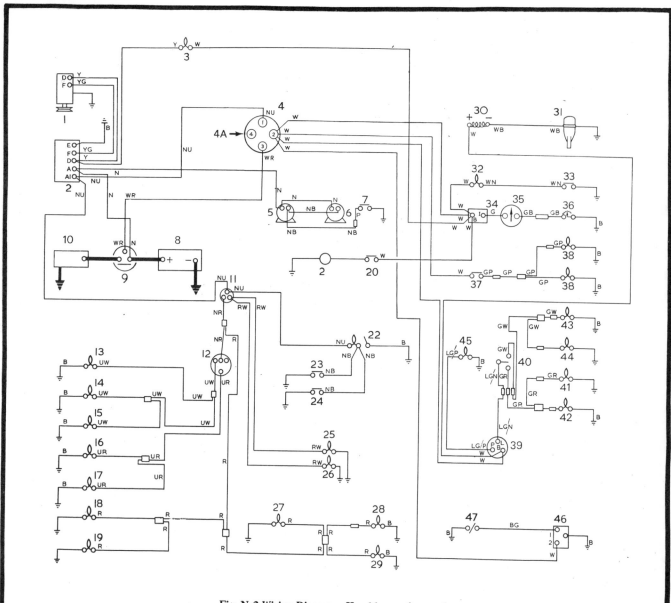

Fig. N:2 Wiring Diagram - Herald negative earth

1. Generator	16. Dip beam	32. Oil pressure warning light
2. Control box	17. Dip beam	33. Oil pressure switch
3. Ignition warning light	18. Front parking lamp	34. Voltage stabilizer
4. Ignition/starter switch	19. Front parking lamp	35. Fuel indicator
4A. Ignition/starter switch radio supply connector	20. Heater switch	36. Fuel tank unit
	21. Heater motor	37. Stop lamp switch
5. Horn	22. Facia lamp	38. Stop lamp
6. Horn	23. Door switch	39. Flasher unit
7. Horn push	24. Door switch	40. Flasher switch
8. Battery	25. Instrument illumination	41. L.H. Flasher lamp
9. Starter solenoid	26. Instrument illumination	42. L.H. Flasher lamp
10. Starter motor	27. Plate illumination lamp	43. R.H. Flasher lamp
11. Master light switch	28. Tail lamp	44. R.H. Flasher lamp
12. Column light switch	29. Tail lamp	45. Flasher warning light
13. Main beam warning light	30. Ignition coil	46. Windscreen wiper motor
14. Main beam	31. Ignition distributor	47. Windscreen wiper switch
15. Main beam		

COLOUR CODE

N.	Brown	LG.	Light Green
U.	Blue	W.	White
R.	Red	Y.	Yellow
P.	Purple	S.	Slate
G.	Green	B.	Black

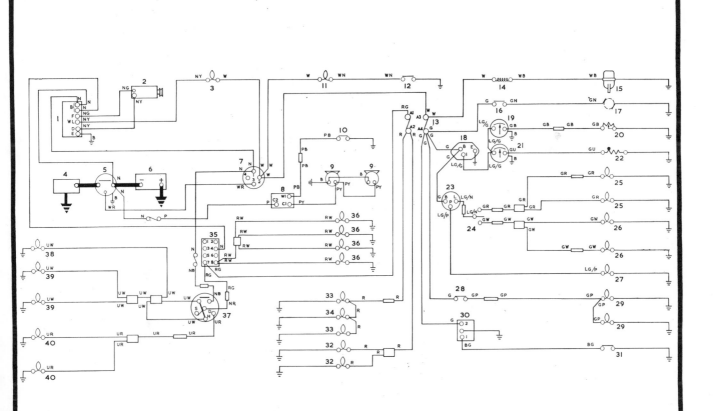

Fig. N:3 Wiring Diagram - Spitfire 4, Mk I & Mk II

1. Control box
2. Generator
3. Ignition warning lamp
4. Starter motor
5. Starter solenoid
6. Battery
7. Ignition/starter switch
8. Horn fuse
9. Horns
10. Horn push
11. Oil warning lamp
12. Oil pressure switch
13. Fuse unit
14. Ignition coil

15. Distributor
*16. Heater blower switch
*17. Heater blower motor
18. Voltage stabilizer
19. Fuel indicator
20. Fuel tank unit
21. Temperature indicator
22. Temperature transmitter
23. Flasher unit
24. Turn signal switch
25. Turn signal lamps, left-hand side
26. Turn signal lamps, right-hand side
27. Turn signal motor
28. Brake/stop lamp switch

29. Brake/stop lamps
30. Windscreen wiper motor
31. Wiper motor switch
32. Front parking lamps
33. Tail lamps
34. Plate illumination lamps
35. Master lighting switch
36. Instrument illumination
37. Steering column light switch
38. Main beam warning lamp
39. Headlamp main beams
40. Headlamp dipped beams

* Special Accessory

CABLE COLOUR CODE

B. Black	G. Green	L. Light	N. Brown	R. Red	U. Blue	Y. Yellow
D. Dark	K. Pink	M. Medium	P. Purple	S. Slate	W. White	

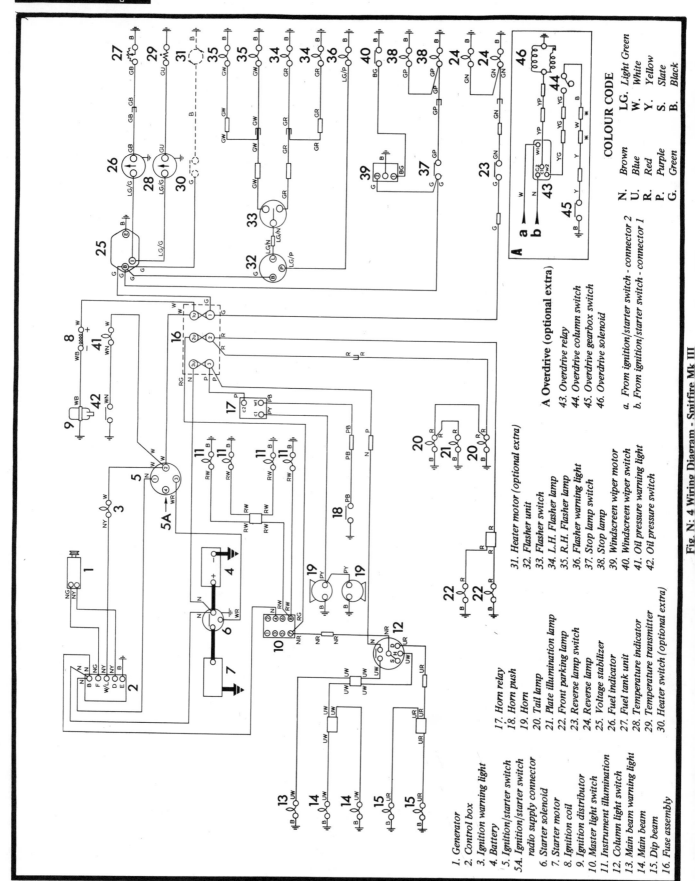

Fig. N: 4 Wiring Diagram - Spitfire Mk III

1. Generator
2. Control box
3. Ignition warning light
4. Battery
5. Ignition/starter switch
5A. Ignition/starter switch radio supply connector
6. Starter solenoid
7. Starter motor
8. Ignition coil
9. Ignition distributor
10. Master light switch
11. Instrument illumination
12. Column light switch
13. Main beam warning light
14. Main beam
15. Dip beam
16. Fuse assembly
17. Horn relay
18. Horn push
19. Horn
20. Tail lamp
21. Plate illumination lamp
22. Front parking lamp
23. Reverse lamp switch
24. Reverse lamp
25. Voltage stabilizer
26. Fuel indicator
27. Fuel tank unit
28. Temperature indicator
29. Temperature transmitter
30. Heater switch (optional extra)
31. Heater motor (optional extra)
32. Flasher unit
33. Flasher switch
34. L.H. Flasher lamp
35. R.H. Flasher lamp
36. Flasher warning light
37. Stop lamp switch
38. Stop lamp
39. Windscreen wiper motor
40. Windscreen wiper switch
41. Oil pressure warning light
42. Oil pressure switch

A Overdrive (optional extra)
43. Overdrive relay
44. Overdrive column switch
45. Overdrive gearbox switch
46. Overdrive solenoid
a. From ignition/starter switch - connector 2
b. From ignition/starter switch - connector 1

COLOUR CODE

N. Brown   LG. Light Green
U. Blue   W. White
R. Red   Y. Yellow
P. Purple   S. Slate
G. Green   B. Black

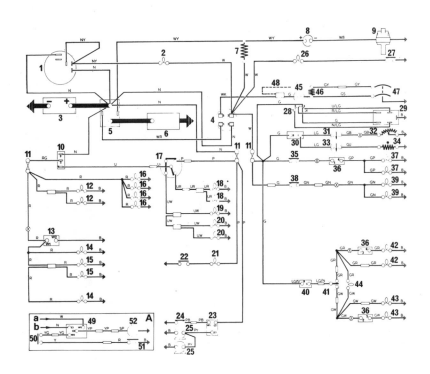

Fig. N:5 Wiring Diagram - Spitfire Mk IV

1. Alternator
2. Ignition warning light
3. Battery
4. Ignition/starter switch
5. Starter solenoid
6. Starter motor
7. Ballast resistor
8. Ignition coil - 6 volt
9. Ignition distributor
10. Master light switch
11. Fuse
12. Front parking lamp
13. Night dimming relay winding
14. Tail lamp
15. Plate illumination lamp
16. Instrument illumination
17. Column light switch
18. Dip beam
19. Main beam warning light
20. Main beam

21. Courtesy light
22. Door switch
23. Horn relay
24. Horn push
25. Horn
26. Oil pressure warning light
27. Oil pressure switch
28. Windscreen wiper switch
29. Windscreen wiper motor
30. Voltage stabilizer
31. Fuel indicator
32. Fuel tank unit
33. Temperature indicator
34. Temperature transmitter
35. Stop lamp switch
36. Night dimming relay
37. Stop lamp
38. Reverse lamp switch
39. Reverse lamp
40. Turn signal flasher unit

41. Turn signal switch
42. L.H. flasher lamp
43. R.H. flasher lamp
44. Turn signal warning light
45. Heater motor
46. Heater rheostat
47. Heater switch
48. Radio facility

A Overdrive (optional extra)

49. Overdrive relay
50. Overdrive gearbox switch
51. Overdrive gear lever switch
52. Overdrive solenoid

a From ignition/starter switch - terminal 3
b From ignition/starter switch - terminal 2

Trouble Shooting

Engine

SYMPTOMS

	a	b	c	d	e	f	g	h	i	j	k	l	m	n	o	p	q	r	s	t	u	v
ENGINE WILL NOT CRANK	*	*	*	*																		
ENGINE CRANKS SLOWLY	*	*	*																			
ENGINE CRANKS BUT DOES NOT START					*	*	*	*								*						
ENGINE STARTS BUT RUNS FOR SHORT PERIODS ONLY									*	*												
ENGINE MISFIRES AT LOW SPEED					*	*					*	*										
ENGINE MISFIRES AT HIGH SPEED					*	*					*	*										*
ENGINE MISFIRES AT ALL SPEEDS					*	*	*				*	*				*						*
ENGINE MISFIRES ON ACCELERATION AND FAILS TO REV.					*	*						*										*
ROUGH IDLE					*	*	*	*	*	*	*	*	*	*	*							*
RUNS ROUGH AT HIGH SPEED							*	*	*	*	*	*	*	*	*							*
LACK OF POWER					*	*	*	*	*		*		*	*		*						
POOR ACCELERATION					*	*	*	*	*		*		*	*		*						
LACK OF TOP SPEED					*	*	*		*		*		*	*		*						
EXCESSIVE FUEL CONSUMPTION					*	*					*		*									
EXCESSIVE OIL CONSUMPTION																*	*	*	*			
PINKING	*				*	*																
COMPRESSION LEAK								*			*	*	*			*					*	

SYMPTOMS

	a	b	c	d	e	f	g	h	i	j	k	l	m	n	o	p	q	r	s	t	u	v

PROBABLE CAUSE

a. Fault in the starting system - Refer to the ELECTRICAL EQUIPMENT section for diagnosis.
b. Engine oil too thick.
c. Stiff engine.
d. Mechanical seizure.
e. Fault in the ignition system - Refer to the IGNITION SYSTEM section for diagnosis.
f. Fault in the fuel system - Refer to the FUEL SYSTEM section for diagnosis.
g. Incorrect valve timing.
h. Compression leak.
i. Air leak at inlet manifold.
j. Restriction in exhaust system.
k. Poor valve seating.
l. Sticking valves.
m. Leaking cylinder head gasket.
n. Worn camshaft lobes.
o. Incorrect tappet clearances.
p. Worn or damaged cylinder bores, pistons and/or piston rings.
q. Worn valve guides.
r. Damaged valve stem seals.
s. Leaking oil seal or gasket.
t. Incorrectly installed spark plug.
u. Cracked cylinder.
v. Broken or weak valve springs.

REMEDIES

b. Drain oil and replace with correct oil.
c. Add small quantity of oil to the fuel and run engine gently.
d. Strip engine and renew parts as necessary.
g. Retime engine.
h. Trace and seal.
i. Trace and seal.
j. Remove restriction.
k. Regrind seats.
l. Free and trace cause.
m. Renew gasket.
n. Fit new camshaft.
o. Adjust tappets.
p. Exchange engine.
q. Replace valve guides.
r. Replace seals.
s. Replace gasket.
t. Replace plug with correct one.
u. Renew cylinder block.
v. Replace springs.

Lubrication System

SYMPTOMS

	a	b	c	d	e	f	g	h	i	j	k	l	m	n
EXCESSIVE OIL CONSUMPTION	*	*	*	*										
LOW OIL PRESSURE	*				*	*	*	*	*	*	*	*		*

PROBABLE CAUSE

a. Worn or damaged cylinder bores, pistons and/or piston rings.
b. Worn valve guides.
c. Damaged valve stem seals.
d. Leaking oil seal or gasket.
e. Faulty oil pressure gauge, switch or wiring.
f. Relief valve defective.
g. Oil pick-up pipe strainer blocked.
h. Oil filter over-flow valve defective.
i. Worn oil pump.
j. Damaged or worn main and/or big-end bearings.
k. Incorrect grade of engine oil.
l. Oil level low.
m. Oil level too high.
n. Oil leak or the pressurised side of the lubrication system.

REMEDIES

a. Regrind cylinder bores and fit new oversize pistons and rings.
b. Replace valves and guides.
c. Replace seals.
d. Seal leak or replace gasket.
e. Trace and rectify.
f. Check and replace if necessary.
g. Remove blockage.
h. Check and replace if necessary.
i. Replace pump or parts.
j. Renew bearings.
k. Replace oil with correct grade.
l. Top up oil.
m. Drain off surplus oil.
n. Trace and remedy.

Cooling System

SYMPTOMS

	a	b	c	d	e	f	g	h	i	j	k	l	m	n	o
OVERHEATING	*	*	*	*	*	*		*	*	*	*	*	*	*	
ENGINE FAILS TO REACH NORMAL OPERATING TEMPERATURE							*								*

PROBABLE CAUSE

a. Insufficient coolant.
b. Drive belt slipping or broken.
c. Radiator fins clogged.
d. Cooling fan defective.
e. Water pump defective.
f. Thermostat jammed shut.
g. Thermostat jammed open.
h. Ignition timing too far retarded.
i. Excessive vehicle load or dragging brakes.
j. Internal passage in the engine and/or radiator blocked.
k. Hoses blocked.
l. Carburettor mal-adjustment.
m. Excessive carbon deposit in the cylinders.
n. Insufficient engine oil or use of inferior grade of oil.
o. Excessive radiator area.

REMEDIES

a. Top up radiator.
b. Tighten belt or renew.
c. Unclog fins.
d. Trace fault, rectify or renew.
e. Replace water pump.
f. Replace thermostat.
g. Replace thermostat.
h. Retime ignition.
i. Unload car, check brakes.
j. Trace and clear.
k. Trace and clear blockage.
l. Adjust correctly.
m. Decarbonise engine, top overhaul.
n. Top up with correct grade. Drain if necessary.
o. Partially blank off in winter only.

Trouble Shooting

Fuel System

SYMPTOMS

	a	b	c	d	e	f	g	h	i	j	k	l	m	n	o	p	q	r	s	t	u	v
ENGINE CRANKS BUT DOES NOT START	*	*	*	*	*	*	*															
ENGINE STARTS BUT RUNS FOR SHORT PERIODS ONLY	*	*	*	*	*	*	*												*	*		
ENGINE MISFIRES AT LOW SPEED				*	*							*										
ENGINE MISFIRES AT HIGH SPEED				*	*							*										
ENGINE MISFIRES AT ALL SPEEDS	*	*	*	*																		
ENGINE MISFIRES ON ACCELERATION AND FAILS TO REV.	*		*						*	*	*	*	*	*	*							*
ROUGH IDLE		*								*	*	*	*	*	*							*
ENGINE RUNS ROUGH AT HIGH SPEED		*									*			*								*
LACK OF POWER		*									*			*								*
POOR ACCELERATION		*									*			*		*						*
LACK OF TOP SPEED		*										*		*								*
EXCESSIVE FUEL CONSUMPTION	*	*									*	*		*								*
PINKING															*					*		
BACKFIRE																				*	*	

PROBABLE CAUSE

a. Fuel tank empty.
b. Fuel line blocked.
c. Fuel pump defective.
d. Blockage in carburettor.
e. Air lock in fuel line.
f. Fuel filter blocked.
g. Carburettor needle valve jammed.
h. Water in carburettor.
i. Erratic fuel flow due to blockage.
j. Idling speed too low.
k. Incorrect setting of choke control.
l. Incorrect carburettor fuel/float level.
m. Carburettor icing.
n. Air leak at inlet manifold.
o. Incorrect grade of fuel.
p. Carburettor accelerator pump defective.
q. Throttle linkage mal-adjusted.
r. Incorrect adjustment of idling mixture.
s. Air filter clogged.
t. Incorrect ignition timing.
u. Carburettor piston sticking.
v. Wrong carburettor jets fitted.

REMEDIES

a. Fill tank.
b. Blow out obstruction with compressed air.
c. Replace pump.
d. Remove blockage.
e. Trace and bleed out.
f. Clean filter.
g. Free needle.
h. Drain out water, dry out.
i. Remove blockage.
j. Adjust throttle stop screw.
k. Reset control.
l. Adjust level.
m. Wait for ice to melt. If persistent, trace cause.
n. Trace leak and seal.
o. Dilute fuel with highest octane rating obtainable.
p. Trace fault and rectify.
q. Adjust correctly.
r. Adjust mixture control.
s. Clean filter.
t. Retime ignition.
u. Oil carburettor.
v. Replace with correct jets.

Ignition System

SYMPTOMS

	a	b	c	d	e	f	g	h	i	j	k	l	m	n	o	p	q	r
ENGINE CRANKS BUT DOES NOT START	*	*	*	*	*	*	*	*	*	*	*							
ENGINE STARTS BUT RUNS FOR SHORT PERIODS ONLY	*		*							*	*	*	*	*				
ENGINE MISFIRES AT LOW SPEED		*	*								*							
ENGINE MISFIRES AT HIGH SPEED		*	*	*	*		*				*	*						
ENGINE MISFIRES AT ALL SPEEDS		*	*	*	*	*	*				*	*	*					
ENGINE MISFIRES ON ACCELERATION AND FAILS TO REV.		*			*						*				*			
ROUGH IDLE		*	*	*		*		*	*	*								
ENGINE RUNS ROUGH AT HIGH SPEED		*	*	*	*	*		*			*				*		*	
LACK OF POWER		*	*		*	*		*			*				*			*
POOR ACCELERATION		*			*	*		*							*	*		
LACK OF TOP SPEED		*			*	*		*							*			*
EXCESSIVE FUEL CONSUMPTION		*			*	*		*										*
PINKING							*	*							*			*

PROBABLE CAUSE

a. Battery discharged or defective.
b. Contact breaker points need cleaning or renewing.
c. Incorrect contact breaker points.
d. Contact breaker spring weak.
e. Spark plugs need cleaning or renewing.
f. Incorrect spark plug gaps.
g. Wrong type of spark plug fitted.
h. Static ignition timing incorrect.
i. Coil or capacitor defective.
j. Open circuit or loose connection in the L.T. circuit.
k. Open circuit, short to earth or loose connection on the coil H.T. lead.
l. Open circuit, short to earth or loose connection on the spark plug leads.
m. Plug leads incorrectly connected.
n. H.T. leak on coil distributor cap or rotor, due to oil, dirt, moisture or damage.
o. Centrifugal advance not functioning correctly.
p. Vacuum advance not functioning correctly.
q. Worn distributor cam or distributor shaft bush.
r. Using wrong grade of fuel.

REMEDIES

a. Recharge or replace battery.
b. Clean or renew.
c. Fit correct points.
d. Renew contact breaker set.
e. Clean or renew plugs.
f. Adjust gaps.
g. Fit correct plugs.
h. Retime ignition.
i. Replace as necessary.
j. Trace and rectify.
k. Trace and rectify.
l. Trace and rectify.
m. Connect correctly.
n. Clean with dry lint free rag.
o. Examine and oil sparingly.
p. Check and rectify.
q. Replace defective parts.
r. Change to correct grade of fuel.

Steering

SYMPTOMS

	a	b	c	d	e	f	g	h	i	j	k	l	m	n	o	p	q	r	s
STEERING STIFFNESS	*	*	*	*	*	*													
STEERING SLACK					*	*	*	*	*	*	*	*							
STEERING WANDER				*		*	*	*	*	*	*	*							
WHEEL SHIMMY	*			*			*	*		*				*	*				
CAR PULLS TO ONE SIDE	*			*											*		*	*	
POOR RECOVERY OF STEERING	*	*	*	*	*	*													
WHEEL TO CENTRE				*	*								*					*	
EXCESSIVE OR ABNORMAL TYRE WEAR	*			*				*	*					*	*				*

| | a | b | c | d | e | f | g | h | i | j | k | l | m | n | o | p | q | r | s |

PROBABLE CAUSE

a. Tyre pressures incorrect or uneven.
b. Lack of lubricant in steering gear.
c. Lack of lubrication at steering linkage ball joints.
d. Incorrect wheel alignment.
e. Incorrectly adjusted steering gear.
f. Steering column bearings too tight or column bent.
g. Steering linkage joints worn or loose.
h. Front wheel bearings worn or incorrectly adjusted.
i. Slackness in front suspension.
j. Road wheel nuts loose.
k. Steering wheel loose.
l. Steering gear mounting bolts loose.
m. Steering gear worn.
n. Shock absorbers defective or mountings loose.
o. Road wheels imbalanced or tyres unevenly worn.
p. Suspension springs weak or broken.
q. Brakes pulling on one side.
r. Chassis frame or suspension misaligned.
s. Improper driving.

REMEDIES

a. Inflate and balance tyres.
b. Inject lubricant.
c. Lubricate.
d. Check steering geometry.
e. Adjust correctly.
f. Adjust renew defective parts.
g. Tighten or replace joints.
h. Adjust or renew bearings.
i. Tighten to correct torque.
j. Tighten nuts to correct torque.
k. Tighten to correct torque.
l. Tighten to correct torque.
m. Replace worn parts.
n. Replace with new.
o. Balance wheels.
p. Renew springs.
q. Balance brakes.
r. Realign.
s. Arrange tuition on driving.

Braking System

SYMPTOMS

	a	b	c	d	e	f	g	h	i	j	k	l	m	n	o	p	q	r	s	t	u	v	w
BRAKE FAILURE	*					*	*	*												*		*	*
BRAKES INEFFECTIVE	*	*	*	*	*	*	*	*												*		*	*
BRAKES GRAB OR PULL TO ONE SIDE		*	*	*							*		*	*		*							
BRAKES BIND									*	*					*		*	*	*				
PEDAL SPONGY							*	*															
PEDAL TRAVEL EXCESSIVE	*					*	*	*									*	*		*			
EXCESSIVE PEDAL PRESSURE REQUIRED		*	*						*									*				*	*
HYDRAULIC SYSTEM WILL NOT MAINTAIN PRESSURE								*												*	*		*
BRAKE SQUEAL DEVELOPS	*	*	*	*								*	*			*							
BRAKE SHUDDER DEVELOPS				*								*	*	*		*							
HANDBRAKE INEFFECTIVE OR REQUIRES EXCESSIVE MOVEMENT																	*	*					

| | a | b | c | d | e | f | g | h | i | j | k | l | m | n | o | p | q | r | s | t | u | v | w |

PROBABLE CAUSE

a. Brake shoe linings or friction pades excessively worn.
b. Incorrect brake shoe linings or friction pads.
c. Brake shoe linings or friction pads contaminated.
d. Brake drums or discs scored.
e. Incorrect brake fluid.
f. Insufficient brake fluid.
g. Air in the hydraulic system.
h. Fluid leak in the hydraulic system.
i. Fluid line blocked.
j. Mal-function in the brake pedal linkage.
k. Unequal tyre pressures.
l. Brake disc or drum distorted or cracked.
m. Brake back plate or calliper mounting bolts loose in the suspension.
n. Wheel bearings incorrectly adjusted.
o. Weak, broken or improperly installed shoe return springs.
p. Uneven brake lining contact.
q. Incorrect brake lining adjustment.
r. Pistons in wheel cylinder or calliper seized.
s. Weak or broken pedal return spring.
t. Master cylinder defective.
u. Fluid reservoir overfilled or reservoir air vent restricted.
v. Servo vacuum hose disconnected or restricted, or servo defective.
w. Wheel cylinder or calliper defective.

REMEDIES

a. Replace linings or pads.
b. Replace with correct linings or pads.
c. Clean thoroughly.
d. Renew drums or discs.
e. Bleed out old fluid and replace with correct.
f. Top up reservoir.
g. Bleed brake system.
h. Trace and seal.
i. Trace and clear blockage.
j. Correct as necessary.
k. Adjust and balance tyre pressures.
l. Renew disc or drum.
m. Tighten as necessary to correct torque.
n. Adjust wheel bearings.
o. Renew or install correctly.
p. Trace cause and remedy.
q. Adjust correctly.
r. Free and clean.
s. Renew spring.
t. Replace master cylinder and seals.
u. Lower fluid level. Clear air vent.
v. Check and replace hose. Renew servo unit if defective.
w. Replace as necessary.

Lubricate and Clean

		No.	MO 6 12 36 / MI 6 12 36 / KM 10 20 60
CAR UP			
ENGINE	Drain oil	1	●●● ✳
Filter	Change element	2	●●
	Clean element	3	
GEARBOX	Check oil/top up	4	●●●
	Change oil	5	
Overdrive Filter	Clean element	6	
AUTOMATIC TRANSM.	Drain fluid	7	
Filter	Clean element	8	
DIFFERENTIAL	Check oil/top up	9	●●●
	Change oil	10	
Limited Slip Differential	Check oil/top up	11	
	Change oil	12	
Sliding Joints(Drive Shaft)	Check oil/top up	13	
	Change oil	14	
SHOCK ABSORBERS	Check oil/top up	15	
PROP./DRIVE SHAFT(S)	Lubricate	16	
GREASE GUN POINTS	Lubricate	17	●●● ✳
PEDAL SHAFT(S)	Lubricate	18	●●
HANDBRAKE	Lubricate	19	●●
GEAR LINKAGE	Lubricate	20	
CAR LOWERED – WHEELS FREE			
WHEEL BEARINGS-Front	Repack	21	●●
WHEEL BEARINGS-Rear	Repack	22	●●
BRAKE FLUID	Renew/bleed syst.	23	●
CAR DOWN – BONNET OPEN			
ENGINE	Refill with oil	24	●●●
	Check oil level	25	
Breather Cap	Clean	26	●●●
Air Cleaner	Service element(s)	27	●●● ✳
	Replace element(s)	28	●
PCV-System	Clean filter	29	
	Clean valve/hose(s)	30	●●● ✳
	Replace valve	31	
Carburettor(s)	Clean jets/bowl	32	
	Top up pist. damper	33	●●● ✳
	Lubricate linkages	34	●●●
Fuel Bowl/Filter(s)	Clean/replace	35	●●
Fuel Injection Pump	Check oil level	36	
Filter(s)	Clean/replace	37	
AUTOMATIC TRANSM.	Refill with fluid	38	
	Check fluid level	39	
DISTRIBUTOR	Clean cap & ign.coil	40	●●●
Spindle/Cam	Lubricate	41	●●●
COOLING SYSTEM	Check/top up	42	●●●
	Flush system	43	
Corrosion Inhibitor	Check solution	44	
Anti-Freeze	Check	45	
Water Pump	Lubricate	46	●●
SCREENWASHER	Check/top up	47	
BATTERY	Check/top up	48	
	Check spec. gravity	49	●●●
Connections	Clean, grease	50	●●●
GENERATOR	Lubricate	51	●●
STEERING	Check/top up	52	●● ✳
Power Steering	Check/top up fluid	53	
	Grease ram	54	
	Clean filter	55	
CLUTCH/BRAKE	Check/top up fluid	56	●●●
BRAKE SERVO	Clean filter	57	
	Renew filter	58	
HYDR. SUSPENSION	Check/top up fluid	59	
	Renew fluid	60	
	Clean filter	61	
CAR DOWN – EXTERNAL			
LOCKS, HINGES, ETC.	Lubricate	62	●●●
Door Drain Holes	Clean	63	
WIPER SPINDLES	Lubricate	64	

EVERY

MOnths
MIles (1000)
KMs (1000)

whichever comes first

1200 - 12/50

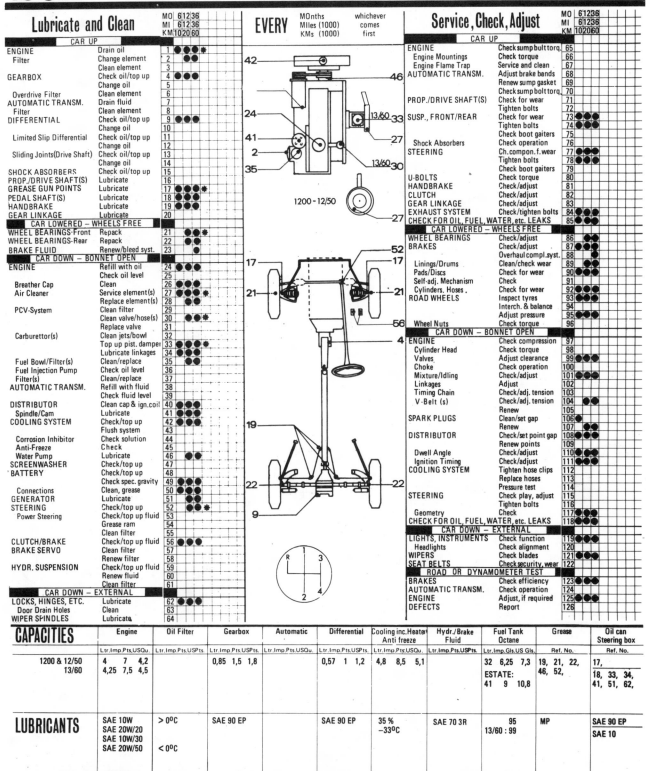

Service, Check, Adjust

		No.	MO 6 12 36 / MI 6 12 36 / KM 10 20 60
CAR UP			
ENGINE	Check sump bolt torq.	65	
	Check torque	66	
Engine Mountings			
Engine Flame Trap	Service and clean	67	
AUTOMATIC TRANSM.	Adjust brake bands	68	
	Renew sump gasket	69	
	Check sump bolt torq.	70	
PROP./DRIVE SHAFT(S)	Check for wear	71	
	Tighten bolts	72	
SUSP., FRONT/REAR	Check for wear	73	●●●
	Tighten bolts	74	●●●
	Check boot gaiters	75	
Shock Absorbers	Check operation	76	
STEERING	Ch. compon. f. wear	77	●●●
	Tighten bolts	78	●●●
	Check boot gaiters	79	
U-BOLTS	Check torque	80	
HANDBRAKE	Check/adjust	81	
CLUTCH	Check/adjust	82	
GEAR LINKAGE	Check/adjust	83	
EXHAUST SYSTEM	Check/tighten bolts	84	●●●
CHECK FOR OIL, FUEL, WATER, etc. LEAKS		85	●●●
CAR LOWERED – WHEELS FREE			
WHEEL BEARINGS	Check/adjust	86	●●
BRAKES	Check/adjust	87	●●●
	Overhaul compl.syst.	88	
Linings/Drums	Clean/check wear	89	●●
Pads/Discs	Check for wear	90	●●●
Self-adj. Mechanism	Check	91	
Cylinders, Hoses.	Check for wear	92	●●
ROAD WHEELS	Inspect tyres	93	●●●
	Interch. & balance	94	
	Adjust pressure	95	●●●
Wheel Nuts	Check torque	96	●●●
CAR DOWN – BONNET OPEN			
ENGINE	Check compression	97	
Cylinder Head	Check torque	98	
Valves	Adjust clearance	99	●●●
Choke	Check operation	100	
Mixture/Idling	Check/adjust	101	●●●
Linkages	Adjust	102	
Timing Chain	Check/adj. tension	103	
V-Belt (s)	Check/adj. tension	104	●●●
	Renew	105	
SPARK PLUGS	Clean/set gap	106	●
	Renew	107	●
DISTRIBUTOR	Check/set point gap	108	●●●
	Renew points	109	
Dwell Angle	Check/adjust	110	●●●
Ignition Timing	Check/adjust	111	●●●
COOLING SYSTEM	Tighten hose clips	112	
	Replace hoses	113	
	Pressure test	114	
STEERING	Check play, adjust	115	
	Tighten bolts	116	
Geometry	Check	117	●●●
CHECK FOR OIL, FUEL, WATER, etc. LEAKS		118	●●●
CAR DOWN – EXTERNAL			
LIGHTS, INSTRUMENTS	Check function	119	●●●
Headlights	Check alignment	120	
WIPERS	Check blades	121	●●●
SEAT BELTS	Check security, wear	122	
ROAD OR DYNAMOMETER TEST			
BRAKES	Check efficiency	123	●●●
AUTOMATIC TRANSM.	Check operation	124	
ENGINE	Adjust, if required	125	●●●
DEFECTS	Report	126	

CAPACITIES

	Engine	Oil Filter	Gearbox	Automatic	Differential	Cooling inc.Heater Anti freeze	Hydr./Brake Fluid	Fuel Tank	Grease	Oil can Steering box
	Ltr.Imp.Pts.USQu.	Ltr.Imp.Pts.USPts.	Ltr.Imp.Pts.USPts.	Ltr.Imp.Pts.USQu.	Ltr.Imp.Pts.USPts.	Ltr.Imp.Pts.USQu.	Ltr.Imp.Pts.USPts.	Ltr.Imp.Gls.US Gls.	Ref. No.	Ref. No.
1200 & 12/50	4 7 4,2		0,85 1,5 1,8		0,57 1 1,2	4,8 8,5 5,1		32 6,25 7,3	19, 21, 22, 46, 52,	17,
13/60	4,25 7,5 4,5							ESTATE: 41 9 10,8		18, 33, 34, 41, 51, 62,

LUBRICANTS

	Engine		Gearbox		Differential	Cooling	Hydr./Brake Fluid	Fuel Tank Octane	Grease	Oil can Steering box
	SAE 10W SAE 20W/20 SAE 10W/30 SAE 20W/50	> 0°C / < 0°C	SAE 90 EP		SAE 90 EP	35% −33°C	SAE 70 3R	95 13/60 : 99	MP	SAE 90 EP SAE 10

AUTOSERVICE DATA CHART

Lubricate and Clean

Intervals: MO 6 12 36 · MI 6 12 36 · KM 10 20 60

Item	Operation	No.	Marks
CAR UP			
ENGINE	Drain oil	1	●●● *
Filter	Change element	2	●●
	Clean element	3	
GEARBOX	Check oil/top up	4	
	Change oil	5	
Overdrive Filter	Clean element	6	
AUTOMATIC TRANSM.	Drain fluid	7	
Filter	Clean element	8	
DIFFERENTIAL	Check oil/top up	9	●●●
	Change oil	10	
Limited Slip Differential	Check oil/top up	11	
	Change oil	12	
Sliding Joints(Drive Shaft)	Check oil/top up	13	
	Change oil	14	
SHOCK ABSORBERS	Check oil/top up	15	
PROP./DRIVE SHAFT(S)	Lubricate	16	
GREASE GUN POINTS	Lubricate	17	●●● *
PEDAL SHAFT(S)	Lubricate	18	●●●
HANDBRAKE	Lubricate	19	●●●
GEAR LINKAGE	Lubricate	20	
CAR LOWERED – WHEELS FREE			
WHEEL BEARINGS-Front	Repack	21	●● *
WHEEL BEARINGS-Rear	Repack	22	
BRAKE FLUID	Renew/bleed syst.	23	
CAR DOWN – BONNET OPEN			
ENGINE	Refill with oil	24	●●●
	Check oil level	25	●●●
Breather Cap	Clean	26	●●●
Air Cleaner	Service element(s)	27	●●●
	Replace element(s)	28	●●●
PCV-System	Clean filter	29	
	Clean valve/hose(s)	30	●● *
	Replace valve	31	
Carburettor(s)	Clean jets/bowl	32	
	Top up pist. damper	33	●●●
	Lubricate linkages	34	●●●
Fuel Bowl/Filter(s)	Clean/replace	35	●●
Fuel Injection Pump	Check oil level	36	
Filter(s)	Clean/replace	37	
AUTOMATIC TRANSM.	Refill with fluid	38	
	Check fluid level	39	
DISTRIBUTOR	Clean cap & ign.coil	40	●●●
Spindle/Cam	Lubricate	41	●●●
COOLING SYSTEM	Check/top up	42	●●●
	Flush system	43	
Corrosion Inhibitor	Check solution	44	
Anti-Freeze	Check	45	
Water Pump	Lubricate	46	●●
SCREENWASHER	Check/top up	47	
BATTERY	Check/top up	48	●●●
	Check spec. gravity	49	●●●
Connections	Clean, grease	50	●●●
GENERATOR	Lubricate	51	
STEERING	Check/top up	52	●● *
Power Steering	Check/top up fluid	53	
	Grease ram	54	
	Clean filter	55	
CLUTCH/BRAKE	Check/top up fluid	56	●●●
BRAKE SERVO	Clean filter	57	
	Renew filter	58	
HYDR. SUSPENSION	Check/top up fluid	59	
	Renew fluid	60	
	Clean filter	61	
CAR DOWN – EXTERNAL			
LOCKS, HINGES, ETC.	Lubricate	62	●●●
Door Drain Holes	Clean	63	
WIPER SPINDLES	Lubricate	64	

EVERY

MOnths / MIles (1000) / KMs (1000) — whichever comes first

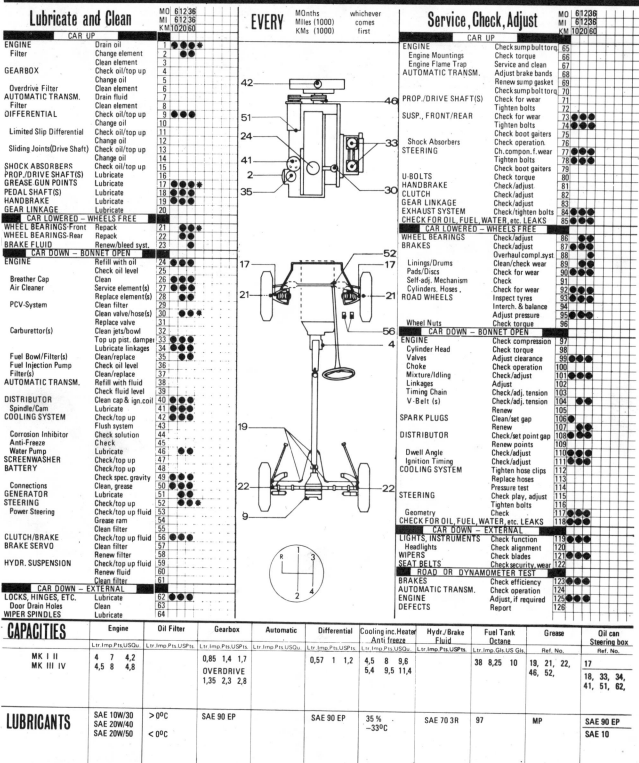

Service, Check, Adjust

Intervals: MO 6 12 36 · MI 6 12 36 · KM 10 20 60

Item	Operation	No.	Marks
CAR UP			
ENGINE	Check sump bolt torq.	65	
Engine Mountings	Check torque	66	
Engine Flame Trap	Service and clean	67	
AUTOMATIC TRANSM.	Adjust brake bands	68	
	Renew sump gasket	69	
	Check sump bolt torq	70	
PROP./DRIVE SHAFT(S)	Check for wear	71	
	Tighten bolts	72	
SUSP., FRONT/REAR	Check for wear	73	●●●
	Tighten bolts	74	●●●
	Check boot gaiters	75	
Shock Absorbers	Check operation.	76	
STEERING	Ch.compon.f.wear	77	●●●
	Tighten bolts	78	●●●
	Check boot gaiters	79	
U-BOLTS	Check torque	80	
HANDBRAKE	Check/adjust	81	
CLUTCH	Check/adjust	82	
GEAR LINKAGE	Check/adjust	83	
EXHAUST SYSTEM	Check/tighten bolts	84	●●●
CHECK FOR OIL, FUEL, WATER, etc. LEAKS		85	●●●
CAR LOWERED – WHEELS FREE			
WHEEL BEARINGS	Check/adjust	86	
BRAKES	Check/adjust	87	
	Overhaul compl.syst	88	
Linings/Drums	Clean/check wear	89	●●●
Pads/Discs	Check for wear	90	●●
Self-adj. Mechanism	Check	91	
Cylinders, Hoses.	Check for wear	92	●●●
ROAD WHEELS	Inspect tyres	93	●●●
	Interch. & balance	94	
	Adjust pressure	95	●●●
Wheel Nuts	Check torque	96	
CAR DOWN – BONNET OPEN			
ENGINE	Check compression	97	
Cylinder Head	Check torque	98	
Valves	Adjust clearance	99	●●●
Choke	Check operation	100	
Mixture/Idling	Check/adjust	101	●●●
Linkages	Adjust	102	
Timing Chain	Check/adj. tension	103	
V-Belt (s)	Check/adj. tension	104	●●
	Renew	105	
SPARK PLUGS	Clean/set gap	106	●
	Renew	107	
DISTRIBUTOR	Check/set point gap	108	●
	Renew points	109	
Dwell Angle	Check/adjust	110	●●●
Ignition Timing	Check/adjust	111	●●●
COOLING SYSTEM	Tighten hose clips	112	
	Replace hoses	113	
	Pressure test	114	
STEERING	Check play, adjust	115	
	Tighten bolts	116	
Geometry	Check	117	
CHECK FOR OIL, FUEL, WATER, etc. LEAKS		118	●●●
CAR DOWN – EXTERNAL			
LIGHTS, INSTRUMENTS	Check function	119	
Headlights	Check alignment	120	
WIPERS	Check blades	121	●●
SEAT BELTS	Check security, wear	122	
ROAD OR DYNAMOMETER TEST			
BRAKES	Check efficiency	123	
AUTOMATIC TRANSM.	Check operation	124	
ENGINE	Adjust, if required	125	●●●
DEFECTS	Report	126	

CAPACITIES

	Engine	Oil Filter	Gearbox	Automatic	Differential	Cooling inc. Heater Anti freeze	Hydr./Brake Fluid	Fuel Tank Octane	Grease	Oil can Steering box
	Ltr.Imp.Pts.USQu.	Ltr.Imp.Pts.USPts.	Ltr.Imp.Pts.USPts.	Ltr.Imp.Pts.USQu.	Ltr.Imp.Pts.USPts.	Ltr.Imp.Pts.USPts.	Ltr.Imp.Pts.USPts.	Ltr.Imp.Gls.US Gls.	Ref. No.	Ref. No.
MK I II	4 7 4,2		0,85 1,4 1,7		0,57 1 1,2	4,5 8 9,6		38 8,25 10	19, 21, 22, 46, 52,	17
MK III IV	4,5 8 4,8		OVERDRIVE 1,35 2,3 2,8			5,4 9,5 11,4				18, 33, 34, 41, 51, 62

LUBRICANTS

	Engine	Oil Filter	Gearbox		Differential	Cooling inc. Heater Anti freeze	Hydr./Brake Fluid	Octane	Grease	Oil can Steering box
	SAE 10W/30 SAE 20W/40 (>0°C) SAE 20W/50 (<0°C)	>0°C <0°C	SAE 90 EP		SAE 90 EP	35 % −33°C	SAE 70 3R	97	MP	SAE 90 EP SAE 10

AUTOSERVICE DATA CHART